I, Too, Sing America

THE · AFRICAN · AMERICAN · BOOK · OF · DAYS

By Paula L. Woods and
Felix H. Liddell

· WORKMAN PUBLISHING ·

Slipcase and cover art: *Wrapping It Up at the Lafayette,* by Romare Bearden; collage, acrylic and lacquer, 1974.
© The Cleveland Museum of Art, Mr. and Mrs. William H. Marlatt Fund, 85.41.

Workman calendars and diaries are available at special discounts when purchased in bulk
for premiums and sales promotions as well as for fund-raising or educational use.
Special editions can also be created to specification.
For details, contact the Special Sales Director at the address below.

ISBN: 1-56305-250-4

Workman Publishing Company, Inc.
708 Broadway
New York, NY 10003

Printed in Japan   First printing August 1992

10 9 8 7 6 5 4 3

ACKNOWLEDGMENTS

You are holding in your hands a dream that was five years in the making—an African-American book of days that we hope conveys the excitement, the pride, the irony of the days in *our* lives. With almost 1,500 entries, *I, Too, Sing America* was a massive undertaking that we could not have possibly completed without the help and support of many people.

Our heartfelt thanks go to the staff of the Moorland-Spingarn Research Center, especially to Esme Bhan and Malik Azeez, who introduced us to their vast archives and an impressive collection of African-American calendars, some dating back to the 1920's; to noted art historian David C. Driskell, who acted as an adviser in the selection of art for the book; to historian John Hope Franklin, for his early encouragement; to Professor Arnold Rampersad, who provided a useful critique of an early version of the manuscript; to Deborah Willis, Jim Huffman and the Prints and Photography staff of the Schomburg Center for Research in Black Culture; to Frank Driggs and his marvelous collection of vintage photographs; and to Sam Daniels, Evelyn Overmiller and the Library of Congress staff for their diligence in helping us uncover many of the wonderful historical images that appear in the book. And to the museums, private galleries, individual collectors and artists, and most notably the National Museum of American Art at the Smithsonian Institution, the Museum of African-American Art in Los Angeles, and Thurlow Tibbs of the Evans-Tibbs Collection—your generosity of spirit and willingness to allow your treasures to enrich the pages of this book are deeply appreciated.

We were assisted by a capable group of individuals whose thoroughness in checking facts and making a recognizable manuscript of the thousands of entries assembled are deeply appreciated. Thank you Susan Freitas, Kathleen Prampin, Ann Wang, Sharion Tytus Rasmussen, Alexandra Pollyea, and Sandra Jones for being there over the long haul.

And special thanks go to the many fine people at Workman Publishing who have brought this book to life: to Peter Workman for his vision and leadership; to Ruth Sullivan, who served not only as our editor but as a sounding board and champion; and to Ira Teichberg, Kathryn Wolgast and Sheilah Scully-Daly for their sensitivity, creativity, and perseverance in what we know has been a challenging project.

And last, to our family and friends, who have withstood our absence and preoccupation until this book came to life—we thank you.

Marcus Garvey once said "a people without the knowledge of their past history, origin and culture is like a tree without roots." We hope that, whoever you are, you read this book in celebration of African-American roots and recognize that our history, our accomplishments and our art are an integral part of the very fabric of this country.

April 1992

I, Too

I, too, sing America

I am the darker brother.
They send me to eat in the kitchen
When company comes,
But I laugh,
And eat well,
And grow strong.

Tomorrow,
I'll sit at the table
When company comes.
Nobody'll dare
Say to me,
"Eat in the kitchen,"
Then.

Besides,
They'll see how beautiful I am
and be ashamed—

I, too, am America.

from *The Weary Blues*, Langston Hughes, Alfred A. Knopf, New York, copyright © 1926. Reprinted by permission of Alfred A. Knopf.

WE, TOO, SING AMERICA!

The idea for the book, I, TOO, SING AMERICA was born at an exhibit of African-American art and photography that we attended five years ago. Among the few attendees in the Museum of African-American Art in Los Angeles, we were struck by the power of the works displayed and wondered how many people knew of the vast contributions of our people to the arts.

Coincidentally, a friend had given Paula a book of days that captured the lives and activities of writers. A quick scan of the book revealed that just *three* African-Americans were included! While we respected them immensely, we knew that Langston Hughes, Toni Morrison, and Richard Wright were only part of a rich African-American literary heritage. We wanted more people to know of the authors who sustained us, who inspired us in our lives. We began to dream of a living chronicle of our contributions, our culture, and our heroes that was not relegated to the margins of history.

As Langston Hughes so powerfully described in the poem from which this book takes its title, too long have our history and art been kept "in the kitchen." And yet pioneering historians like Carter G. Woodson fought that dismissal by a society enamored of its racist view of Americans of African descent. One of Woodson's most enduring accomplishments was the establishment of Negro History Week in 1927 to celebrate the achievements of black people. A ringing success, since 1976 we have been deluged with information on black history for an *entire month* (a great improvement, to be sure), yet relatively little the rest of the year.

But the simple truth is that African-American history is not a February media event, but a *daily part* of the fabric of this country. In recognition and celebration of this fact, we compiled I, TOO, SING AMERICA, a unique book that shows how black history is an African-AMERI-CAN phenomenon, rich in contributions to what has made this country great and full of milestones that deserve every American's contemplation.

Certainly politics, history, and religion are covered, but so too are African-Americans' contributions in education, medicine, science, business, literature, sports, and entertainment. I, TOO, SING AMERICA celebrates over 500 years of familiar dates in black history and little known facts, such as the achievement of African-American inventors who are responsible for providing the sugar we use, fountain pens, golf tees, and many more innovative and useful products. Or how the "Negro National Anthem" came to be written. Or the African ancestry of such notable men of arts and letters as John James Audubon, Aleksandr Pushkin, and Alexandre Dumas.

I, TOO, SING AMERICA also includes many ironies in African-American history, such as the death of noted antilynching advocate Ida B. Wells-Barnett on the same day as the Scottsboro Boys' arrest; the deaths of noted Harlem Renaissance poets Claude McKay and Langston Hughes on the same day nineteen years apart; the shared birthdays of noted African-American men of letters W.E.B. DuBois and Haki Mahubuti and poets Gwendolyn Brooks and Nikki Giovanni; or the withdrawal from office of the first appointed African-American governor, P.B.S. Pinchback of Louisiana, on the same day that the only elected African-American governor, L. Douglas Wilder of Virginia, took office 117 years later.

Equally important, I, TOO, SING AMERICA is filled with African-American art that for almost 200 years has defied notions of what we are capable of achieving despite the crushing oppression of racism and discrimination. I, TOO, SING AMERICA rings out with the stories of Henry Ossawa Tanner, an Impressionist who left the racism of America to paint in France; of Edward Bannister, who won and was almost denied his medal at the 1876 Centennial Exhibition in Philadelphia when the judges saw the color of his skin; or Horace Pippin, his right hand crippled in World War I, who nonetheless painted art prized by museums and collectors all over this land. Stories and fine art reproductions of the giants are blended with art from modern masters like the late Romare Bearden, Claude Clark, Sr., Elizabeth Catlett, Richard Mayhew, and many others.

More than 60 fine art and photography reproductions grace the pages of I, TOO, SING AMERICA, together with over 300 pictures and 1,500 entries. And whether you use this book to record the births, anniversaries, and milestones in your family's history, as a diary, appointment book, or for your coffee table, I, TOO, SING AMERICA proves that black history is a 365-day-per-year affair, a celebration we can all share with pride. ◆

—PAULA L. WOODS AND
FELIX H. LIDDELL

1

2

1804 Haiti achieves independence from France.

1808 The slave trade is outlawed in the U.S.

1831 William Lloyd Garrison publishes the first issue of *The Liberator* in Boston. The newspaper will become a major influence in the movement to abolish slavery in the U.S.

1863 President Abraham Lincoln issues the Emancipation Proclamation, declaring freedom for slaves living in the states that joined the rebellion that will become known as the Civil War.

1916 The first issue of the *Journal of Negro History* is published with Carter G. Woodson as editor.

1917 Ulysses Simpson Kay is born in Tuscon, Ariz. He will become a classical composer and one of the first American composers to travel to the Soviet Union. He will be known for his works for orchestra, piano, and chamber ensemble.

The last day of Kwanzaa, called Imani ("Faith"), is celebrated today. Culminating in a community feast, Imani commemorates "belief in our people, parents, teachers, leaders and the righteousness and victory of our struggle."

1837 The first National Negro Catholic Congress is held in Washington, D.C.

1915 John Hope Franklin is born in Rentiesville, Okla. He will become a scholar and historian most famous for his book *From Slavery to Freedom: A History of Negro Americans*, which will sell over two million copies.

1965 Led by Martin Luther King, Jr., the Selma, Ala., voter registration drive begins.

1977 Erroll Garner, pianist and composer, dies in Los Angeles, Calif. He was considered the best-selling jazz pianist in the world, most famous for the jazz standard "Misty."

Meanwhile, Ellis Wilson dies. An artist known best for his striking paintings of African-Americans, his work had been exhibited at the New York World's Fair of 1939, the Harmon Foundation, and the Detroit Institute of Arts. Among his best-known works are *Funeral Procession, Field Workers,* and *To Market.*

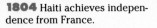

John Hope Franklin

Loïs Mailou Jones, *Jardin du Luxembourg*, ca. 1948. Oil on canvas. National Museum of American Art, Smithsonian Institution, gift of Gladys P. Payne in honor of Alice P. Moore.

3

4

1945 The Albany Institute of History and Art in New York State opens its exhibit *The Negro Artist Comes of Age: A National Survey of Contemporary American Artists*. The show includes works by Aaron Douglas, William H. Johnson, Palmer Hayden, Eldzier Cortor, Lois M. Jones, and others and will run for five weeks.

1947 The National Association for the Advancement of Colored People's annual report calls 1946 "one of the grimmest years in the history of the NAACP." The report details violence and atrocities heaped upon "Negro veterans freshly returned from a war to end torture and racial extermination."

1969 Louis Stokes is sworn in as the first African-American congressman from the State of Ohio. He will serve more than ten terms in Congress and be distinguished by his leadership of the 1977 Select Committee on Assassinations and chairmanship of the House Commit-

tee on Standards of Official Conduct (Ethics Committee).

1989 *The Arsenio Hall Show* premieres. It is the first regularly scheduled nightly talk show to star an African-American.

Arsenio Hall

1787 Prince Hall, founder of the first African-American Masonic lodge, and others petition the Massachusetts legislature for funds to return to Africa. The plan is the first recorded effort by African-Americans to return to their homeland.

1935 Boxer Floyd Patterson is born in Waco, N.C. A gold medal winner in the 1952 Summer Olympic Games in the middleweight class, he will be the first gold medalist to win a world professional title.

William H. Gray

1985 Congressman William H. Gray is elected chairman of the House Budget Committee, the highest congressional post held by an African-American.

Meanwhile, in New York, Leontyne Price makes her farewell appearance with the Metropolitan Opera, singing the title role of *Aïda*.

5

6

1804 Ohio begins the restriction of the rights and movements of free African-Americans by passing the first of several "Black laws." It is a trend that will be followed by most Northern states.

1911 Kappa Alpha Psi fraternity is founded on the campus of Indiana University by Elder Watson Diggs, Byron Kenneth Armstrong, and eight others. It will be the first African-American fraternity to be chartered as a national organization.

1943 George Washington Carver dies of anemia. He was a pioneering plant chemist and agricultural researcher noted for his work with the peanut and soil restoration while at Tuskegee Institute.

1948 A commemorative stamp of George Washington Carver is issued by the U.S. Postal Service. The posthumous honor bestowed upon the famed agricultural expert and researcher is only one of the many awards he received, including the 1923 Spingarn Medal and membership in the NYU Hall of Fame.

George Washington Carver

1773 "Felix," a Boston slave, and others petition Massachusetts Governor Hutchinson for their freedom. It is the first of eight similar petitions filed during the Revolutionary War.

1882 Thomas Boyne receives the Congressional Medal of Honor for bravery in two New Mexico battles while a sergeant in Troop C, 9th U.S. Cavalry.

1966 Harold R. Perry becomes the second African-American Roman Catholic bishop and the first in the 20th century.

1984 Pennsylvania Supreme Court Justice Robert N.C. Nix, Jr. is inaugurated as Chief Justice. The Philadelphia native, former deputy attorney general of the state, and thirteen-year veteran of the Court, is the first African-American to head a state Supreme Court.

1989 Elizabeth Koontz dies. She was a noted educator and first African-American president of the National Education Association.

Harold R. Perry

EDWARD MITCHELL BANNISTER, *Newspaper Boy,* 1869. Oil on canvas. National Museum of American Art, Smithsonian Institution, gift of the Harmon Foundation.

7

8

1890 William B. Purvis is awarded patent #419,065 for a fountain pen.

1891 Zora Neale Hurston, who will become a brilliant folklorist, novelist, and short story writer, is born in Eatonville, Fla. She will be one of the more influential writers of the Harlem Renaissance, known for her novel *Their Eyes Were Watching God* and her folklore collections, including *Mules and Men*.

1950 The James Weldon Johnson Collection officially opens at Yale University. Established in 1941 through a gift by Grace Nail Johnson, widow of the famed author, diplomat, and NAACP official, the collection will eventually include the papers of Johnson, Langston Hughes, W.E.B. Du Bois, Richard Wright, Jean Toomer, Zora Neale Hurston, and many other writers of the Harlem Renaissance.

Zora Neale Hurston

1955 Marian Anderson appears as Ulrica in Verdi's *Un Ballo in Maschera* with the New York Metropolitan Opera. In her debut performance at the Met, Anderson becomes the first African-American ever to sing with the company.

1811 A slave rebellion begins 35 miles outside of New Orleans, La. U.S. troops will be called to put down the uprising of over 400 slaves, which will last three days.

1867 Overriding President Andrew Johnson's veto, Congress passes legislation giving African-Americans in the District of Columbia the right to vote.

1922 Colonel Charles Young dies in Lagos, Nigeria. He was one of the first African-American graduates of West Point, the first to achieve the rank of colonel in the U.S. Army, and the second winner of the NAACP's Spingarn Medal (1916).

Colonel Charles Young

1975 The state-owned Alabama Educational Television Commission has its application for license renewal denied by the Federal Communications Commission because of racial discrimination against African-Americans in employment and programming.

9

10

1866 Fisk College is established in Nashville, Tenn.

1901 Edward Mitchell Bannister dies in Providence, R.I. Challenged to become an artist after reading a newspaper article deriding African-Americans' ability to produce art, he disproved that statement throughout a distinguished art career.

1914 Phi Beta Sigma fraternity is founded at Howard University.

1935 Earl G. Graves is born in Brooklyn, N.Y. He will become president and chief executive officer of Earl G. Graves, Ltd., the publisher of *Black Enterprise* magazine, a successful entrepreneur, and one of the strongest advocates for African-American business.

Earl Graves

1989 Time, Inc. agrees to sell NYT Cable for $420 million to Comcast Corporation, Lenfest Communications, and an investment group led by African-American entrepreneur J. Bruce Llewellyn. It is the largest cable TV acquisition by an African-American.

1768 James Varick is born in Orange County, N.Y. Racism in New York City will lead Varick, a licensed clergyman, and 30 other African-Americans to leave the famous and predominantly white John Street Methodist Episcopal Church and establish the first African-American church in New York City. He will later become the founder and first bishop of the African Methodist Episcopal Zion Church.

1925 Drummer Max Roach is born in New Land, N.C. He will become an influential figure in the development of modern jazz, playing with Charlie Parker, Dizzy Gillespie, and Clifford Brown before forming his own groups in the 1950's. He will achieve wide acclaim for his superb musical innovation.

Julian Bond

1966 The Georgia House of Representatives refuses to seat African-American legislator Julian Bond, SNCC communications director, because of his opposition to U.S. involvement in the Vietnam War. He will be seated almost one year later, after a legal battle that will eventually be resolved by the U.S. Supreme Court.

11

12

1902 Acknowledging the increasing attention African-American athletes receive, the Baltimore *Afro-American* states, "Mr. [Joe] Gans gets more space in the white papers than all the respectable colored people in the state." Gans is the world lightweight boxing champion and first native African-American world title holder.

1961 Rioting erupts on the University of Georgia campus. African-American students Charlayne Hunter and Hamilton Holmes are suspended but will be reinstated by a federal court order. Hunter-Gault will become an Emmy award-winning journalist with *The MacNeil/Lehrer NewsHour*.

1985 Reuben V. Anderson is appointed a judge on the Mississippi Supreme Court. Anderson is the first African-American named to the court.

Charlayne Hunter-Gault

1890 Mordecai W. Johnson is born in Paris, Tenn. He will become the first African-American president of Howard University in 1926, a position he will hold for 34 years. He will also be a recipient of the NAACP's Spingarn Medal in 1929.

1959 Berry Gordy borrows $800 from a family loan fund to form Motown Records. The record company's first releases will appear on the Tamla label.

1965 Noted playwright Lorraine Hansberry dies of cancer in New York City at the age of 34 while her second play, *The Sign in Sidney Brustein's Window*, is playing on

Broadway. Her first and most famous work, *A Raisin in the Sun*, brought her wide acclaim on Broadway, earned her the New York Drama Critics Circle Award for best play, and became a motion picture starring Sidney Poitier, Ruby Dee, and Claudia McNeill.

1982 A commemorative stamp of Ralph Bunche is issued by the U.S. Postal Service as part of its Great Americans series.

13

14

_____
_____
_____
_____
_____
_____
_____
_____

1873 P.B.S. Pinchback steps down as the first African-American governor of Louisiana, a position he held for one month after replacing the impeached Governor H.C. Warmouth.

1913 Delta Sigma Theta sorority is founded by 22 undergraduates at Howard University. The sorority will grow to have 175,000 members in over 800 chapters in the U.S., West Germany, the Caribbean, Liberia, and the Republic of Korea.

1979 A commemorative stamp of Martin Luther King, Jr. is issued by the U.S. Postal Service as part of its Black Heritage USA commemorative series. The stamp of the slain civil rights leader is the second in the series.

L. Douglas Wilder

1990 Lawrence Douglas Wilder of Virginia is inaugurated as the first African-American to be elected governor in the U.S. Wilder won the election in Virginia by a mere 7,000 votes in a state once the heart of the Confederacy. Later in the year, he will receive the NAACP's Spingarn Medal for his lifetime achievements.

1916 Author John Oliver Killens is born in Macon, Ga. Among his works will be the novels _Youngblood_ and _And Then We Heard the Thunder_, biographies of Denmark Vesey, John Henry, and Aleksandr Pushkin, and the script for _Odds Against Tomorrow_, a 1959 movie starring Harry Belafonte.

1975 William T. Coleman is named Secretary of Transportation by President Gerald R. Ford. He is the second African-American to hold a Cabinet-level position.

1981 James Frank, president of Lincoln University in Jefferson City, Mo., is installed as the first African-American president of the National Collegiate Athletic Association.

William T. Coleman

1987 The National Urban League's report "State of Black America" blasts President Ronald Reagan's policies, stating, "Black Americans enter 1987 besieged by the resurgence of raw racism, persistent economic depression and the continued erosion of past gains."

Horace Pippin, *Two Roses,* 1940. Oil on canvas. Private collection.

15

16

Martin Luther King Jr.

Black Heritage USA 15c

1908 Alpha Kappa Alpha sorority is founded at Howard University in Washington, D.C. The culmination of efforts by Ethel Hedgeman and eight other undergraduates, it is the first Greek-letter organization for African-American women.

1929 Michael Luther King is born in Atlanta, Ga. Better known as Martin, a name he will formally adopt, King will become a Baptist minister,

world-renowned civil rights leader, and an advocate of non-violence. His efforts, beginning with the Montgomery bus boycott in 1955 and continuing for the next 13 years, will fundamentally change civil rights for African-Americans and earn him a number of honors and awards, including the Nobel Peace Prize (1964), Medal of Freedom, and Spingarn Medal (1957).

1968 Reporting the results of a *Jet* magazine poll, *The New York Times* article "Negro History Week Stirs Up Semantic Debate" indicates that 59% of those polled prefer the term Afro-American or black to Negro.

1970 Atlanta's Ebenezer Baptist Church, the nearby crypt containing the remains of Martin Luther King, Jr., and his boyhood home are dedicated as part of a memorial to be known as the Martin Luther King, Jr. Center for Nonviolent Change.

1865 General William T. Sherman issues Field Order No. 15, which sets aside parts of South Carolina and Florida for exclusive settlement by African-Americans, each family being given a maximum of 40 acres of land. Many will never see their land because President Andrew Johnson will reverse the policy implemented by the Freedman's Bureau.

1938 Benny Goodman leads a historic jazz concert at Carnegie Hall in New York City. Later considered one of the first "serious" jazz concerts, Goodman refused to perform without two African-American members of his band, Teddy Wilson on piano and Lionel Hampton on vibraphone. Hall officials relented and the integrated band performs to critical praise.

1941 The 99th Pursuit Squadron, an all-African-American unit, is formed and the Tuskegee Training Program is established. The 99th will fly more

than 500 missions and more than 3,700 sorties during one year of combat before being combined with the 332nd Fighter Group.

1978 NASA names Major Frederick D. Gregory, Major Guion Bluford, and Dr. Ronald McNair to its astronaut program.

Frederick D. Gregory

17

18

Muhammad Ali

Robert Weaver

1759 Paul Cuffe is born in Cuttyhunk, Mass. He will become a successful shipowner, philanthropist, and a force in the movement for African-Americans' repatriation to Africa.

1924 Jewel Plummer Cobb is born in Chicago, Ill. She will be a prominent cancer research biologist before becoming a professor and administrator at Connecticut College and Rutgers University and, in 1981, president of California State University, Fullerton, the first African-American woman to hold such a position in the CSU system.

1931 James Earl Jones is born in Arkabutla, Miss. He will become renowned as an actor, both on the stage and the screen, earning a Tony award in 1969 for his portrayal of boxing great Jack Johnson in *The Great White Hope* as well as acclaim for his Broadway roles in *A Lesson From Aloes*, *Fences*, and many others. Among his film and television credits will be the voice of Darth Vader in *Star Wars* and leading roles in *Paris* and *Gabriel's Fire*.

1942 Cassius Marcellus Clay, Jr. is born in Louisville, Ky. Early in his boxing career, Clay converts to Islam. As Muhammad Ali, he is one of the first African-American athletes to intermingle political and social consciousness with sports.

1949 Congressman William Dawson is elected chairman of the House Expenditure Committee. He is the first African-American to head a standing committee of Congress.

1966 Robert Weaver takes the oath of office as Secretary of the Department of Housing and Urban Development. Appointed by President Lyndon B. Johnson, Weaver becomes the first African-American to serve in a U.S. President's Cabinet.

1990 Washington, D.C., mayor Marion Barry is arrested for allegedly purchasing and using crack cocaine in a Washington, D.C., hotel room. The circumstances surrounding his arrest, trial, and conviction on one count of misdemeanor cocaine possession will be hotly debated by African-American and white citizens of the District and elsewhere.

WILLIAM H. JOHNSON, *Young Pastry Cook,* ca. 1928–1930. Oil on canvas. National Museum of American Art, Smithsonian Institution, gift of the Harmon Foundation.

19

20

_____
_____
_____
_____
_____
_____
_____
_____
_____

1854 Biddy Mason and her children are granted their freedom by the courts of Los Angeles County after three years in the state. Mason will become a major landowner in Los Angeles known for her philanthropy to the poor.

1887 Clementine Hunter is born in Natchitoches, La. She will become a painter in the 1930's after spending years working on the Melrose Plantation, a haven for many rural Southern artists. Her folk-art style will earn her the nickname "the Black Grandma Moses."

1959 In a letter to her mother shortly before the opening of her first play, *A Raisin in the Sun*, Lorraine Hansberry says, "Mama, it is a play that tells the truth about people Negroes and life and I think it will help a lot of people to understand how we are just as complicated as they are—and just as mixed up—but above all, that we have among our miserable and downtrodden ranks—people who are the very essence of human dignity. That is what, after all the laughter and tears, the play is supposed to say."

1983 In its "State of Black America" annual report, the National Urban League warns that the recession had disproportionately hurt African-Americans: "A major question facing the nation in 1983 is whether the inevitable restructuring of the American economy will include black people."

Hiram Rhoades Revels

1788 The first African Baptist Church is organized in Savannah, Ga., with Andrew Bryan ordained as its pastor.

1870 Hiram Rhoades Revels is chosen by the Mississippi legislature to fill the U.S. Senate seat of Confederate president Jefferson Davis. Although he will be challenged by the Senate, Revels will take his seat one month later, becoming the first African-American U.S. senator.

1895 Eva Jessye is born in Coffeyville, Kans. She will become an influential choral director, working in King Vidor's *Hallelujah* and the original production of George Gershwin's *Porgy and Bess*.

1977 Clifford Alexander, Jr. is sworn in as the first African-American Secretary of the Army.

1986 The inaugural issue of *American Visions* magazine hits newsstands nationwide. The magazine is dedicated to exposing its readers to African-American contributions to history, literature, music, and the arts.

21

22

1913 Fannie Muriel Jackson Coppin dies in Washington, D.C. She was a pioneering educator and missionary and one of the first African-American women to graduate from an American college (Oberlin, 1865).

1920 James Farmer, founder of the Congress of Racial Equality (CORE), is born in Marshall, Tex.

1938 Jack and Jill of America, Inc. is founded in Philadelphia, Pa., by Marion Turner Stubbs Thomas. Dedicated to providing educational, cultural, civic, and social programs for African-American youth, Jack and Jill will grow to have 180 chapters nationwide.

1964 Carl T. Rowan is named director of the U.S. Information Agency, the highest federal position ever held by an African-American. By virtue of his position, he also becomes the first African-American to sit on the National Security Council.

1990 Quincy Jones is awarded the French Legion of Honor for his contributions to music as a trumpeter, composer, arranger and record producer.

Carl T. Rowan

1906 Twenty-eight-year-old Meta Vaux Warrick's sculpture *Portraits from Mirrors* is exhibited at the 101st Annual Exhibition at the Pennsylvania Academy of the Fine Arts in Philadelphia, Pa. Although it is one of the first major American showings of her work, the young Warrick (later Fuller) has already studied sculpture with the legendary Auguste Rodin and had her work exhibited in Paris at S. Bing's Gallery Nouveau.

1935 Singer Sam Cooke is born in Chicago, Ill. Best known for his recordings "You Send Me" and "Twistin' the Night Away," Cooke will become one of the most popular singers of the 1960's.

Sam Cooke

1981 Samuel Pierce is named Secretary of Housing and Urban Development (HUD). One of the few African-Americans in the Reagan Administration, there will be high expectations for his potential to effect change, but Pierce's leadership will be severely questioned as scandal rocks his department in 1989. An estimated $2 billion will be lost due to fraud and mismanagement during Pierce's tenure.

23

24

1837 Amanda Berry Smith is born into slavery in Maryland. Unable to preach in the AME Church, which did not ordain women ministers, Smith will become an independent missionary and travel throughout the U.S. and three other continents.

1891 The first African-American hospital, Provident Hospital, in Chicago, Ill., is founded by Daniel Hale Williams, M.D. At the same time, he establishes the Provident Hospital School of Nursing because Emma Reynolds, an African-American, has been denied admission to every school of nursing in Chicago.

1945 As a result of pressure placed upon it by the National Association of Colored Nursing Graduates (NACGN) and others, the Army Nurse Corps drops its color bar and admits nurses without regard to race.

1964 The 24th Amendment, which abolishes the poll tax, is ratified. The poll tax had been used extensively in the South as a means of preventing African-Americans from voting.

1977 The first episode of *Roots*, adapted from *The New York Times* bestseller by Alex Haley, is aired on ABC. Over the next several nights, 130 million Americans will be transfixed before their televisions as the story of Kunta Kinte is told.

1989 In *City of Richmond v. J.A. Croson Co.*, the U.S. Supreme Court invalidates the city's minority set-aside program, a major setback for the concept's proponents.

Alex Haley

1985 Four-term Los Angeles mayor Tom Bradley receives the NAACP's Spingarn Medal for his long career as a public servant and for "demonstrating … that the American dream not only can be pursued but realized."

1988 Forty-eight African-American writers and literary critics sign a controversial statement that appears in *The New York Times Book Review* supporting author Toni Morrison and protesting her failure to win "the keystone honors of the National Book Award or the Pulitzer Prize."

Tom Bradley

1989 Reverend Barbara Harris's election as suffragan bishop is ratified by the Diocese of Massachusetts. Her election and consecration occur amid widespread controversy regarding the role of women bishops in the Episcopal Church.

25

1890 The National Afro-American League is founded at an organizing meeting in Chicago, Ill. Joseph C. Price is elected the first president of what will come to be considered a pioneering African-American protest organization.

1966 Constance Baker Motley becomes the first African-American woman to be appointed to a federal judgeship.

1972 Congresswoman Shirley Chisholm begins her campaign for President of the U.S. Although she will ultimately be unsuccessful, she will make known the concerns of African-Americans across the country.

1980 Black Entertainment Television, better known as BET, begins broadcasting from Washington, D.C. Robert L. Johnson, who established the company with a $15,000 personal loan, will make BET one

Robert L. Johnson

of the most successful cable television networks, with 25 million subscribers by its tenth anniversary and, in 1991, the first black-owned company to be listed on the New York Stock Exchange.

26

1863 The War Department authorizes the governor of Massachusetts to enlist Negro troops to fight in the Civil War. The 54th and 55th Volunteer Infantry are the result.

1928 Eartha Mae Kitt is born in North, S.C. She will start her career as a professional dancer with the Katherine Dunham Dance Troupe, which will take her to Paris, where she will tour as a nightclub singer. She will eventually return to the U.S. and roles on Broadway and in films.

1940 Sherian Grace Cadoria is born in Marksville, La. She will make her career in the Army, and in 1985, will be promoted to brigadier general, the highest-ranking African-American in the nation.

1944 Angela Yvonne Davis is born in Birmingham, Ala. Active in civil rights demonstrations and in SNCC, she will be fired twice from UCLA because of her Communist Party affiliation

Sherian Grace Cadoria

and she will successfully sue for reinstatement. A philosopher and author, she will flee the law after being implicated in the 1970 Soledad Brothers shooting. After 16 months in jail, she will be acquitted of all charges.

1958 Anita Baker is born in Toledo, Ohio. A singer of ballads and jazz-inspired R & B, her 1986 album *Rapture* will sell five million copies and earn her a 1987 Grammy. She will win two more in 1989.

1990 Elaine Weddington is named assistant general manager of the Boston Red Sox.

RICHMOND BARTHÉ, *Portrait of Rose McClendon,* 1933. Plaster. Permanent collection, Carl Van Vechten Gallery of Fine Arts, Fisk University of Nashville, Tennessee.

27

28

1869 Will Marion Cook, who will become a noted composer and conductor, is born. Studying the violin at age 13, at 15 Cook will win a scholarship to study at the Berlin Conservatory. Among other accomplishments, he will introduce syncopated ragtime to New York City theatergoers in his operetta *Clorinda*. Duke Ellington will call him the "master of all masters of our people."

1952 Ralph Ellison's powerful novel *Invisible Man* wins the National Book Award.

Ralph Ellison

1961 Leontyne Price makes her Metropolitan Opera House debut as Leonora in Verdi's *Il Trovatore*.

1972 Mahalia Jackson dies in Evergreen Park, Ill. Born in New Orleans, La., she began her singing career with the Salem Baptist Choir in Chicago, Ill. She achieved national fame with her recording of "Move on up a Little Higher," which sold over a million copies. Many considered her rich contralto voice the best in gospel music.

Mahalia Jackson

1901 Richmond Barthé is born in Bay Saint Louis, Miss. Educated at the Art Institute of Chicago, he will begin to attain critical acclaim as a sculptor at 26. His first commissions will be of Henry O. Tanner and Toussaint L'Ouverture. He will also become the first African-American commissioned to produce a bust for the NYU Hall of Fame (of Booker T. Washington).

1944 Matthew Henson is a recipient of a joint medal by Congress for his role as codiscoverer of the North Pole. It is the U.S. government's first official recognition of the explorer who accompanied Commander Robert Peary on his 1909 expedition.

1958 Roy Campanella is paralyzed from the chest down, ending his ten-year career with the Dodgers, where he had been named the National League's MVP three times.

1972 Scott Joplin's Opera *Treemonisha*, published 61 years earlier, has its world premiere with Robert Shaw and Katherine Dunham directing.

1986 The space shuttle *Challenger* explodes after lift-off at Cape Canaveral, Fla. One of the seven crew members killed is physicist Dr. Ronald McNair, the only African-American aboard.

Dr. Ronald McNair

29

30

1837 Aleksandr Sergeyevich Pushkin, a Russian of African ancestry who was considered the "Shakespeare of Russian Literature," is killed in a duel. Technically one-eighth African or an octoroon, Pushkin was by all accounts Negroid in his appearance. His verse novel *Eugene Onegin* and other works are considered classics of Russian literature and inspiration for later great Russian writers such as Gogol, Dostoyevski, and Tolstoy.

1926 Violette Neatley Anderson is the first African-American women admitted to practice before the U.S. Supreme Court.

1954 Oprah Winfrey is born in Kosciusko, Miss. She will become the first African-American woman to host a nationally syndicated talk show and will be nominated for an Academy Award for best supporting actress in 1985 for her role in *The Color Purple*. Following in the footsteps of Oscar Micheaux

Oprah Winfrey

and others, she will also form her own film and television production company, Harpo Studios, in Chicago, Ill.

1981 William R. "Cozy" Cole dies in Columbus, Ohio. A jazz drummer who played with Cab Calloway and Louis Armstrong, he was known as a versatile percussionist who played in big bands, comedy jazz groups, and Broadway musicals. In 1958, his recording of "Topsy" became the only drum solo to sell more than one million records.

1844 Richard Theodore Greener becomes the first African-American to graduate from Harvard University.

1858 William Wells Brown publishes the first drama by an African-American, *Leap to Freedom*. Brown is an escaped slave who will also become noted as an abolitionist and author of several early historical publications.

1927 The Harlem Globetrotters, considered by many the most popular basketball team in the world, is formed by Abe Saperstein. Originally called the Savoy Big Five after their home court, the Savoy Ballroom, in Chicago, Ill., the team's name will be changed to the Harlem Globetrotters.

1944 Sharon Pratt is born in Washington, D.C. In 1990, as Sharon Pratt Dixon, she will be elected the first woman mayor of Washington, D.C. Her defeat of incumbent Marion Barry coupled with her years of commu-

nity involvement and activism will raise the beleaguered city's hopes for positive change.

1945 Floyd Flake is born in Los Angeles, Calif. He will become a congressman from New York's 6th District.

1979 Franklin A. Thomas becomes the first African-American to head a major U.S. charitable foundation when he is named president of the Ford Foundation.

Franklin A. Thomas

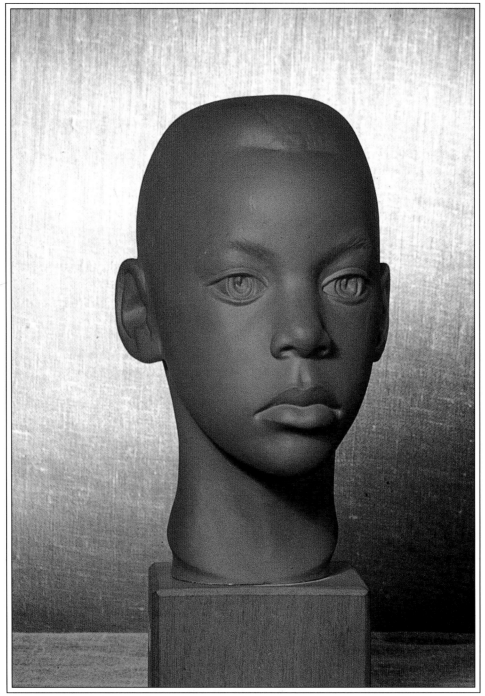

WILLIAM E. ARTIS, *Eddie,* ca. 1950. Terra-cotta. Hampton University Museum, Hampton, Virginia.

31

1

1919 Jackie Robinson, the first African-American to break racial barriers in major league baseball, is born in Cairo, Ga. He will start playing baseball in the Negro Leagues in preparation for a career as a phys ed coach. His major league baseball career with the Brooklyn Dodgers will begin in 1947 and he will play for nine years before leaving baseball to become a bank official, land developer, and director of programs to fight drug addiction. Among his honors will be the NAACP's Spingarn Medal in 1956.

1934 Etta Moten sings for President and Mrs. Franklin D. Roosevelt at a White House dinner for family and friends. Moten, a stage and screen star, sings songs from her role in the movie *Golddiggers of 1933* and *Swing Low Sweet Chariot*. It is the first time an African-American actress performs at the White House.

1963 James Baldwin's influential collection of essays *The Fire Next Time* is published.

1988 Washington Redskins quarterback Doug Williams is named Most Valuable Player for leading his team to a 42–10 win over the Denver Broncos in Super Bowl XXII. He is the first African-American quarterback to play in a Super Bowl game.

Jackie Robinson

1865 John Rock becomes the first African-American lawyer to practice before the U.S. Supreme Court.

1870 Jonathan Jasper Wright is elected to the South Carolina Supreme Court. He is the first African-American to hold a major judicial position.

1871 Jefferson Franklin Long, Republican congressman from Georgia, makes the first speech by an African-American on the floor of Congress.

1902 Langston Hughes is born in Joplin, Mo. He will be known as one of the most prolific American poets of the 20th century and a leading voice of the Harlem Renaissance. In addition to his poetry, Hughes will achieve success as an anthologist and juvenile author, will write plays and librettos, found theater groups, and be a widely read columnist and humorist. Among his honors will be the NAACP's Spingarn Medal (1960).

1960 A Greensboro, N.C., protest begins the sit-in movement when four African-American college students from North Carolina A&T College sit at a "whites-only" Woolworth's lunch counter and refuse to leave when denied service.

1978 The first stamp of the U.S. Postal Service's Black Heritage USA series honors Harriet Tubman, famed abolitionist and "conductor" on the Underground Railroad.

2

1914 William Ellisworth Artis is born in Washington, N.C. Educated at Syracuse University and a student of Augusta Savage, Artis's sculptures will exhibit a strong originality and a romantic, almost spiritual appeal. His works will be exhibited at Atlanta University, the Whitney Museum, the *Two Centuries of Black American Art* exhibit and collected by Fisk University, Hampton University, the North Carolina Museum of Art, and private collectors.

1938 Operatic baritone Simon Estes is born in Centerville, Iowa. He will be noted for his leading roles in Wagnerian operas and will sing at the opening of the 1972 Summer Olympic Games in Munich, Germany.

1948 President Harry S Truman sends a message to Congress pressing for civil rights legislation, including antilynching, fair employment practices, and anti-poll tax provisions.

1988 A commemorative stamp of James Weldon Johnson is issued by the U.S. Postal Service as part of its Black Heritage USA series.

Simon Estes

3

Blanche Kelso Bruce

1939 The Baltimore Museum of Art exhibit *Contemporary Negro Art* opens. The exhibit, which will run for 16 days, will feature works by Richmond Barthé, Aaron Douglas, Archibald Motley, Jr., and Jacob Lawrence's *Toussaint L'Ouverture* series.

1874 Blanche Kelso Bruce is elected to the U.S. Senate from Mississippi. He will be the first African-American senator to serve a full term and the first to preside over the Senate during a debate.

1948 Laura Wheeler Waring, portrait painter and illustrator, dies. Trained at the Pennsylvania Academy of the Fine Arts, she received the Harmon Award in 1927 for achievement in the fine arts and, with Betsey Graves Reyneau, completed a set of 24 renderings of their works titled *Portraits of Outstanding Americans of Negro Origins* for the Harmon Foundation in the 1940's.

1981 The Air Force Academy drops its ban on applicants with sickle-cell trait. The ban was considered by many a means of stigmatizing African-Americans.

1989 Former Saint Louis Cardinals first baseman Bill White is named president of the National League. He is the first African-American to head a major sports league.

4

5

1794 France abolishes slavery. The nation will have a lukewarm commitment to abolition and will, under Napoleon, reestablish slavery in 1802 along with the reinstitution of the "Code noir," prohibiting blacks, mulattoes and other people of color from entering French colonial territory or intermarrying with whites.

1913 Rosa Parks is born in Tuskegee, Ala. When the seamstress and NAACP member refuses to yield her seat to a white on a Montgomery bus in 1955, her actions will spark a 382-day boycott of the buses in Montgomery, halting business and services in the city and becoming the initial act of nonviolent disobedience of the American civil rights movement. She will be honored with the NAACP's Spingarn Medal for her heroism and later work with Detroit youth (1979) and be called the "Mother of the Civil Rights Movement."

1986 A stamp of Sojourner Truth is issued by the the U.S. Postal Service as part of its Black Heritage USA commemorative series. Truth was an abolitionist and a famous "conductor" on the Underground Railroad.

Sojourner Truth
22
Black Heritage USA

1934 Henry (Hank) Aaron is born in Mobile, Ala. After starting his major league baseball career with the Milwaukee Braves in 1954, he will distinguish himself as a home-run specialist and will break Babe Ruth's record in 1974.

1958 Clifton W. Wharton, Sr. becomes the first African-American to head a U.S. European embassy when he is confirmed as ambassador to Romania.

1968 Students in Orangeburg, S.C., try to end the discriminatory practices of a local bowling alley. Their confrontation with police and the National Guard, and the subsequent death of three students, creates widespread outrage among students across campuses in the South.

1969 Cinque Gallery is incorporated by African-American artists Romare Bearden, Ernest Crichlow, and Norman Lewis. Located in the SoHo district of

Henry "Hank" Aaron

New York City, the nonprofit gallery's mission is to assist in the growth and development of minority artists and to end the cycle of exclusion of their work from the mainstream artistic community.

1972 Robert Lewis Douglas, founder and coach of the Rens, is inducted into the Basketball Hall of Fame.

6

7

Melvin Tolson

1820 The first organized emigration to Africa begins when 86 free African-Americans leave New York Harbor aboard the *Mayflower of Liberia.* They are bound for the British colony of Sierra Leone, which welcomes free African-Americans and fugitive slaves.

1867 The Peabody Fund is established to provide monies for construction, endowments, scholarships, teacher and industrial education for newly freed slaves.

1898 Melvin B. Tolson, author and educator, is born in Moberly, Mo. Educated at Fisk, Lincoln, and Columbia universities, his first volume of poetry, *Rendezvous with America,* will be published in 1944. He will be best known for *Libretto for the Republic of Liberia,* published in 1953.

1931 The Harlem Experimental Theatre Group performs its first plays at St. Philips Parish House. The group's advisory board includes famed actress Rose McClendon, author Jesse Fauset, and Grace Nail.

1961 The "jail-in" movement starts in Rock Hill, S.C., when arrested students demand jail rather than fines.

Carter G. Woodson

Black Heritage USA 20c

1926 The first Negro History Week begins. Originated by Carter G. Woodson and the Association for the Study of Negro Life and History, the Sunday kickoff celebration involves ministers, teachers, professionals, and business people in highlighting the "achievements of the Negro." The concept will win increasing popularity and be expanded in 1976 to an entire month of local and national events exploring African-American culture.

1974 Grenada achieves its independence from Great Britain.

Once a year we go through the charade of February being 'Black History Month.' Black History Month needs to be a 12-MONTH THING. When we all learn about our history, about how much we've accomplished while being handicapped with RACISM, it can only inspire us to greater heights, knowing we're on the giant shoulders of our ANCESTORS.
—Spike Lee

Laura Wheeler Waring, *Still Life,* 1928. Oil on canvas. The Evans-Tibbs Collection, Washington, D.C.

8

_____
_____
_____
_____
_____
_____
_____
_____

9

_____
_____
_____
_____
_____
_____

1894 Congress repeals the Enforcement Act, which makes it easier for some states to disenfranchise African-American voters.

1925 Marcus Garvey is sent to federal prison in Atlanta for mail fraud in connection with the sale of stock in his Black Star Line. His prosecution was vigorously advocated by several prominent African-American leaders, including Robert Sengstacke Abbott and others.

1944 Harry S. McAlpin of the *Daily World* in Atlanta, Ga., is the first African-American accredited to attend White House press conferences.

1968 Gary Coleman is born in Zion, Ohio. He will become a child actor in the television series *Diff'rent Strokes* from 1978 to 1986.

1906 Poet and author Paul Laurence Dunbar dies in Dayton, Ohio, at the age of 34. Never fully recovering from a bout of pneumonia in 1899, he nonetheless produced three novels (including *The Sport of the Gods*), three books of verse, three collections of short stories, two unpublished plays, and lyric pieces set to music by Will Marion Cook.

1944 Alice Walker is born in Eatonton, Ga. Best known for *The Color Purple,* which will win the American Book Award and the Pulitzer Prize, she will also write a variety of other critically praised and award-winning works including poetry and children's books and edit a book on Zora Neale Hurston, whom she will credit as her role model.

Meanwhile, John Rozelle is born in Saint Louis, Mo. He will become an artist and professor at the Art Institute of Chicago. His work reflects his self-identification as an

Gary Franks

"African-American sentinel," or visual historian, guide, and advocate of contemporary African-American culture.

1953 Gary Franks is born in Waterbury, Conn. In 1990, he will be elected to Congress from Connecticut's 5th District and become the first African-American Republican congressman since Oscar De Priest left office in 1934.

10

11

1927 Leontyne Price, who will be acclaimed as one of the world's greatest operatic talents, is born in Laurel, Miss. She will amass many operatic firsts, being the first African-American to sing opera on network TV and the first to receive the Presidential Medal of Freedom. Among her honors will be the NAACP's Spingarn Medal, three Emmys, and Kennedy Center Honors.

1939 Roberta Flack is born in Asheville, N.C. She will begin her professional singing career in Washington, D.C., win Grammys for "The First Time Ever I Saw Your Face," "Where Is the Love," and "Killing Me Softly with His Song."

1942 Mary Lovelace O'Neal is born in Jackson, Miss. Educated at Howard and Columbia universities, she will become a professor of fine arts and painter who will exhibit her work in museums in the U.S., Morocco, and Chile.

1943 Eta Phi Beta, the national business and professional sorority, is incorporated in Detroit, Mich. It will have chapters throughout the U.S. and number among its members civil rights activist Daisy Bates and artist Margaret T. Burroughs.

1989 Ronald H. Brown, who had served as Jesse Jackson's campaign manager, becomes chairman of the Democratic National Committee, the first African-American to hold the position in either party.

1961 Robert Weaver becomes the highest-ranking African-American in the federal government as he is sworn in as administrator of the Housing and Home Finance Agency.

1990 Nelson Mandela is released from prison after being held for nearly 27 years without trial by the South African government. The founder and unofficial leader of the African National Congress, Mandela became, during his imprisonment, a symbol for the struggle of black South Africans to overcome apartheid.

Meanwhile, James "Buster" Douglas defeats Mike Tyson in a stunning upset in Tokyo to win the heavyweight boxing championship. Almost two years later to the day, Tyson will be convicted of rape and two related charges filed by a Miss Black America contestant in Indianapolis, Ind.

Robert Weaver

ELLIS WILSON, *Chinese Lily,* ca. 1934. Oil on canvas. DuSable Museum of African-American History, Chicago, Illinois.

12

13

1793 The first fugitive slave law is passed by Congress, which makes it a crime to hide or protect a runaway slave.

1900 For a Lincoln birthday celebration, James Weldon Johnson writes the lyrics for "Lift Every Voice and Sing." With music by his brother, J. Rosamond, the song is first sung by 500 children in Jacksonville, Fla. It will become known as the "Negro National Anthem."

1909 W.E.B. Du Bois and others, including whites, meet in Springfield, Ill., and advocate a militant civil rights organization to combat the growing violence against African-Americans. The meeting becomes the catalyst for the founding of the National Association for the Advancement of Colored People.

1951 Sergeant Cornelius H. Charlton is posthumously awarded the Congressional Medal of Honor for bravery during the Korean War.

James W. Johnson

1983 Eubie Blake dies at the age of 100 in New York City. Blake was one of the last ragtime pianists and composers whose most famous songs included "I'm Just Wild About Harry." With Noble Sissle, Blake was the composer of the first all-African-American Broadway musical, *Shuffle Along,* which opened on Broadway in 1921.

1818 Absalom Jones, the first African-American Episcopal priest ordained in the U.S., dies in Philadelphia, Pa. He was an instrumental force in the development of the early African-American church and benevolent society movements.

1892 The first African-American performers, the World's Fair Colored Opera Company, appear at New York City's Carnegie Hall less than one year after the hall's opening. In the company is concert singer Matilda Sissieretta Jones, who will have her solo debut at Carnegie Hall two years later.

1907 Wendell P. Dabney establishes *The Union.* The Cincinnati, Ohio, paper's motto is "For no people can become great without being united, for in union there is strength."

1957 The Southern Leadership Conference is founded at a meeting of ministers in New Orleans, La. Martin Luther King, Jr. is elected its first president. Later in the year its name will be changed to the Southern Christian Leadership Conference.

Wendell P. Dabney

14

15

1760 Richard Allen, founder and first bishop of the AME Church, is born into slavery in Philadelphia, Pa.

1817 The birth of Frederick Douglass in Tuckahoe, Md., is attributed to this date. He will state, "I have no accurate knowledge of my age, never having seen any authentic record containing it … and it is the wish of most masters within my knowledge to keep their slaves thus ignorant."

1946 Gregory Hines is born in New York City. A child tap-dancing star in the group Hines, Hines, and Dad, Hines will lead a new generation of tap dancers that will benefit from the advice and teaching of such tap legends as Henry Le Tang, "Honi" Coles, Sandman Sims, the Nicholas Brothers, and Sammy Davis, Jr. Hines will also become a successful actor in movies including *White Knights, Tap,* and *A Rage in Harlem.*

FREDERICK DOUGLASS
25¢ U.S. POSTAGE

1978 Maxima Corporation, a computer systems and management company, is incorporated. Headquartered in Lanham, Md., it will become one of the largest African-American-owned companies and earn its founder, chairman and CEO, Joshua I. Smith, chairmanship of the U.S. Commission on Minority Business Development.

1964 Louis Armstrong's "Hello Dolly," a song the world-renowned trumpeter recorded and almost forgot, becomes the number-one record on Billboard's Top 40 charts, replacing The Beatles' "I Want to Hold Your Hand." It is Armstrong's first and only number-one record.

1968 Henry Lewis becomes the first African-American to lead a symphony orchestra in the U.S. when he is named director of the New Jersey Symphony.

1969 Noted historian John Henrik Clarke, speaking before the Jewish Currents Conference in New York City, says, "You cannot subjugate a man and recognize his humanity, his history… so systematically you must take this away from him. You begin by telling lies about the man's role in history."

1992 At memorial services attended by over 1,600 in Memphis, Tenn., author Alex Haley (*Roots, Autobiography of Malcolm X*) is eulogized by his wife, who says, "Thank you, Alex, you have helped us know who we truly are."

Louis Armstrong

16

17

1923 Bessie Smith makes her first recording for Columbia Records. The record, "Down Hearted Blues," written by Alberta Hunter and Lovie Austin, will sell an incredible 800,000 copies and be Columbia's first popular hit.

1951 The New York City Council passes a bill prohibiting discrimination in city-assisted housing.

1972 Wilt Chamberlain scores his 30,000th point in a basketball game between the Los Angeles Lakers and the Phoenix Suns. He is the first player in the NBA to score 30,000 points.

1918 Charles Hayes is born in Cairo, Ill. He will be elected to the House of Representatives succeeding Harold Washington in 1983.

1936 Jim Brown is born in Saint Simons, Ga. He will be considered one of the greatest offensive backs in the history of football, establishing records while with the Cleveland Browns for most yards gained and most touchdowns. Brown will also develop a film career, establish the Negro Industrial and Economic Union, and work with African-American youth.

1938 Mary Frances Berry is born in Nashville, Tenn. She will be an influential force in education and civil rights, become the first woman of any race to serve as chancellor of a major research university

(University of Colorado in 1976), and a member of the U.S. Commission on Civil Rights.

1942 Huey P. Newton, a co-founder and minister of defense for the Black Panther Party, is born in Monroe, La.

1963 Michael Jeffrey Jordan, who will be a star basketball player for the University of North Carolina, the 1984 Olympic gold medal team and the Chicago Bulls, is born in Brooklyn, N.Y. Jordan's phenomenal style and scoring ability will earn him universal acclaim and selection on six all-star NBA teams and twice the NBA's Most Valuable Player.

Bessie Smith

Jim Brown

18

19

Toni Morrison

1867 Augusta Institute, later Morehouse College, is founded in Atlanta, Ga.

1894 Paul Revere Williams is born in Los Angeles, Calif. He will become one of the most famous African-American architects, designer of private residences in Los Angeles, the Hollywood YMCA, the Beverly

Regent Hotel, UCLA's Botany Building and many others. Among his many awards will be the NAACP's Spingarn Medal.

1931 Toni Morrison is born in Lorain, Ohio. She will become one of the most celebrated modern novelists of the 20th century, winning the National Book Critics Award in 1978 for *Song of Solomon* and the Pulitzer Prize for Fiction in 1988 for *Beloved*.

1973 Palmer Hayden dies in New York City. One of the principal artists of the Harlem Renaissance who, like Henry O. Tanner and others, studied in Paris, his most enduring work often depicted everyday scenes of African-American life.

1919 The first Pan-African Congress, organized by W.E.B. Du Bois, opens in Paris. Fifty-seven delegates from 16 countries and colonies will meet for three days and declare: "The natives of Africa must be

allowed to participate in the government as fast as their development permits."

1940 William "Smokey" Robinson is born. As part of the Motown group The Miracles and in his solo career, Robinson will be an enduring R & B and pop performer.

1987 Rioting erupts in Tampa, Fla., after a young African-American man dies from a police chokehold.

1992 John Singleton is nominated for two Academy Awards for best director and best screenplay for his first film, *Boyz N the Hood*. Singleton is the first African-American director ever to be nominated for the Academy Award.

Smokey Robinson

PALMER HAYDEN, *Fetiche et Fleurs,* 1932–1933. Oil on canvas. From the collection of the Museum of African-American Art, Los Angeles, California. Gift of Miriam A. Hayden.

20

21

1927 Sidney Poitier is born in Miami, Fla. He will become one of the modern movies' leading men, making his screen debut in 1950 and earning praise in such films as *Cry the Beloved Country, Blackboard Jungle, Porgy and Bess, A Raisin in the Sun, To Sir With Love, Heat of the Night,* and *Guess Who's Coming to Dinner.* His 1965 role in *Lilies of the Field* will earn him an Oscar, the first for an African-American in a starring role.

1929 Writer Wallace Thurman's play *Harlem* opens in New York City. It is the first successful play by an African-American playwright.

1937 Nancy Wilson is born in Chillicothe, Ohio. She will become a well-known jazz

and pop singer, singing with Cannonball Adderly, George Shearing, Art Farmer and Chick Corea, among others. She will make more than 50 albums, including *With My Lover Beside Me,* featuring the lyrics of Johnny Mercer and the music of Barry Manilow.

1991 African-Americans win eight Grammys including Mariah Carey for best new artist and female pop vocal, Anita Baker for female R & B vocal, Luther Vandross for male R & B vocal, Living Colour for best hard rock performance, Hammer for best rap solo and best R & B song for "U Can't Touch This," and Chaka Khan and Ray Charles for best R & B vocal by a duo or group.

Nancy Wilson

1933 Nina Simone is born in Tryon, N.C. She will begin her entertaining career in 1954 and bolstered by critical praise for her 1959 recording of "I Loves You, Porgy," she will tour in the U.S. and Europe during the 1960's and early 1970's. Returning to the concert stage and recording studio in 1977, she will be called the "High Priestess of Soul."

1936 Barbara Jordan is born in Houston, Tex. The first African-American state senator in the Texas legislature since 1883 and a three-term congresswoman, she will play a key role in the 1974 Watergate hearings. In 1976, she will be the first woman and first African-American to make a keynote speech before the Democratic National Convention.

1940 John Lewis is born in Troy, Ala. He will become founder and chairman of SNCC, organizer of the Selma-to-Montgomery March in 1965, executive director of the Voter

Barbara Jordan

Education Project, and congressman from Georgia's 5th District. Lewis's power will continue to be felt when he is named Democratic deputy whip by Speaker of the House Thomas S. Foley in 1991.

1965 Malcolm X is assassinated at the Audubon Ballroom in Harlem. One of the most charismatic leaders of the civil rights and black power movements, he was best known for his doctrine of self-determination for African-American people, including their right to fight for their rights and protect themselves in a hostile America by "whatever means necessary."

22

23

1841 Grafton Tyler Brown is born in Harrisburg, Pa. A lithographer and painter, he will be considered to be one of the first African-American artists in California. His paintings will be collected by the Oakland (California) Museum of Art, Washington State Museum, and private individuals.

1888 Horace Pippin is born in West Chester, Pa. His right arm crippled in World War I (where he earned a Purple Heart), Pippin will paint holding the wrist of his practically useless right arm in his left fist. The self-taught artist will win wide acclaim for the primitive style and strong emotional content of his work.

1938 Ishmael Reed is born in Chattanooga, Tenn. He will become a poet (nominated for the National Book Award for *Conjure*), novelist (*Yellow Back Radio Broke Down, Mumbo Jumbo, Flight to Canada*), and anthologist of the well-received

19 Necromancers from Now and *The Yardbird Reader, Volume I.*

1950 Julius Erving is born in Roosevelt, N.Y. He will become a star basketball player, first for the ABA's Virginia Squires and later for the NBA's Philadelphia 76ers.

Julius Erving

1868 William Edward Burghardt (W.E.B.) Du Bois is born in Great Barrington, Mass. He will become one of the greatest men of letters of his time, serving as an editor, teacher, political theorist, and novelist. His accomplishments will include founding and editing *Crisis* magazine, writing the influential *Souls of Black Folk,* being one of the founding fathers of the NAACP, and being the first African-American to become a member of the National Institute of Arts and Letters.

1942 Don Lee (Haki Mahubuti) is born. He will become a major African-American literary critic, author of nonfiction and poetry, and founder of the influential Third World Press.

1979 Frank E. Peterson is named the first African-American general in the Marine Corps.

Comer Cottrell

1990 Comer J. Cottrell, President of Pro-Line Corporation, pays $1.5 million for the Bishop College campus, traditionally an African-American college, in a bankruptcy auction. Cottrell's actions result in the relocation of Paul Quinn College in Waco, another African-American campus, to the Dallas site.

GRAFTON TYLER BROWN, *Mt. Tacoma at Sunset from Lake Washington, W.T.,* 1884. Oil on canvas. Courtesy Washington State Capitol Museum, Olympia, Washington.

24

25

1811 Daniel A. Payne, educator, clergyman, bishop, historian of the AME Church, and the first African-American to become a college president, is born in Charleston, S.C.

1842 James Forten, Sr. dies in Philadelphia, Pa. A businessman who amassed a fortune as a sailmaker, Forten was one of the most influential abolitionists of the first half of the 19th century and chairman of the first Negro Convention.

1980 Willie Davenport and Jeff Gadley, the first African-Americans to represent the U.S. in the Winter Olympics, place 12th in the four-man bobsled competition. Davenport had been a medal winner in the 1968 and 1976 Summer Games.

1982 Quincy Jones wins five Grammys for *The Dude,* including producer of the year.

Quincy Jones

1992 Edward Perkins is nominated UN ambassador by President George Bush. Perkins had formerly served as director-general of the US Foreign Service and ambassador to the Republic of South Africa.

1964 Muhammad Ali, considered by many the greatest heavyweight champion of all time, wins his first world heavyweight championship title by defeating Sonny Liston in Miami.

1978 Daniel "Chappie" James, Jr. dies at 58 in Colorado Springs, Colo. James was an early graduate of the Tuskegee Institute Flying School and flew more than 100 missions during the Korean War. He was the first African-American to achieve the rank of four-star general.

1980 Robert E. Hayden, African-American poet and former poetry consultant to the Library of Congress, dies in Ann Arbor, Mich. Hayden's most notable works include *Words in Mourning Time* and *Angle of Ascent: New and Selected Poems.*

1991 Adrienne Mitchell becomes the first African-American woman to die in combat in the Persian Gulf War when she is killed in her military barracks in Dharan, Saudi Arabia.

1992 Natalie Cole, Patti LaBelle, Lisa Fischer, Luther Vandross, B.B. King, Boyz II Men, and James Brown, among others, win Grammy awards in ceremonies hosted by Whoopi Goldberg.

Robert Hayden

26

_____
_____
_____
_____
_____
_____
_____
_____

1844 James Edward O'Hara, two-term congressman from North Carolina, is born in New York City.

1928 Antoine "Fats" Domino is born in New Orleans, La. He will be a pioneering R & B pianist whose hits will include "Ain't That A Shame" and "Blueberry Hill."

1930 *The Green Pastures* opens on Broadway at the Mansfield Theater with Richard B. Harrison as "De Lawd."

1946 A race riot in Columbia, Tenn., results in two deaths and ten injuries.

1964 Boxer Cassius Clay converts to Islam, adopting the name Muhammad Ali, saying, "I believe in the religion of Islam … I believe in Allah and peace…."

1966 Andrew Brimmer becomes the first African-American governor of the Federal Reserve Board when he is appointed by President Lyndon B. Johnson.

Andrew Brimmer

27

_____
_____
_____
_____
_____
_____
_____
_____

Debi Thomas

1872 Charlotte Ray graduates from Howard Law School. She is the first African-American woman lawyer in the U.S.

1902 Marian Anderson is born in Philadelphia, Pa. She will become the first modern African-American to win international renown as an opera singer and will be considered one of the great operatic voices of the century. Singing at a time of great social upheaval for African-Americans, Anderson's professional career will contain many operatic and civil rights milestones and recognition, including Kennedy Center Honors in 1978.

1942 Charlayne Hunter is born in Due West, S.C. One of the first students to integrate the University of Georgia, Charlayne Hunter-Gault will become a print and broadcast journalist and win two Emmy awards for her work on public TV's *The MacNeil/Lehrer NewsHour.*

1988 Debi Thomas, a world-class figure skater, wins a bronze medal in the Winter Olympic Games in Calgary. She is the first African-American ever to win a medal in the Winter Games.

28

29

Leap Year

John Sengstacke

1776 George Washington, in his letter of acknowledgment to Phillis Wheatley for a poem she wrote for his birthday, says, "I thank you most sincerely for … the elegant line you enclosed … the style and manner exhibit a striking proof of your poetic talents."

1942 Riots against African-Americans occur in Detroit at the Sojourner Truth Homes.

1977 Eddie "Rochester" Anderson dies. Born in Oakland, Calif., to a theatrical family, Anderson's guest appearance on a 1937 Jack Benny Easter show grew to be a 30-year career on the popular radio, and later television, program.

1991 *The Content of our Character*, the controversial book on affirmative action and race relations by Shelby Steele, wins the National Book Critics Circle Award.

Eddie "Rochester" Anderson

1892 Augusta Savage is born in Green Springs, Fla. She will become a sculptor, teacher, and one of the most influential forces among Harlem Renaissance artists.

1940 Robert Sengstacke Abbott, newspaper editor and publisher of the *Chicago Defender,* dies in Chicago. His newspaper became a bold voice for African-Americans in the North, advocating during the wave of lynchings after World War I the slogan "if you must die, take at least one with you," later simplified to "an eye for an eye." Abbott dies as his nephew, John Sengstacke, is establishing the National Newspaper Publishers Association in Washington, D.C.

Meanwhile, in Hollywood, Hattie McDaniel receives an Academy Award for best supporting Actress for her role in *Gone With the Wind.* She is the first African-American to win an Oscar. Often criticized for her portrayal of maids, she will say, "It's much better to play a maid than to be one. The only choice permitted me is either to be a servant $7.00 a week or portray one for $700.00 a week."

1968 The National Advisory Commission on Civil Disorders, convened by President Lyndon B. Johnson after riots occur in major cities throughout the U.S., issues its report. In it, the so-called Kerner Commission concludes that white racism is one of the fundamental causes of riots in the U.S.

1

2

1780 Pennsylvania becomes the first state to abolish slavery.

1864 Rebecca Lee graduates from the New England Female Medical College. She, along with Rebecca Cole and Susan McKinney, is one of the first African-American female physicians.

1875 The Civil Rights Bill is passed by Congress. The bill, which gives African-Americans equal rights in inns, theaters, public transportation, and other public amusements, will be overturned by the Supreme Court in 1883.

1914 Ralph Waldo Ellison, who will become the author of *Invisible Man* (winner of the 1952 National Book Award), is born in Oklahoma City, Okla.

1927 Harry Belafonte is born in New York City. He will become a successful folk singer, actor, and winner of the first Emmy awarded to an African-American. His commitment to civil and human rights will lead him to march with Martin Luther King, Jr. in Montgomery, Selma, and Washington, D.C. Among his achievements will be Kennedy Center Honors in 1989.

Harry Belafonte

1867 Howard University is chartered by Congress in Washington, D.C.

1919 Claude A. Barnett establishes the Associated Negro Press (ANP), the first national news service for African-American newspapers. The goal of the ANP is to provide national news releases to African-American publishers. The ANP will operate for the next 48 years and have, at one time, 95% of all African-American newspapers as subscribers.

1921 Harry Pace establishes Pace Phonograph Corporation to produce records on the Black Swan label. It is the first African-American-owned and -operated record company and will record blues, jazz, spirituals, and operatic arias.

1962 Philadelphia 76er Wilt Chamberlain scores 100 points in an NBA game against the New York Knicks. It is a feat Chamberlain will repeat but

Claude Barnett

one which will never be equalled by another NBA player.

1986 Sidney Barthelemy is elected mayor of New Orleans, La., succeeding Ernest Morial as the second African-American mayor of the city.

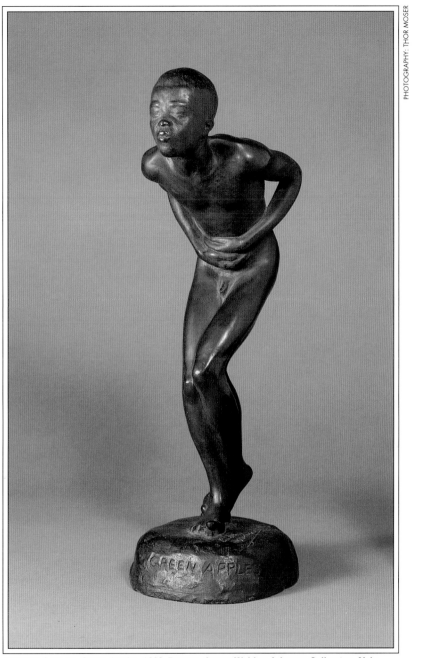

AUGUSTA SAVAGE, *Green Apples,* 1928. Bronze. James Weldon Johnson Collection. Yale University Collection of American Literature, Beinecke Rare Book and Manuscript Library, New Haven, Connecticut.

3

4

1820 The Missouri Compromise becomes law in an attempt to resolve the conflict between pro- and antislavery forces. In the final law, Missouri joins the Union as a slave state while Maine joins as a free one.

1821 Thomas L. Jennings receives a patent for an invention to dry scour clothes. It is the earliest known patent granted to an African-American.

1865 Congress establishes the Bureau of Refugees, Freedmen, and Abandoned Lands, commonly known as the Freedman's Bureau, to provide health and education to newly freed slaves displaced by the Civil War.

1896 The South Carolina legislature passes a measure creating the Colored Normal Industrial, Agricultural and Mechanical College (later South Carolina State) in Orangeburg.

1962 Jacqueline Joyner is born in East Saint Louis, Ill. Joyner-Kersee becomes an

Jackie Joyner-Kersee

Olympic champion, winning two medals (silver in 1984 and gold in 1988) in the heptathlon and another gold in the long jump at the 1988 Games in Seoul, South Korea.

1988 Juanita Kidd Stout becomes the first African-American woman to serve on a state supreme court when she is sworn in as an associate justice of the Supreme Court of Pennsylvania.

1897 Willie Covan is born in Atlanta, Ga. He will become one of the earliest successful tap dancers, appearing in the original production of *Shuffle Along* as well as with the Four Covans.

1922 Theater legend Bert Williams dies at 46 in New York City. He was considered the foremost African-American vaudeville performer, teaming first with George Walker in 1895, most notably in *In Dahomey,* and later as a soloist with the Ziegfeld Follies.

1932 Miriam Zensi Makeba is born in Prospect Township, South Africa. Although exiled from her homeland, Makeba will become an internationally known singer and critic of apartheid.

1968 In New York, Joe Frazier wins the heavyweight boxing title when he defeats Manuel Ramos by a technical knockout in the second round.

Miriam Makeba

5

6

1770 Crispus Attucks becomes the first African-American martyr in the American Colonies when he is killed during the Boston Massacre.

1897 The American Negro Academy is founded by Alexander Crummel. The purpose of the organization is the promotion of literature, science, art, the fostering of higher education, and the defense of the Negro.

1920 Leontine Turpeau Current Kelly is born in Washington, D.C. In 1984, she will become the first African-American woman to be named a bishop of a major religious organization, the United Methodist Church.

1985 The Mary McLeod Bethune commemorative stamp is issued by the U.S. Postal Service as the eighth stamp in its Black Heritage USA series.

Mary McLeod Bethune

Black Heritage USA 22

1857 The U.S. Supreme Court rules against citizenship for African-Americans in the Dred Scott decision. The Court rules that Dred Scott, a slave, cannot sue for his freedom in a free state because he is property and, as such, "has no rights a white man has to respect."

1901 Virginia State University in Petersburg, Va., is founded.

1923 Charles Ethan Porter dies in Rockville, Conn. A student of the National Academy of Design in New York City, the first African-American artist in the U.S. to graduate from a four-year school of art, and member of the Connecticut Academy of Fine Arts, Porter did not receive the recognition that contemporaries Edward Bannister and Henry Ossawa Tanner won. He will be best known for the paintings *Still Life (Crock With Onions), Strawberries,* and *Daisies,* but there will not be a major retrospective of his work until 1987.

1957 Ghana becomes the first African nation to achieve freedom from colonial rule when the Ashanti, Northern Protectorates, the Gold Coast and British Togoland declare their independence. The celebration ceremonies are attended by a number of American dignitaries, including African-American leaders Ralph Bunche, A. Philip Randolph, Adam Clayton Powell, Jr., Martin Luther King, Jr., and Coretta Scott King.

Dred Scott

Hale Aspacio Woodruff, *Caprice,* 1962. Oil on canvas. The Evans-Tibbs Collection, Washington, D.C.

7

8

1917 Janet Collins is born in New Orleans, La. She will become a prima ballerina and the first African-American to perform on the stage of the Metropolitan Opera House in New York City.

1927 In *Nixon v. Hearn*, the U.S. Supreme Court strikes down a Texas law prohibiting African-Americans from voting in a "white" primary.

1942 The first five cadets graduate from the Tuskegee Flying School: Captain Benjamin O. Davis, Jr. and Second Lieutenants Mac Ross, Charles DeBow, L.R. Curtis, and George S. Roberts. They will become part of the famous 99th Pursuit Squadron.

1945 Photographer Anthony Bonair is born in Trinidad. A photographer since the early 1970's, Bonair's work explores dance, Carnival, and the streets as well as new directions utilizing multiple-exposure techniques.

99th Pursuit Squadron

1985 The record "We Are the World" is released as a single. The song, whose proceeds benefit African famine relief efforts, is written by Lionel Richie and Michael Jackson and produced by Quincy Jones, with the singing participants organized by Jones, Harry Belafonte, and Ken Kragen.

1825 Alexander Thomas Augusta is born free in Norfolk, Va. A surgeon and practicing physician, he will become the first African-American faculty member of an American medical school, Howard University.

1876 The U.S. Senate refuses to seat P.B.S. Pinchback of Louisiana because of alleged election irregularities.

1945 Phyllis Mae Daley, a graduate of Lincoln School for Nurses in New York, receives her commission as an ensign in the Navy Nurse Corps. She is the first of four African-American Navy nurses (including Helen Turner, Ella Lucille Stimley, and Edith De Voe) to serve in active duty in World War II.

1971 Joe Frazier defeats Muhammad Ali in a heavyweight boxing championship billed as the "fight of the century."

1991 *New Jack City*, a film directed by Mario Van Peebles, actor and son of director Melvin Van Peebles, premieres. Produced by African-Americans George Jackson and Doug McHenry, the film, which tells the violent story of the rise and fall of a drug lord played by Wesley Snipes, will suffer from widespread violence among moviegoers.

Alexander T. Augusta

9

1841 Joseph Cinque and 37 African slaves who revolted on the ship *Amistad* are ordered freed by the U.S. Supreme Court and returned to Africa after successfully appealing their mutiny conviction on grounds that they were kidnaped by outlawed slave traders. Their defense attorney is John Quincy Adams, former President of the U.S. and a Massachusetts senator.

1871 Oscar De Priest, who will be the first congressman elected from a Northern state, is born in Florence, Ala. He will represent Illinois and be an active advocate for pensions for African-American ex-slaves, lynching prevention, and civil rights improvements.

1891 North Carolina Agricultural & Technical State University is founded in Greensboro.

1914 The new Southern University campus opens near Baton Rouge, La., with nine teachers and 47 students.

Joseph Cinque

1953 Larry Doby signs a contract with the Cleveland Indians and becomes the first African-American to play in baseball's American League. Doby will later become baseball's second African-American manager when he signs with the Chicago White Sox in 1978.

10

1850 Hallie Quinn Brown is born in Pittsburgh, Pa. She will become the author of *Homespun Heroines and Other Women of Distinction*, a 1926 collection of biographical sketches of notable African-American women.

1913 Harriet Tubman dies in Auburn, N.Y. An escaped slave, Tubman was known to the Underground Railroad as "Black Moses" for her heroic trips south to free hundreds of slaves. Later in her life she served as a scout, spy, cook, and nurse during the Civil War.

1969 James Earl Ray pleads guilty in the first degree to the murder of Martin L. King, Jr. and will be sentenced to 99 years in prison. The House Select Committee on Assassinations will later state that although it believes Ray shot King, Ray was part of a larger conspiracy.

Hallie Q. Brown

11

12

1884 William Edward Scott is born in Indianapolis, Ind. He will study with Henry O. Tanner at the Art Institute of Chicago and become best known for his portrait studies of Haitians, rural life, and landscapes.

1926 Ralph David Abernathy is born in Linden, Ala. He will become a famed minister, civil rights advocate, and confidant of Martin L. King, Jr. After King's assassination, he will become the president of the Southern Christian Leadership Conference and write an autobiography that will attract widespread criticism for his comments on King's alleged womanizing.

1931 *Conjure Man Dies*, a play by Rudolph Fisher, premieres on Broadway at the Lafayette Theatre. Fisher, who had died over a year before the play's premiere, had adapted the play from his 1932 short story *The Conjure-Man Dies: A Mystery Tale of Dark Harlem*, considered the first detective fiction by an African-American.

Lorraine Hansberry

1950 Bobby McFerrin is born in New York City. He will be known for his versatile and innovative a cappella jazz vocals and for his hit song "Don't Worry Be Happy," which will sell over ten million copies and earn him three Grammy awards in 1989 in addition to a Grammy for best jazz vocalist.

1959 *A Raisin in the Sun* becomes the first play written by an African-American woman, Lorraine Hansberry, to open on Broadway. The play will run for 19 months, be named best play by the New York Drama Critics Circle, and bring Lloyd Richards to Broadway as the first black director in modern times.

1888 Hall Johnson is born in Athens, Ga. In 1925, he will organize and direct the Hall Johnson Choir as well as have significant success as an arranger. One of his early successes on the stage will be as choral director for the 1930 Broadway play *The Green Pastures* and the 1933 play *Run Little Chillun*, for which he will write the book and music. Johnson and his choir will move to Hollywood in 1936 to make the film version of *The Green Pastures*.

1926 The Savoy Ballroom, nicknamed the "Home of Happy Feet," opens in New York City.

1932 Andrew Young is born in New Orleans, La. He will become a minister, influential leader in the civil rights movement, first African-American ambassador to the UN, and mayor of Atlanta.

Andrew Young

1936 Virginia Hamilton is born in Yellow Springs, Ohio. She will become an award-winning author of juvenile fiction including *House of Dies Drear, M.C. Higgins the Great,* and *Sweet Whispers, Brother Rush*.

1982 Charles Fuller wins the Pulitzer Prize for *A Soldier's Play*.

13

14

1914 James Reese Europe explains the significance of his Clef Club Symphony Orchestra, consisting of the best African-American musicians in New York City: "...we colored people have our own music that is a part of us It's the product of our souls; it's been created by the sufferings and miseries of our race."

James Reese Europe's Clef Club Band

Harlem Hospital and Metropolitan Hospital in New York City, exhibit his work at the Atlanta University annuals, the Art Institute of Chicago, and the Whitney Museum and be represented in museums in the U.S. and Europe. Among his major works will be *Safari, Eve,* and *Quarter Horse.*

1918 John Rhoden is born in Birmingham, Ala. An art student who will study with Richmond Barthé and at Talladega College, Rhoden's sculptures will have strong romantic and classical elements. He will receive commissions for

1930 Richard Allen "Blue" Mitchell is born in Miami, Fla. The trumpeter will make his name as a member of Horace Silver's Quintet. From 1974 he will play as a soloist or as an accompanist for Tony Bennett and Lena Horne.

1917 The first training camp for "colored" officers is established by the U.S. Army in Des Moines, Iowa, after a long lobbying effort by the NAACP, led by Joel E. Spingarn and James Weldon Johnson. The camp will issue 678 officer commissions to African-Americans, compared to 380,000 African-American enlisted men mobilized in World War I.

1933 Quincy Delight Jones is born in Chicago, Ill. A trumpeter and record producer, he will collaborate with many major American and French recording artists, including Michael Jackson on the latter's *Thriller* and *Bad* albums, two of the most successful records during the 1980's. A musical innovator, in 1991 Jones will receive two Grammy awards for producer of the year and album of the year for *Back on the Block.*

1947 William J. Jefferson is born in Lake Providence, La. He will become a Louisiana state senator in 1979 and, in 1990, the first congressman elected from the state since Charles Edmund Nash left office in 1876.

William J. Jefferson

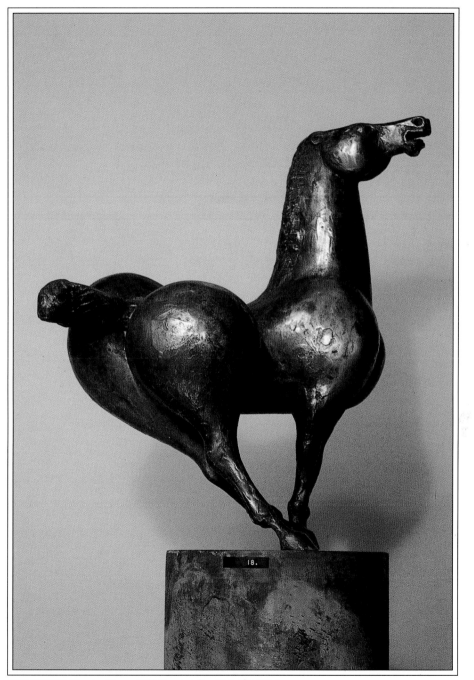

JOHN RHODEN, *Quarter Horse,* 1958. Bronze. Courtesy the artist.

15

1842 Robert C. DeLarge is born in Aiken, S.C. He will defeat a white opponent by 986 votes out of 32,000 cast to earn a seat as a South Carolina representative to the U.S. Congress.

1912 Sam Hopkins is born in Centerville, Tex. He will become a blues guitarist, better known as "Lightnin" Hopkins, and be considered one of the last blues singers in the grand tradition of "Blind" Lemon Jefferson, with whom he played as a child.

1938 Emilio Cruz is born in New York City. He will become a painter who will study in his teens with the influential African-American artist Bob Thompson, study European masters in Italy, Paris, London, and Amsterdam and become noted in the U.S. for both his figurative and abstract paintings. His work will be exhibited or collected by the Museum of Modern Art, National Museum of American Art, the Studio

Lester Young

Museum of Harlem, and prestigious private galleries.

1959 Saxophonist and major influence on the "Cool School" of jazz, Lester "Prez" Young dies at 50 in New York City.

1969 St. Clair Drake is named director of the African and Afro-American Studies program at Stanford University. Drake's accomplishments in the position will form a model for such programs across the country.

16

1827 With the assistance of James Varick, Richard Allen, Alexander Crummel, and others, Samuel E. Cornish and John B. Russwurm publish *Freedom's Journal* in New York City. Operating from space in Varick's Zion Church, *Freedom's Journal* is the first African-American newspaper. Russwurm says of the establishment of the newspaper, "We wish to plead our own cause. Too long have others spoken for us."

1870 Senator Hiram R. Revels argues against Georgia's re-admission to the Union without safeguards for black citizens. It is the first official speech by an African-American before Congress.

1960 San Antonio, Tex., becomes the first major Southern city to integrate lunch counters.

1988 President Ronald Reagan vetoes a civil rights bill that would restore protections invalidated by the U.S. Supreme Court's 1984 ruling in *Grove City College v. Bell*. Reagan's veto will be overridden by Congress less than a week later.

1989 The U.S. Senate agrees to try U.S. District Court Judge Alcee Hastings on fraud, corruption, and perjury charges stemming from a 1981 bribery conspiracy case. Hastings, appointed by President Jimmy Carter as the first judge to serve on the federal bench in Florida, will be convicted of eight of the original articles and impeached in October.

17

18

Nat King Cole

1806 Norbert Rillieux is born a free man in New Orleans, La. Rillieux will become best known for his revolutionary improvements in sugar refining methods. Awarded his second patent for an evaporator, the invention will be widely used throughout Louisiana and the West Indies, dramatically increasing and modernizing sugar production.

1865 Aaron Anderson wins the Navy's Medal of Honor for his heroic actions aboard the *USS Wyandank* during the Civil War.

1891 West Virginia State College is founded in Institute.

1919 Nathaniel Adams Coles is born in Montgomery, Ala. Better known as Nat "King" Cole, he will start his musical career in a band with his brother Eddie and in a production of *Shuffle Along.* Leader of the King Cole Trio, he will achieve international acclaim as a jazz pianist before becoming an even more popular balladeer known for such songs as "Mona Lisa," "The Christmas Song" and "Unforgettable." Cole will also have the distinction of being the first African-American to host a network television series (1956–1957), a pioneer in breaking down racial barriers in Las Vegas, and a founding member of the National Academy of Recording Arts and Sciences, which will honor him with a posthumous Lifetime Achievement Grammy in 1989.

1901 William Henry Johnson is born. The Florence, S.C., native will leave his home for New York and Europe where he will develop a deliberate and controversial primitive painting style. Among his more famous works will be *Chain Gang, Calvary,* and *Descent from the Cross.*

1939 Charley Pride is born in Sledge, Miss. Intent on a career in baseball, he will begin his country music career in 1960 singing between innings at a company-sponsored baseball game where he is a player. A recording contract will follow in 1964 and a debut with the "Grand Ole Opry" in 1967. Pride will become the first African-American to become a successful country music star. His awards will include a 1972 Grammy.

1943 William Hastie wins the NAACP's Spingarn Medal. A former federal judge and law school dean, Hastie, a civilian aide to Secretary of War Henry L. Stimson, had resigned his position earlier in the year over the armed forces' discriminatory practices.

1972 The *USS Jesse L. Brown,* the first U.S. naval ship to be named after an African-American naval officer, is launched at Westwego, La. Brown was the first African-American pilot in the U.S. Naval Reserve and was killed in the Korean War.

William H. Johnson

WILLIAM H. JOHNSON, *Still Life*, ca. 1923–1926. Oil on canvas. National Museum of American Art, Smithsonian Institution, gift of the Harmon Foundation.

19

20

The Count Basie Orchestra

1930 Ornette Coleman is born in Fort Worth, Tex. He will become a noted avant-garde jazz saxophonist and composer.

1937 The Count Basie Orchestra, with vocalists Billie Holiday and Jimmy Rushing, opens at the Apollo Theatre in Harlem.

1939 The New Negro Theater is founded in Los Angeles, Calif., by Langston Hughes. The company stages as its first performance Hughes's play *Don't You Want to be Free?*

1968 Students take over the Administration Building at Howard University demanding resignation of university officials and a stronger orientation to black culture in the curriculum. It is the first of many college protests over black studies programs on African-American and white college campuses across the nation.

1852 *Uncle Tom's Cabin*, by white abolitionist Harriet Beecher Stowe, is published. The controversial novel will be credited by many, including Abraham Lincoln, with sparking the Civil War.

1883 Jan Matzeliger receives patent #274,207 for his shoe lasting machine. His invention will revolutionize the shoe industry, allowing for the first mass production of shoes.

1950 Dr. Ralph Bunche receives the Nobel Peace Prize for his work as a mediator in the Palestine crisis. He is the first African-American to be so honored.

1957 Spike Lee is born in Atlanta, Ga. His films, among them *She's Gotta Have It, Do the Right Thing* and *Jungle Fever*, explore the social, political, and interpersonal relationships between African-Americans and whites not seen since the work of director Oscar Micheaux.

1987 *Hollywood Shuffle* premieres. The film is directed by, produced by, and stars Robert Townsend. Townsend also used his own money to bring his comedic vision to the screen.

Jan E. Matzeliger
Shoe Lasting Machine   No.274,207
Patented March 20,1883
29
Black Heritage USA

21

22

1949 The Rens, originally from New York but now representing Dayton, Ohio, play their last game against the Denver Nuggets. Their lifetime record, amassed over 26 years, is 2,318 wins and 381 losses. Their opponents, the Nuggets, will become the first NBA team to be owned by African-Americans when Bertram Lee and Peter Bynoe lead a group of investors that buys the club in 1989.

1955 NAACP chairman, author, and civil rights pioneer Walter White dies in New York City.

1960 Police in Sharpeville, near Johannesburg, fire on black South Africans protesting racial pass laws. A protest strategy devised by the Pan-African Congress to flood South African jails with pass violators, the protesters will suffer 72 deaths and over 200 injuries in the two days of violence that will become known as the Sharpeville Massacre.

Walter White

1965 A freedom march from Selma to Montgomery, Ala., dramatizes the denial of voting rights for African-Americans. Led by Martin Luther King, Jr., thousands of marchers are protected by U.S. Army troops and National Guardsmen because of violence encountered earlier, including the fatal beating of a white minister, Reverend James J. Reeb.

1882 African-American Shakespearean actor Morgan Smith dies in Sheffield, England. Smith had emigrated to England in 1866, where he performed in Shakespeare's *Richard III, Macbeth, Hamlet,* and *The Merchant of Venice,* as well as *Othello.*

1931 Richard Berry Harrison receives the NAACP's Spingarn Medal for his role as "De Lawd" in *The Green Pastures* and for his "long years ... as a dramatic reader and entertainer, interpreting to the mass of colored people in church and school the finest specimens of English drama from Shakespeare down."

1943 George Benson is born in Pittsburgh, Pa. He will begin singing in nightclubs as a child and form a rock group at age 17. An early jazz guitarist, his addition of soul elements and scat-influenced vocals will win him wide recognition and acclaim and numerous Grammy awards.

George Benson

23

24

1784 Tom Molineaux, who will become America's most celebrated early boxing success, is born into slavery in Georgetown, D.C. Emigrating to London after winning money to purchase his freedom in a fight, Molineaux challenges champion Tom Cribb in a fight attended by 10,000 spectators in 1810, which he will apparently win but is ruled against by a partisan referee. After a subsequent loss to Cribb in 1811, Molineaux will sink into alcoholism and die penniless in Ireland at the age of 34.

1938 Maynard Jackson is born in Dallas, Tex. He will be elected the first African-American mayor of Atlanta, Ga. for two terms, 1974 to 1982, and be re-elected in 1989 for an unprecedented third term.

1873 Slavery is abolished in Puerto Rico.

1953 Yvette Marie Stevens is born. She will become better known as Chaka Khan, lead singer of the rock group Rufus (winner of a 1974 Grammy) and a three-time Grammy-winning soloist.

1912 Dorothy Irene Height is born in Richmond, Va. She will become the president of the National Council of Negro Women and one of the strongest advocates for the needs of African-American women and families.

1941 *Native Son*, a play adapted from Richard Wright's novel of the same name, opens at the St. James Theatre in New York City.

1958 Bill Russell, center for the Boston Celtics, becomes the NBA's MVP. He is again named in 1961, 1962, 1963 and 1965.

1968 In New York City, Bob Foster wins the light heavyweight championship by knocking out Dick Tiger in four rounds.

1972 Z. Alexander Looby, the first African-American to serve on the Nashville City Council, dies in Nashville, Tenn.

1975 Muhammad Ali beats Chuck Wepner in a 15-round bout to retain his world heavyweight crown.

Dorothy Height

25

26

1931 Ida B. Wells-Barnett, journalist, militant African-American rights and antilynching advocate, and founder of the NAACP, dies in Chicago.

Meanwhile, nine African-American youths are arrested in Scottsboro, Ala., for allegedly raping two white women. Although they will be quickly convicted in a trial that outraged African-Americans and much of the nation, the case will be appealed and the "Scottsboro Boys" retried several times.

1939 Toni Cade Bambara is born in New York City. She will become a noted writer of such fiction as *Gorilla, My Love,* and *The Salt Eaters.*

1942 Aretha Franklin is born in Memphis, Tenn. From her first singing experiences in her father's church through a singing career and 21 gold records, she will earn the title "Queen of Soul."

Aretha Franklin

1975 Salem Poor, who fought alongside other colonists during the Battle of Bunker Hill, is honored as one of four "Contributors to the Cause," a commemorative issue of the U.S. Postal Service.

1991 Whoopi Goldberg wins the Academy Award for best actress in a supporting role for *Ghost.* Also winning an Oscar is Russell Williams II, for best sound editing for the movie *Dances with Wolves.* It is Williams's second Oscar in a row (the first was for *Glory*), a record for an African-American.

1937 William Hastie is appointed to a federal judgeship in the Virgin Islands. With the appointment, Hastie becomes the first African-American to serve on the federal bench in the U.S. or its territories.

1944 Diana Ross is born in Detroit, Mich. Ross, with Mary Wilson and Florence Ballard, will form the Supremes in 1961 and have 15 consecutive smash-hit singles with the group. Ross will also pursue an acting career in such movies as *Lady Sings the Blues* and receive a Tony Award for her Broadway show *An Evening with Diana Ross.* Both with the Supremes and as a solo artist, she will have more number-one records than any other artist in the history of the charts.

1950 Theodore Pendergrass is born in Philadelphia, Pa. He will become a lead singer for Harold Melvin and the Blue Notes and pursue an active solo career interrupted by an auto accident that will leave him paralyzed from the chest down.

1991 The Reverend Emmanuel Cleaver becomes the first African-American mayor of Kansas City, Mo.

Emanuel Cleaver

EDMONIA LEWIS, *Moses* (after Michelangelo), 1875. Carved marble. National Museum of American Art, Smithsonian Institution, gift of Mr. and Mrs. Alfred T. Morris, Jr.

27

28

1872 Cleveland Luca, a musician, member of the famous musical Luca Family Quartet and composer of the Liberian National Anthem, dies in Liberia.

1924 Sarah Vaughan is born in Newark, N.J. On a dare, she will enter a 1943 amateur contest at the Apollo Theatre in Harlem and be hired by Earl "Fatha" Hines as a result of her performance. She will begin recording in 1945, be considered one of the finest jazz vocalists, and earn the nickname "The Divine One."

1934 Arthur Mitchell is born in New York City. The first male recipient of the dance award from the High School of Performing Arts in 1951, he will be the first African-American dancer to become a principal artist in the New York City Ballet Company and will found the highly influential Dance Theatre of Harlem.

1972 Fleeta Drumgo and John Cluchette are acquitted by an all-white jury of the murder of a white guard at Soledad prison. George Jackson, the third "Soledad Brother," was killed in the alleged escape attempt.

Sarah Vaughan

1925 Sculptor Ed Wilson is born in Baltimore, Md. He will study at the University of Iowa, receive sculpture awards from the Carnegie Foundation, Howard University and the State University of New York, and have his work shown at *Two Centuries of Black American Art,* and other exhibitions. Among his major works will be *Cybele.*

1966 Bill Russell is named head coach of the Boston Celtics, the first African-American to coach an NBA team.

1984 Educator and civil rights activist Benjamin Mays dies in Atlanta, Ga. Mays had served as

Benjamin Mays

dean of the School of Religion at Howard University and president of Morehouse College, where he served as the mentor to the young Martin Luther King, Jr.

29

30

1918 Pearl Mae Bailey is born in Newport News, Va. She will achieve tremendous success as a stage and film actress, recording artist, nightclub headliner, and television performer. Among her most notable movies will be *Porgy and Bess* and *Carmen Jones* and she will receive a Tony Award for her starring role in an all-African-American version of *Hello Dolly*. Bailey will be widely honored, including being named special advisor to the U.S. Mission to the UN and receiving the Presidential Medal of Freedom.

1945 Walt Frazier is born in Atlanta, Ga. He will become a basketball player and, as a guard for the New York Knicks, lead his team to NBA championships in 1970 and 1973. He will also earn the nickname "Clyde" (from the movie *Bonnie and Clyde*) for his stylish wardrobe and flamboyant lifestyle off the court.

Pearl Bailey

1869 The 15th Amendment to the Constitution is ratified, which guarantees the right to vote regardless of "race, color or previous condition of servitude." Despite ratification of the amendment, it will be almost 100 years before African-Americans become universally enfranchised.

1923 Zeta Phi Beta sorority is incorporated. It was founded in 1920 at Howard University.

1932 The New York Rens, one of the best-known African-American basketball teams, beat the Boston Celtics by three points to win their first world professional championship. It is the first world championship won by an African-American team in any sport.

1946 *St. Louis Woman* opens on Broadway. Based on a book by Arna Bontemps and Countee Cullen from Bontemps's novel *God Sends Sunday*, the play brought to wide attention to supporting actress Pearl Bailey,

Naomi Sims

who stopped the show nightly with her renditions of "Legalize My Name" and "A Woman's Prerogative."

1948 Naomi Sims is born in Oxford, Miss. She will become a trailblazing fashion model and founder of a beauty company that will bear her name.

ANTHONY BONAIR, Untitled, Multiple-exposure photography. Courtesy the photographer.

31

1853 At concert singer Elizabeth Taylor Greenfield's New York debut in Metropolitan Hall, African-Americans are not allowed to attend. Angered and embarrassed at the exclusion of her race, Greenfield will perform in a separate concert at the Broadway Tabernacle for five African-American congregations.

1871 Jack Johnson, the first African-American to be crowned heavyweight champion, is born in Galveston, Tex.

1949 William Grant Still's opera *Troubled Island* receives its world premiere at the New York City Opera. In addition to marking Robert McFerrin's debut as the first African-American male to sing with the company, the opera is the first ever written by an African-American to be produced by a major opera company.

William Grant Still

1980 Larry Holmes wins the vacant world heavyweight title by knocking out Leroy Jones in the eighth round.

1988 Toni Morrison wins the Pulitzer Prize for *Beloved*, a powerful novel of a runaway slave who murders her daughter rather than see her raised in slavery.

1

1868 Hampton Institute is founded in Hampton, Va., by General Samuel Chapman Armstrong.

1917 Scott Joplin dies in New York City. One of the early developers of ragtime and the author of "Maple Leaf Rag," Joplin also created several ragtime and grand operas, the most noteworthy of which, *Treemonisha*, consumed his later years in an attempt to have it published and performed.

1951 Oscar Micheaux dies in Charlotte, N.C. Micheaux formed his own film production company, Oscar Micheaux Corporation, to produce his novel *The Homesteader* and over 30 other movies, notably *Birthright*, which was adapted from a novel by Pulitzer Prize–winning author T.S. Stribling, and *Body and Soul*, which marked the film debut of Paul Robeson.

1966 The first World Festival of Negro Arts opens in Dakar, Senegal, with the U.S. African-American delegation having one of the largest number of representatives. First prizes are won by poet Robert Hayden, engraver William Majors, actors Ivan Dixon and Abbey Lincoln, gospel singer Mahalia Jackson, jazz trumpeter Louis Armstrong, and sociologist Kenneth Clark.

2

3

1855 John Mercer Langston is elected clerk of Brownhelm, Ohio, township. He will be considered the first African-American elected to public office.

1918 Charles White is born in Chicago, Ill. An artist who will work with traditional materials (pen, ink, oil on canvas and lithography), White will transform the image of African-Americans and earn praise from critics and artists alike. White will receive dozens of awards and his work will be collected by museums on three continents and major corporations.

1932 Bill Pickett, well-known cowboy who was acclaimed by President Theodore Roosevelt as "one of the best trained ropers and riders the West has produced," dies. Pickett performed as a bulldogger in Europe, Mexico, and the U.S., where he was often assisted by two relatively unknown white cowboys, Tom Mix and Will Rogers.

1939 Marvin Gaye is born in Washington, D.C. He will sign with Motown in 1962 and begin a 22-year career that includes hits "Pride and Joy," duets with Mary Wells and Tammi Terrell, as well as best-selling albums exploring his social consciousness (*What's Going On*) and sexuality (*Let's Get It On, Midnight Love*).

Charles White

1934 Richard Mayhew is born in Amityville, N.Y. A student at the Art Students League, Brooklyn Museum Art School, and Columbia University, as well as the Academia in Florence, Italy, Mayhew will be one of the most respected and revolutionary landscape artists of the 20th century. He will also form—with fellow artists Romare Bearden, Charles Alston, Hale Woodruff, and others—Spiral, a forum for artistic innovation and exploration of African-American artists' relationships to the civil rights movement.

1961 Eddie Murphy is born in Brooklyn, N.Y. A stand-up comedian before pursuing a movie career, Murphy will be the largest African-American box-office draw. Among his most successful movies will be *48 Hours*, *Trading Places*, *Beverly Hills Cop*, *Coming to America*, and *Harlem Nights*.

1963 Led by Martin Luther King, Jr., the Birmingham anti-segregation campaign begins.

Before it is over, more than 2,000 demonstrators, including King, will be arrested. The Birmingham Manifesto, issued by Fred Shuttlesworth of the Alabama Christian Movement for Human Rights the morning of the campaign, summarizes the frustration and hopes of the protesters: "The patience of an oppressed people cannot endure forever.... This is Birmingham's moment of truth in which every citizen can play his part in her larger destiny."

1964 Malcolm X speaks at a CORE–sponsored meeting on "The Negro Revolt—What Comes Next?" In his speech "The Ballot or Bullet," X warns of a growing black nationalism that will no longer tolerate patronizing white political action.

1984 John Thompson of the Georgetown Hoyas basketball team coaches the Patrick Ewing–led squad to an NCAA championship. It is a first for an African-American coach.

4

5

1915 McKinley Morganfield is born in Rolling Fork, Miss. He will be better known as Muddy Waters, a blues singer.

1928 Maya Angelou is born in Saint Louis, Mo. Noted as the author of a multivolume autobiographical series, as well as several volumes of poetry, she was also the first African-American streetcar conductor in San Francisco, a dancer, nightclub singer, editor, and teacher of music and drama in Ghana and professor of American Studies at Wake Forest University.

1938 Vera Mae Smart Grosvenor, who will become the author of the popular and influential cookbook *Vibration Cooking* (1970), is born in Fairfax, S.C.

1942 Richard Parsons is born in New York City. In 1990, he will be named chief executive officer of Dime Savings Bank, the first African-American CEO

Maya Angelou

of a large, nonminority U.S. savings institution.

1968 Acknowledged leader of the U.S. civil rights movement Martin Luther King, Jr. is assassinated in Memphis, Tenn. His death will result in a national day of mourning and the postponement of the baseball season. Over 30,000 people will form a funeral procession behind his coffin, pulled by two Georgia mules. King's death will also set off summer riots in 160 cities leaving 82 people dead and causing $69 million in property damage.

1839 Robert Smalls is born into slavery in Beaufort, S.C. He will become a Civil War hero by sailing an armed Confederate steamer out of Charleston Harbor and presenting it to the Union Navy and be a three-term congressman from his state.

1910 Charles W. Follis is born in Cloverdale, Va. He is the first African-American to play professional football.

1937 Colin Powell is born in New York City. He will become a highly decorated Army officer, receiving the Bronze Star and Purple Heart and a promotion to four-star general in 1988. He will also be the first African-American to serve as the Chief of Staff for the Armed Forces.

1958 Booker T. Washington becomes the only African-American honored twice on a U.S. postage stamp. To commemorate the centennial of his birth, the U.S. Postal Service issues a stamp depicting the cabin where he was born.

1990 Seven African-American journalists are inducted into the newly created Hall of Fame of the National Association of Black Journalists in Washington, D.C. Dubbed "pioneers of mainstream journalism," the inductees include Dorothy Butler Gilliam of the *Washington Post*, Malvin R. Goode of ABC News, Mal H. Johnson of Cox Broadcasting, Gordon Parks of *Life* magazine, Ted Poston of the *New York Post*, Norma Quarles of Cable News Network, and Carl T. Rowan of King Features Syndicate. Twelve Pulitzer Prize winners are also honored at the awards ceremonies.

U.S. POSTAGE 3¢
CENTENNIAL OF BOOKER T. WASHINGTON

6

7

Robert E. Peary, Matthew Henson

1798 James P. Beckwourth is born in Fredericksburg, Va. He will become a noted scout and will discover a pass in the Sierra Nevadas between the Feather and Truckee rivers that will bear his name.

1865 Writing in the *Philadelphia Press* under the pen name "Rollin," Thomas Morris Chester describes the Union Army's triumphant entry into the city of Richmond, Va., during the closing days of the Civil War. Rollin is the only African-American newspaperman writing for a mainstream daily. There will be no others for almost 70 years.

1909 Matthew Henson, accompanying Commander Robert Peary, discovers the North Pole. Although in later years Henson will be called Peary's servant or merely "one Negro" on the expedition, Henson is a valuable colleague and codiscoverer of the pole. Peary says,

"I couldn't get along without him."

1937 Billy Dee Williams is born in Harlem. He will become one of the most romantic leading men of film and television. Among his best known roles will be football great Gale Sayers in the TV movie *Brian's Song* as well as leading parts in the movies *Lady Sings the Blues* and two *Star Wars* films.

1971 *Contemporary Black Artists in America* opens at the Whitney Museum of American Art in New York City. The exhibit includes the work of 58 master painters and sculptors such as Jacob Lawrence, Charles White, Alma Thomas, Betye Saar, David Driskell, Richard Hunt, and others.

1712 Slave riots in New York City result in the death of eight whites. Twenty-five slaves will be killed or commit suicide for their part in the riot.

1867 Johnson C. Smith University is founded in Charlotte, N.C.

1872 William Monroe Trotter is born near Chillicothe, Ohio. Editor of the Boston *Guardian*, he will also be a militant civil rights activist and adversary of Booker T. Washington and his moderate politics.

1915 Eleanor Fagan is born in East Baltimore, Md. As Billie Holiday or "Lady Day," she will become an internationally known jazz and blues singer famous for such songs as "Strange Fruit," "Lover Man," and "God Bless the Child." Troubled in life by drug addiction, Holiday will die of drug and alcohol abuse in 1959.

1938 Trumpeter Frederick Dewayne Hubbard is born in Indianapolis, Ind. From a musical family, Hubbard will play four instruments in his youth and will later play with "Slide" Hampton, Quincy Jones, and Art Blakey. A leader of his own band since the 1960's, he will record the noteworthy albums *Red Clay, First Light* and the Grammy Award–winning *Straight Life*.

1940 The first U.S. stamp ever to honor an African-American is issued bearing the likeness of Booker T. Washington.

Billie Holiday

CHARLES WHITE, *The Prophet #1,* 1975–1976. Color lithograph. Collection of Professor and Mrs. David C. Driskell.

8

9

_____
_____
_____
_____
_____
_____
_____
_____

Marian Anderson

1922 Carmen McRae is born in New York City. She will begin her professional career in her 20's with Benny Carter and be a renowned jazz vocalist for more than 40 years.

Percy Julian

1938 Cornetist and bandleader Joe "King" Oliver dies in Savannah, Ga. He was considered one of the leading musicians of New Orleans–style jazz and served as a mentor to Louis Armstrong, who played with him in 1922.

1974 Hank Aaron of the Atlanta Braves hits his 715th home run against a pitch thrown by Los Angeles Dodger Al Downing at a home game in Fulton County Stadium. Aaron's home run breaks the long-standing record of Babe Ruth.

1987 Los Angeles Dodgers executive Al Campanis is fired for alleged racially biased comments about the managerial potential of African-Americans.

1990 Percy Julian, who helped create drugs to combat glaucoma and methods to mass produce cortisone, and agricultural scientist George Washington Carver are the first African-American inventors admitted into the National Inventors Hall of Fame in the hall's 17-year history.

1898 Paul Robeson is born in Princeton, N.J. The son of an ex-slave turned Methodist minister, Robeson will attend Rutgers University on a full scholarship, where he will excel in four sports, be a member of the debate team, and earn a Phi Beta Kappa key. An attorney, he will later become one of America's foremost actors and singers. He will make 14 films including *The Emperor Jones*, *King Solomon's Mines*, and *Showboat*. An advocate of African-American equality, his public support of Communism will cause the cancellation of concert dates and the revocation of his passport.

1929 Paule Marshall is born in Brooklyn, N.Y. She will be the author of the novels *Browngirl, Brownstones*, *Praisesong for the Widow*, and *Daughters*.

1939 When she is refused admission to the Daughters of the American Revolution's Constitutional Hall to give a planned concert, Marian Anderson performs for 75,000 on the steps of the Lincoln Memorial. Two months later, she will be honored with the NAACP's Spingarn Medal for her talents as "one of the greatest singers of our time" and for "her magnificent dignity as a human being."

1950 Juanita Hall becomes the first African-American to win a Tony award for her role as Bloody Mary in the musical *South Pacific*.

10

11

1926 Johnnie Tillmon (later Blackston) is born in Scott, Ark. A welfare rights champion, Tillmon will become the founding chairperson and director of the National Welfare Rights Organization.

1932 The James Weldon Johnson Literary Guild announces the winners of its first annual nationwide poetry contest for children. The judges—Jessie Fauset and Countee Cullen, among others—select in the teen category a 16-year-old Liberian youth and Margaret Walker of New Orleans, who receives an honorable mention for her poem "When Night Comes."

1943 Arthur Ashe is born in Richmond, Va. One of the first African-American male tennis stars, he will be the first African-American to win a spot on the American Davis Cup tennis team, the first to win the U.S. Open and the men's singles title at Wimbledon, in 1975.

Arthur Ashe

1883 Spelman College is founded in Atlanta, Ga.

1933 Tony Brown is born in Charleston, W.Va. He will become well known as executive producer, host, and moderator of the Emmy–winning television series *Black Journal*.

1955 Roy Wilkins is elected the NAACP's executive secretary following the death of Walter White.

1968 President Lyndon B. Johnson signs what will become known as the 1968 Housing Act, which outlaws discrimination in the sale, rental, or leasing of 80% of the housing in the U.S. Passed by the Senate and submitted by the House to Johnson in the aftermath of the King assassination, the bill also protects civil rights workers and makes it a federal crime to cross state lines for the purpose of inciting a riot.

Roy Wilkins

1972 Benjamin L. Hooks, a Memphis lawyer and Baptist minister, becomes the first African-American to be named to the Federal Communications Commission.

1988 Willie D. Burton becomes the first African-American to win the Oscar for sound when he receives the award for the movie *Bird*.

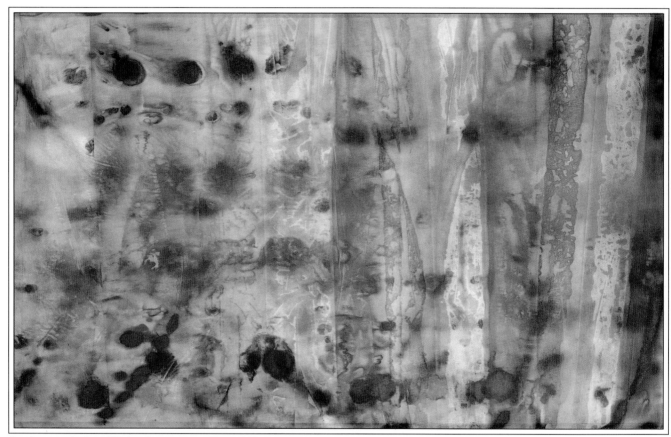

SAM GILLIAM, *April 4,* 1969. Acrylic on canvas. National Museum of American Art, Smithsonian Institution.

12

13

1825 Richard Harvey Cain is born in Greenbrier, Va. He will become an AME minister, publisher, member of the House of Representatives, an AME bishop, and a founder of Paul Quinn College in Waco, Tex.

1861 The Civil War begins as Confederate troops attack Fort Sumter, S.C.

1940 Herbie Hancock is born in Chicago, Ill. He will be one of the most popular jazz artists, known for his compositions "Watermelon Man" and "Chameleon," as well as his musical score for the movie 'Round Midnight, for which he will win an Oscar in 1986.

1966 Emmett Ashford becomes the first African-American major league umpire when he is named to the American League.

August Wilson

1990 August Wilson's *The Piano Lesson* wins the Pulitzer Prize for drama. It is the second Pulitzer Prize for Wilson, who also won one for *Fences* in 1987 and was awarded the New York Drama Critics Award for *Fences*, *Ma Rainey's Black Bottom*, and *Joe Turner's Come and Gone.*

1891 Nella Larsen is born in Chicago, Ill. She will write two important novels of the Harlem Renaissance, *Quicksand* and *Passing.*

1906 Riots occur in Brownsville, Tex., when African-American soldiers retaliate against white citizens for racial slurs.

1907 Harlem Hospital opens in New York with 150 beds. It will become one of the early leading African-American hospitals.

1946 Al Green is born in Forrest City, Ark. He will become one of the most popular soul and pop singers of the 1970's, known for his recordings "Tired of Being Alone" and "I'm Still in Love with You." Green will later become a minister and return to performing as a gospel singer, where he will win numerous Grammy awards.

1963 Sidney Poitier receives an Oscar for best actor for his performance in *Lilies of the Field.* He is the first African-American male to receive the Academy Award. He will later become a director and make 1980's *Stir Crazy*, the largest-grossing movie by an African-American director ever.

Sidney Poitier

14

15

Howardena Pindell

1775 The first U.S. abolitionist society, the Pennsylvania Society for the Abolition of Slavery, is formed in Philadelphia, Pa., by Quakers. Benjamin Franklin serves as its first president.

1943 Artist Howardena Pindell is born in Philadelphia, Pa. A student at Boston and Yale universities, she will receive several art fellowships and travel the world to create art that reflects a clear artistic vision and an intense commitment to issues of racial and social injustice.

1991 A major retrospective of the late Romare Bearden's career and work opens at the Studio Museum of Harlem. Entitled *Memory and Metaphor: The Art of Romare Bearden 1940–1987,* the exhibit includes 140 oil and watercolor paintings as well as numerous collages that chronicle his exploration of abstract expressionism, social realism, and reinterpretation of classical themes in art and literature.

1889 Asa Philip Randolph is born in Crescent Way, Fla. He will become a labor leader, the organizer of the Brotherhood of Sleeping Car Porters in 1925, and a tireless fighter for civil rights.

1919 Elizabeth Catlett is born in Washington, D.C. She will become an internationally known printmaker and sculptor who will emigrate to Mexico and embrace both African and Mexican influences in her art.

1922 Harold Washington is born in Chicago, Ill. He will serve in the Illinois House of Representatives and Senate as well as two terms in Congress before becoming the first African-American mayor of Chicago.

1928 Pioneering architect Norma Merrick (later Sklarek) is born in New York City. Sklarek will be the first licensed woman architect in the U.S. and the first African-American wom-

an to become a fellow in the American Institute of Architects.

1966 The Student Nonviolent Coordinating Committee (SNCC) is formed on the campus of Shaw University in Raleigh, N.C.

A. Philip Randolph
25
Black Heritage USA

16

17

1862 Slavery is abolished in Washington, D.C., when $993,407 in compensation is paid to slave owners for their lost "property."

1869 Ebenezer Don Carlos Bassett is appointed Consul-General to Haiti and the Dominican Republic, the first African-American to serve in a diplomatic position for the U.S. Bassett will hold the post for 12 years.

1947 Kareem Abdul-Jabbar (né Ferdinand Lewis Alcindor) is born in New York City. He will be one of the finest basketball players in history, first with UCLA, then with the Milwaukee Bucks and, from 1975 to his retirement in 1990, with the Los Angeles Lakers. All-time leading scorer in the NBA, Abdul-Jabbar will lead the Lakers to five NBA championships, including back-to-back titles in 1987 and 1988.

Kareem Abdul-Jabbar

1973 Lelia Smith Foley becomes the first African-American female to be elected mayor of a U.S. city when she takes office in the small town of Taft, Okla. She will hold the position for 13 years.

1758 Frances Williams, the first African-American to graduate from a college in the Western Hemisphere, publishes a collection of Latin poems.

1818 For unknown reasons, Daniel Coker is expelled from the AME Church. Coker had been a key organizer in the church's early history and was elected its first bishop, a position he declined possibly because of his fair complexion.

1978 Thomas W. Turner, founder of the Federation of Colored Catholics, civil rights pioneer and charter member of the NAACP, dies in Washington, D.C., at the age of 101.

1980 Zimbabwe, formerly known as Rhodesia, gains its independence. Reggae stars Bob Marley and the Wailers and others perform in the celebration

Robert Mugabe

festivities. Robert Mugabe will be sworn in the following day as prime minister of the newly formed nation.

18

19

1861 Nicholas Biddle becomes the first African-American in uniform to be wounded in the Civil War.

Alice Walker

1864 The First Kansas Colored Volunteers break through Confederate lines at Poison Spring, Ark. The unit will sustain heavy losses when captured African-American soldiers are murdered by Confederate troops as opposed to being taken as POWs, which is the standard treatment for captured whites.

1877 The American Nicodemus Town Company is founded by six African-American settlers in northwestern Kansas. The town will be settled later in the year.

1983 Alice Walker is awarded the Pulitzer Prize for *The Color Purple*. Ten days later, the novel will also win the American Book Award for fiction.

1775 With the assistance of African-American soldiers, Minutemen defeat the British at Concord Bridge in the initial battle of the Revolutionary War.

1837 Cheyney University is founded in Cheyney, Pa.

1942 Atlanta University's first exhibition of African-American art is held. Organized by Hale Woodruff, artist and former professor at the university, it will be popularly known as the Atlanta Annual. Winners in the first show will be Charles Alston and Lois Mailou Jones.

1971 Walter Fauntroy takes office as the first elected Congressional representative from the District of Columbia since Reconstruction.

Walter Fauntroy

1975 James B. Parsons becomes the first African-American chief judge of a federal court, the U.S. District Court in Chicago. In 1961, Parsons became the first African-American district court judge.

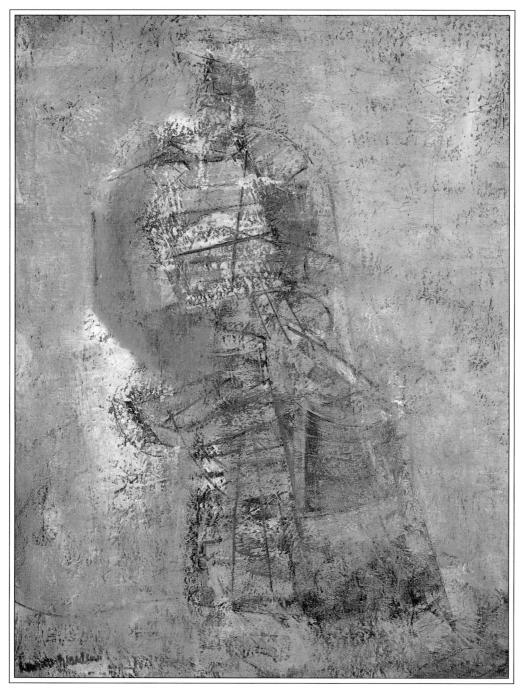

ROMARE BEARDEN, *Blue Lady,* 1955. Oil on canvas. Private collection. Courtesy the Studio Museum of Harlem, New York, New York.

20

James Earl Jones

1909 Lionel Hampton is born in Louisville, Ky. He will become the best-known jazz master of the vibraphone.

1926 Harriet Elizabeth Byrd is born in Cheyenne, Wyo. She will become a teacher and, in 1981, the first African-American legislator in Wyoming's statehood.

1951 Luther Vandross is born in New York City. An early backup singer and commercial jingle writer, his big break as a solo artist will come in 1981 when his album *Never Too Much* will reveal his talents to both R & B and pop audiences. He will make a string of hit albums, earning seven consecutive platinum and double-platinum albums and achieve his greatest crossover success with the albums *The Best of Luther Vandross* and *Power of Love*, which will earn him three Grammy awards.

1969 James Earl Jones wins a Tony for his portrayal of controversial heavyweight champion Jack Johnson in *The Great White Hope*.

21

1878 The ship *Azor* leaves on its first trip carrying African-Americans to Liberia.

1938 The Harlem Suitcase Theatre opens with Langston Hughes's play *Don't You Want to be Free?* The play's star is a young Robert Earl Jones, father of James Earl Jones.

1966 Milton Olive, Jr. becomes the first African-American to win the Congressional Medal of Honor for bravery during the Vietnam War. He will be honored for saving the lives of his fellow soldiers by falling on a live grenade while participating in a search-and-destroy mission near Phu Coung.

1974 By winning the Monsanto Open in Pensacola, Fla., Lee Elder becomes the first African-American professional golfer to qualify for the Masters Tournament. It will be one of four PGA tour victories for the Dallas, Tex., native, including the Houston Open in 1976 and the Greater Milwaukee Open and Westchester Classic in 1978. Elder's career earnings of $2 million will place him among the top three African-American golfers, along with Calvin Peete ($2.3 million and 12 PGA tournament victories) and Charlie Sifford ($1 million).

Lee Elder

22

23

_____
_____
_____
_____
_____
_____
_____
_____

1526 The first recorded slave revolt occurs in Stono, S.C.

1882 Benjamin Brawley is born in Benedict, S.C. He will become a prolific author and educator, serving as a professor of English at Morehouse, Howard, and Shaw universities. He will also serve as dean of Morehouse. His books, among them *A Short History of the American Negro* and *A New Survey of English Literature*, will be landmark texts recommended at several colleges.

1922 Charles Mingus is born in Nogales, Ariz. Raised in Watts, Calif., he will play double bass with Charlie Parker, Duke Ellington, and Bud Powell before becoming a bandleader and composer in his own right. Although not as popular as Miles Davis or Ellington, Mingus, who also will play piano, will be considered one of the principal forces in modern jazz.

Charles Mingus

1856 Granville T. Woods, who will become an inventor of steam boilers, furnaces, incubators and auto air brakes and holder of over 50 patents, is born in Columbus, Ohio.

1913 The National Urban League is incorporated in New York City. The organization was founded in 1910 when the Committee on Urban Conditions Among Negroes met in New York to discuss means to assist rural African-Americans in the transition to urban life. Founders included Mrs. Ruth Standish Baldwin and Dr. George Edmund Haynes, who becomes the league's first executive director.

1941 New Yorkers are treated to a performance of *Café Society* at Carnegie Hall by a group of jazz artists that includes Albert "Jug" Ammons, Hazel Scott, and Art Tatum. It also marks the first performance of Helena (later Lena) Horne, who sings "Summertime," among other songs.

1944 The NAACP Youth Council and Committee for Unity in Motion Pictures selects its first Motion Picture Award recipients. Given to honor actors whose roles advance the image of African-Americans in motion pictures, awards go to Rex Ingram for *Sahara*, Lena Horne for *As Thousands Cheer*, Leigh Whipper for *The Oxbow Incident* and *Mission to Moscow*, Hazel Scott for her debut in *Something to Shout About* and Dooley Wilson for his role as Sam in *Casablanca*, among others. The awards will be the forerunner to the NAACP's Image Awards.

1964 James Baldwin's play *Blues for Mr. Charlie* opens on Broadway. Starring Al Freeman, Jr., Diana Sands, and others, the play reveals the plight of African-Americans in the South.

ELIZABETH CATLETT, *Singing Head,* 1980. Black Mexican marble. National Museum of American Art, Smithsonian Institution.

24

25

1884 The Medico-Chirurgical Society of Washington, D.C., is founded. It is the first African-American medical society.

1886 Augustine Tolton is ordained as a Catholic priest after studying at the College of the Propagation of the Faith in Rome for five years. Tolton will distinguish himself as a speaker and a pastor at Catholic churches in New Jersey, New York City, Chicago, and Quincy, Ill.

1943 Speaking on race relations and racial equality at Wayne State University, Langston Hughes says, "I am for the Christianity that fights poll tax, race discrimination, lynching, injustice and inequality of the masses. I don't feel that religion should be used to beat down Jews [and] Negroes, and to persecute other minority groups."

1944 In *Smith v. Allwright*, the Supreme Court rules that a "white primary" law that excludes African-Americans from

voting is a violation of the 15th Amendment and thus unconstitutional.

1972 James M. Rodger, Jr., of Durham, N.C., is honored in a White House ceremony as National Teacher of the Year. He is the first African-American to receive the honor.

Meanwhile, Robert Wedgeworth is named director of the American Library Association. He is the first African-American to head the organization.

1918 Ella Fitzgerald is born in Newport News, Va. Discovered at an amateur contest at the Apollo Theatre in 1934, Fitzgerald will be a leading jazz vocalist of the swing era. Known for her renditions of such songs as "A Tisket, A Tasket" (her first million-seller), her unique scat styling and series of recordings of great American songwriters will make her an enduring favorite of jazz lovers.

1944 The United Negro College Fund (UNCF) is founded by Dr. Frederick Douglass Patterson, then president of Tuskegee Institute, with 27 charter colleges and universities.

Ella Fitzgerald

1950 At the NBA's annual players draft, the Boston Celtics select Charles "Chuck" Cooper. He is the first African-American ever drafted by an NBA team.

1972 Major General Frederick E. Davidson becomes the first African-American to lead an Army division when he is assigned command of the 8th Infantry Division in Europe.

1990 Tenor saxophonist Dexter Gordon dies in Philadelphia, Pa. A leading influence in the bop movement along with Billy Eckstine and Dizzy Gillespie, Gordon played in London in the early 1960's and stayed until the mid-1970's. Elected to the Jazz Hall of Fame in 1980, his role in the 1986 movie *'Round Midnight* will revive interest in his music and earn him an Academy Award nomination for best actor.

26

27

William L. Dawson

1886 William Levi Dawson is born in Albany, Ga. A graduate of Fisk University, he will move to Chicago, serve in the 365th Infantry in World War I, become an attorney and initially be involved in Republican politics upon his return to the city after the war. Elected to his first term in the U.S. Congress in 1942, he will serve 27 years in the House, where he will become the first African-American representative to chair a committee of Congress, the Committee on Expenditures in Executive Departments, in 1949.

1785 John James Audubon is born in Les Cayes, Saint Dominique (later Haiti), to an African-Caribbean mother and a French father. He will display an early affinity for bird specimens and drawing in France, later emigrating to the U.S., where he will marry a plantation owner's daughter and paint the ground-breaking collection *The Birds of America*.

1991 Maryann Bishop Coffey is named the first woman and the first African-American co-chairman of the National Conference of Christians and Jews.

1927 Coretta Scott is born in Marion, Ala. She will marry Martin Luther King, Jr. in 1953 and be an integral part of his civil rights activities. After his assassination in 1968, she will continue her civil rights activities, founding the Martin Luther King, Jr. Center for Nonviolent Change in Atlanta, Ga.

1960 Togo achieves its independence from France. Sylvanus Olympio serves as its first prime minister.

1961 Sierra Leone obtains its independence from Great Britain with Dr. Milton Margai as its first prime minister.

1972 Artist Charles Alston dies in New York City. After studying at Columbia University and Pratt Institute, he traveled to Europe and the Caribbean before executing murals for Harlem Hospital and Golden State Mutual Life Insurance Company in Los Angeles. A recipient of the National Academy of Design Award, he also re-

Coretta Scott King

ceived the first-place award of the Atlanta University Collection's 1942 show for his gouache *Farm Boy*. Among his other notable works are *School Girl, Frederick Douglass,* and *Nobody Knows.*

28

29

1941 In a famous Jim Crow railroad case brought by congressman Arthur W. Mitchell, the Supreme Court rules that separate facilities must be substantially equal.

1967 Muhammad Ali refuses induction into the U.S. Army and is stripped of his boxing titles by the World Boxing Association and the New York Athletic Association.

Gloria Naylor

1983 Two African-American women, Alice Walker and Gloria Naylor, win prestigious American Book Awards for fiction. Alice Walker's novel *The Color Purple* will be dramatized as a theatrical movie starring Whoopi Goldberg, Danny Glover, and Oprah Winfrey. Naylor's first novel, *The Women of Brewster Place*, will be made into a made-for-television movie and series starring Oprah Winfrey, Jackeé, and Paula Kelly.

1991 Former CORE director and North Carolina judge Floyd McKissick dies in Durham, N.C. He led CORE from 1963 to 1966 during its transformation to a more militant civil rights organization.

Duke Ellington 22 USA

1854 Ashmun Institute, later Lincoln University, is founded in Oxford, Pa.

1881 Julian Francis Abele is born in Philadelphia, Pa. He will become an architect widely believed to have designed Philadelphia's Museum of Art and the Free Library, as well as major buildings on the Duke University campus.

1899 Edward "Duke" Kennedy Ellington is born in Washington, D.C. He will form his first band in 1919, and move to New York

City in 1922. His five-year tenure at the famed Cotton Club will garner him wide acclaim. Scoring both his first musical and making his recording debut in 1924, Ellington will be known as the first conventional jazz composer, although he will also become renowned for his Sacred Concerts in the mid-1960's. His most notable works include "Take the A Train," "Mood Indigo," "Sophisticated Ladies," and "I Got It Bad and That Ain't Good."

1922 Parren James Mitchell is born in Baltimore, Md. In 1971, he will become the first African-American elected to Congress from the State of Maryland.

1948 Willi Smith is born in Philadelphia, Pa. A noted designer, he will take his first job with Arnold Scaasi in New York City and form his own fashion label, Willi Wear Ltd., in 1976. He will be a Coty Award winner in 1983 and will lead his company until his death from AIDS in 1987.

30

1

1931 William Lacy Clay is born in Saint Louis, Mo. He will be a congressman from Missouri and become chairman of the Post Office and Civil Service Committee.

1940 Jesse E. Moorland dies in Washington, D.C. He was a clergyman, key force in fund-raising for black YMCAs, and a board member of Howard University. The donation of his substantial private library to Howard formed the basis of the Moorland-Spingarn Research Center on the university's campus.

1961 Isiah Lord Thomas is born in Chicago, Ill. One of nine children raised by a single mother, Thomas will become a basketball star, first for Indiana University and later for the Detroit Pistons, where he will lead the team to 1989 and 1990 NBA championships.

1983 Robert C. Maynard becomes the first African-American to gain a controlling interest in a major metropolitan newspaper when he buys the *Oakland Tribune* from Gannett.

Jesse E. Moorland

1901 Sterling Brown is born in Washington, D.C. He will become a poet, literary critic, editor of *The Negro in American Fiction* and *Negro Poetry and Drama,* and the coeditor of the anthology *The Negro Caravan.*

1941 A. Philip Randolph issues a call for 100,000 blacks to march on Washington, D.C., to protest armed forces and defense industry discrimination. In response, President Franklin D. Roosevelt, who attempted to persuade Randolph and others to cancel the demonstration, will issue Executive Order 8802, to ban federal discrimination, before Randolph finally yields.

1950 Gwendolyn Brooks becomes the first African-American to win a Pulitzer Prize for her book of poetry *Annie Allen.*

1975 A commemorative stamp of poet Paul Laurence Dunbar is issued by the U.S. Postal Service as part of its American Arts series.

Gwendolyn Brooks

1990 Robert Guillaume, former star of the *Benson* TV series, premieres in the title role in *Phantom of the Opera* at the Music Center in Los Angeles. Guillaume continues the role that had been played to critical acclaim by the English star Michael Crawford.

1991 Rickey Henderson steals his 939th base in the Oakland A's game against the New York Yankees, breaking Lou Brock's record.

ALMA THOMAS, *Leaves Outside a Window in Rain,* 1966. Watercolor. The Evans-Tibbs Collection, Washington, D.C.

2

3

Ralph Abernathy

1844 Elijah McCoy, who will become a master inventor, holder of over 50 patents and source for the phrase "the real McCoy," is born in Ontario, Canada.

1920 The first game of the National Negro Baseball League (NNL) is played in Indianapolis,

Ind. The NNL was formed earlier in the year by Andrew "Rube" Foster and a group of African-American baseball club owners to combat prejudice and further enjoyment of the game.

1968 The Poor People's March, led by Ralph D. Abernathy, begins as caravans from all over the country leave for Washington, D.C., to protest poverty and racial discrimination.

1992 Los Angeles begins a massive cleanup and rebuilding effort after three days of widespread civil unrest. The April 29 acquittal of four police officers in the 1991 beating of motorist Rodney G. King fueled perceptions of unequal justice for African-Americans and sparked multiracial violence that resulted in unprecedented figures of 58 deaths, over 2,000 injuries, over 600 fires, $1 billion in property damage and spread to San Francisco, Las Vegas, Seattle, Atlanta, and Madison (Wisc.), and Toronto.

Jimmy Winkfield

1845 Macon B. Allen becomes the first African-American formally admitted to the bar in Massachusetts when he passes the examination in Worcester. The previous year he was admitted to the bar in Maine, making him the first licensed African-American attorney in the U.S.

1902 Astride Alan-a-Dale, African-American jockey Jimmy Winkfield wins his second Kentucky Derby in a row. With

Winkfield's wins, African-American jockeys have won 15 of 28 Derby races.

1920 Walker Smith, Jr. is born in Detroit, Mich. He will be better know as Sugar Ray Robinson, winner of boxing titles in three weight classes.

1948 In *Shelley v. Kraemer*, the Supreme Court rules that courts cannot enforce segregational housing covenants.

4

5

1937 Sculptor Melvin Edwards is born in Houston, Tex. He will have one-man exhibits at the Santa Barbara Museum of Art, the Walker Art Center in Minneapolis, and the Whitney Museum of American Art in New York City. His work will be represented in private collections as well as that of the Museum of Modern Art, the Schomburg Collection of the New York Public Library, and the Los Angeles County Museum of Art, among others.

1942 Nickolas Ashford is born in Fairfield, S.C. He will become a songwriter who, with his partner and wife Valerie Simpson, will write such hits as "Reach out and Touch (Somebody's Hand)," "Ain't Nothing Like the Real Thing," and "Ain't No Mountain High Enough." Becoming a solo act in 1973, Ashford and Simpson will have a string of successful albums including *Send It*, *Solid*, and *Real Love*.

1943 William Tubman is elected president of Liberia.

1961 Thirteen CORE–sponsored Freedom Riders begin a bus trip throughout the South to force desegregation of terminals. Ten days later, the bus will be bombed and its passengers attacked by white segregationists near Anniston, Ala.

1969 *No Place to Be Somebody* opens at the Public Theatre in New York. Charles Gordone's powerful play will earn its author the 1970 Pulitzer Prize for Drama.

William Stanley Braithwaite

1865 Adam Clayton Powell, Sr. is born in a log cabin in Soak Creek, Va. He will become a social and religious leader at Abyssinian Baptist Church in Harlem.

1905 Robert Sengstacke Abbott founds the *Chicago Defender*, calling it "The World's Greatest Weekly."

1919 The NAACP awards the Spingarn Medal to William Stanley Braithwaite.

Braithwaite's publication of essays and verse in notable mainstream magazines and editorial efforts on three books of verse and poetry anthologies had earned him wide acclaim among African-Americans and whites.

1931 Edwin A. Harleston dies in Charleston, S.C. One of the most popular and influential African-American painters of the day, his work will be exhibited at the Harmon Foundation, the Gallery of Art in Washington, D.C., and in the exhibit *Two Centuries of Black American Art*.

1969 Moneta Sleet becomes the first African-American to win a Pulitzer Prize for his photograph of Mrs. Martin Luther King, Jr. and her daughter at her husband's funeral.

1977 The Afro-American Historical and Genealogy Society is founded in Washington, D.C. The society's mission is to encourage scholarly research in African-American genealogy.

EDWIN HARLESTON, *Portrait of Aaron Douglas*. Oil on canvas. Gibbes Museum of Art, Charleston, South Carolina.

6

7

Charles Gilpin

1787 Prince Hall forms African Lodge 459, the first Black Masonic Lodge in the U.S.

1812 Martin R. Delany is born free in Charlestown, Va. He will become the first African-American field officer to serve in the Civil War, a noted physician, author, explorer, and a newspaper editor.

1930 Noted actor Charles Gilpin dies. The founder and manager of the Lafayette Theatre Company, one of the earliest African-American stock companies in New York, Gilpin achieved fame for his performance as Brutus Jones in Eugene O'Neill's play *The Emperor Jones*. In 1921, he won the NAACP's Spingarn Medal in recognition of his theatrical career.

1960 The Civil Rights Act of 1960 is signed by President Eisenhower. The act acknowledges the federal government's responsibility in matters involving civil rights and reverses its customary "hands-off" policy.

1884 Henrietta Vinton Davis performs scenes from Shakespeare with Powhatan Beaty at Ford's Opera House in Washington, D.C., site of the assassination of President Abraham Lincoln. Vinton's career will span a total of 44 years and will include her involvement with Marcus

Garvey's UNIA, including a vice-presidency of Garvey's doomed Black Star Line.

1931 Literary critic and editor Darwin Turner is born in Cincinnati, Ohio. His major works will include *Black American Literature: Essays, Poetry, Fiction and Drama* (1969) and *Voices from the Black Experience: African and Afro-American Literature* (1972).

1941 *Natural Man*, a play by Theodore Browne, premieres in New York City. It is a production of the American Negro Theatre, founded by Abram Hill and Frederick O'Neal.

1946 William Hastie is inaugurated as the first African-American governor of the Virgin Islands.

William Hastie

8

1771 Phillis Wheatley sails for England. Two years later, her book of poetry, *Poems on Various Subjects, Religious and Moral*, will be published in London.

Phillis Wheatley

1915 Henry McNeal Turner dies in Windsor, Canada. He was an influential minister in the AME Church and was appointed the first African-American chaplain in the U.S. Army.

1917 African-American Jesse Washington is burned alive in a public square in Waco, Tex. Fifteen thousand will look on in the incident known later as the "Waco horror."

1925 A. Philip Randolph organizes the Brotherhood of Sleeping Car Porters after failing to integrate the American Federation of Labor.

1965 The Association for the Advancement of Creative Musicians is founded by Muhal Richard Abrams.

9

Canada Lee

1750 The *South Carolina Gazette* reports that Caesar, a South Carolina slave, has been granted his freedom and a lifetime annuity in exchange for his cures for poison and rattlesnake bite. Caesar and the famous James Derham of New Orleans are two of the earliest known African-American medical practitioners.

1919 James Reese Europe is killed by a crazed band member after a concert at Mechanics Hall in Boston. Europe was one of the preeminent jazz bandleaders of the early 20th century, beginning with his association with the team of

J. Rosamond Johnson and Bob Cole in *The Shoo Fly Regiment* in 1906. Founder of the Clef Club, Europe joined the 15th, and later, 369th Infantry Regiments. The military band he formed during World War I was one of the most popular in all of Europe.

1952 Canada Lee dies in New York. A jockey and amateur boxer before turning to acting, Lee achieved wide acclaim for his portrayal of Bigger Thomas in the 1941 Broadway play *Native Son* and for the film *Cry the Beloved Country*.

1974 The House Judiciary Committee formally opens its impeachment hearings against President Richard M. Nixon with representatives John Conyers, Jr. (D-Mich.) and Barbara Jordan (D-Tex.) among members of the committee. Jordan, in particular, distinguishes herself as an eloquent and incisive contributor to the hearings process.

10

11

1775 Lemuel Haynes, Epheram Blackman, and Primas Black help capture Fort Ticonderoga as members of Ethan Allen's Green Mountain Boys.

1837 Pinckney Benton Steward (P.B.S.) Pinchback is born near Macon, Ga. In 1868, he will be elected to the state legislature as a senator and, in

Jackie Robinson
Black Heritage USA 20c

1871, be elected president of the Louisiana senate, lieutenant governor of Louisiana, and serve briefly as appointed governor. He will be elected to the U.S. Senate in 1873 but never be seated by that body due to supposed election irregularities.

1876 The American Centennial Exposition opens in Philadelphia, Pa. Included are works by four African-American artists, among them Edmonia Lewis's *The Dying Cleopatra* and Edward Bannister's *Under the Oaks*. Bannister's painting will win the bronze medal, a distinct and controversial achievement for the renowned painter.

1950 Jackie Robinson appears on the cover of *Life* magazine. It is the first time an African-American has been featured on the magazine's cover in its 13-year history.

1895 William Grant Still is born in Woodville, Miss. Considered one of the nation's greatest composers, he will begin his career by writing arrangements for W.C. Handy and as musical director for Harry Pace's Phonograph Corporation. One of his most famous compositions, *Afro-American Symphony*, will be the first symphonic work by an African-American to be performed by a major symphony orchestra, the Rochester Philharmonic Symphony, in 1931. He will also be the first African-American to conduct a major U.S. symphony, the Los Angeles Philharmonic, in 1936.

1933 Louis Eugene Walcott is born in New York City. He will be better known as Louis X, minister of the Nation of Islam mosque in Harlem and later as Louis Farrakhan, national representative of the Honorable Elijah Muhammad of a revived Nation of Islam.

Fred Shuttlesworth

1963 One day after Reverend Fred Shuttlesworth announces agreement on a limited integration plan in Birmingham, Ala., his home is bombed and a riot ensues.

1981 Hoyt J. Fuller dies in Atlanta. He was a literary critic and editor of *First World* and *Black World* (formerly *Negro Digest*) magazines.

12

13

1916 Albert Murray is born in Nokomis, Ala. He will become an author of several works of nonfiction, among them the influential collection of essays *The Omni Americans: New Perspectives on Black Experience and American Culture.*

1926 Mervyn Dymally is born in Cedros, Trinidad. He will become the first African-American elected as lieutenant governor of California and will be elected to Congress in 1980, where he will serve for 12 years.

1958 At a summit meeting of national African-American leaders, President Dwight D. Eisenhower is roundly criticized for urging them to "be patient" in their demands for full civil and voting rights.

1967 H. Rap Brown replaces Stokely Carmichael as chairman of SNCC.

Mervyn Dymally

1991 Hampton University students stage a silent protest against President George Bush's commencement address to highlight their opposition to his civil rights policies.

1871 Alcorn A&M College opens in Lorman, Miss.

1891 Isaac Murphy becomes the first jockey to win three Kentucky Derbys as he wins the fabled race astride Kingman. Kingman was trained by Dud Allen, an African-American trainer.

1914 Joseph Louis Barrow is born in Lexington, Ala. "The Brown Bomber" will hold the heavyweight crown from his 1937 title match with James J. Braddock until his first retirement in 1949. In his 71 professional fights, he will amass a record of 68 victories, 54 by knockouts.

1950 Steveland Judkins Morris is born in Saginaw, Mich. As 12-year-old Little Stevie Wonder, he will become a singing and musical sensation notable for "Fingertips, Part 2." Wonder will continue to record throughout adulthood, with the albums *Talking Book*, *Songs in the Key of Life*, *The Woman in Red*, and the soundtrack to the movie *Jungle Fever*. Among other awards he will win 12 Grammys and a 1984 best song Oscar for "I Just Called to Say I Love You."

1979 Max Robinson becomes the first network news anchor when he appears on ABC's *World News Tonight.*

1990 George Stallings is ordained as the first bishop of the African-American Catholic Church. Stallings broke from the Roman Catholic Church in 1989, citing the church's failure to meet the needs of African-American Catholics.

Stevie Wonder

MARTHA JACKSON-JARVIS, *Arc of the Southern Sun,* 1990. Clay, copper, and wood. Courtesy the artist.

14

15

Clara Stanton Jones

1913 Clara Stanton Jones is born in Saint Louis, Mo. She will become the first African-American director of the Detroit Public Library and the first African-American president of the American Library Association.

1959 Soprano saxophonist Sidney Bechet dies in France. A member of both Duke Ellington's and Noble Sissle's orchestras, Bechet moved to France and there achieved the greatest success of his career.

1963 Twenty-year-old Arthur Ashe becomes the first African-American to make the U.S. Davis Cup tennis team.

1969 John B. McLendon becomes the first African-American coach in the ABA when he signs a two-year contract with the Denver Nuggets.

1885 Erskine Henderson wins the Kentucky Derby riding Joe Cotton. The horse's trainer is another African-American, Alex Perry.

1918 In a World War I incident that will later be known as "The Battle of Henry Johnson," the African-American attacks advancing Germans, frees sentry Needham Roberts, and forces the retreat of the enemy troops. Johnson and Roberts will be awarded the Croix de Guerre, France's highest military award. They are the first Americans ever to win the award.

1923 *The Chip Woman's Fortune* by Willis Richardson opens at the Frazee Theatre on Broadway. The play, staged by the Ethiopian Art Theatre of Chicago, is the first dramatic work by an African-American playwright to be mounted on Broadway.

1942 The 93rd Infantry is activated at Fort Huachuca, Ariz. It is the first African-American division formed during World War II and is assigned to combat duty in the South Pacific.

Henry Johnson

1946 Camilla Williams appears in the title role of *Madama Butterfly* with the New York City Opera. She is the first African-American female concert singer to sign a contract with a major American opera company.

16

17

1917 Harry T. Burleigh, composer, pianist, and singer, is awarded the NAACP's Spingarn Medal for excellence in the field of creative music.

1929 John Conyers, Jr. is born in Detroit, Mich. He will be elected to the House of Representatives from Michigan's 1st District in 1964, where he will advocate home rule and Congressional representation for the District of Columbia. He will be the principal sponsor of the 1965 Voting Rights Act and the 1983 Martin Luther King, Jr. holiday bill, as well as a founder of the Congressional Black Caucus.

1930 Betty Carter is born in Flint, Mich. She will become an uncompromising jazz singer who will earn the nickname "Betty Bebop" for her bop improvisational style.

1966 Stokely Carmichael is elected chairman of SNCC, the Student Nonviolent Coordinating Committee, a group formed

John Conyers, Jr.

during the Freedom Marches and dedicated to voter registration in the South.

Meanwhile, Janet Damita Jackson is born in Gary, Ind. Sister of the famous Jacksons of the Jackson 5 singing group, she will have her own successful career, first in acting (*Good Times, Diff'rent Strokes, Fame*), then as a solo recording artist. Her albums *Control* and *Rhythm Nation 1814* will earn her five American Music Awards and a Grammy award.

1875 The first Kentucky Derby is won by African-American jockey Oliver Lewis riding a horse named Aristides. Fourteen of the 15 jockeys in the race are African-Americans.

1915 The National Baptist Convention is chartered.

1954 The Supreme Court outlaws school segregation in *Brown v. Board of Education.* The ruling is a major victory for the NAACP, led by Thurgood Marshall of the Legal Defense Fund, and other civil rights groups.

1956 "Sugar" Ray Charles Leonard is born in Wilmington, S.C. Leonard will win the National Golden Gloves championship at 16, an Olympic gold medal in 1976, and have a successful professional boxing career, winning titles in both the welterweight and middleweight divisions.

1957 The Prayer Pilgrimage, attracting a crowd of over 30,000, is held on the steps of the Lincoln Memorial in Washington, D.C. Timed to coincide with the third anniversary of *Brown v. Board of Education*, the pilgrimage is organized by Martin Luther King, Jr., the NAACP, and others to advocate greater voting and civil rights for African-Americans.

1969 A commemorative stamp of W.C. Handy, "Father of the Blues," is issued by the U.S. Postal Service.

1987 The work of four contemporary African-American artists—Sam Gilliam, Keith Morrison, William T. Williams, and Martha Jackson-Jarvis—is shown in the inaugural exhibition of the new Anacostia Museum in Washington, D.C.

RICHARD MAYHEW, *Sedona,* 1990. Oil on canvas. Courtesy Sherrie Washington Gallery, Detroit, Michigan.

18

19

_____
_____
_____
_____
_____
_____
_____
_____

_____
_____
_____
_____
_____
_____
_____
_____

1652 Rhode Island enacts the first colonial law limiting slavery.

1848 William Leidesdorff dies in San Francisco, Calif. The first man to sail a steamboat into

San Francisco Bay, Leidesdorff developed a successful business empire, including a hotel, warehouse, and other real-estate developments. Active politically, he served on San Francisco's first town council and became city treasurer. A street in the city will be named in his honor.

1880 George Lewis wins the sixth running of the Kentucky Derby astride Fonso.

1896 In _Plessy v. Ferguson_, the U.S. Supreme Court upholds Louisiana's "separate but equal" segregation laws. The ruling is a major setback for integration and marks the beginning of Jim Crow laws.

1946 Reginald Martinez Jackson is born in Wyncote, Pa. He will be better known as Reggie Jackson, star baseball player for the Oakland A's and New York Yankees. He will set or tie seven World Series records.

Reggie Jackson

1925 Malcolm Little, later known as Malcolm X and El Hajj Malik El-Shabazz, is born in Omaha, Nebr. In prison he is introduced to the Nation of Islam and begins studies that will lead him to become one of the most militant and electrifying leaders of the civil rights movement. His story will be immortalized in the book _Autobiography of Malcolm X_, ghostwritten by Alex Haley.

1930 Lorraine Hansberry, noted playwright of _A Raisin in the Sun_ and _The Sign in Sidney Brustein's Window_, is born in Chicago, Ill.

1965 Patricia Harris is named U.S. Ambassador to Luxembourg. She is the first African-American woman to become an ambassador for the U.S.

Malcolm X

1991 Willy T. Ribbs becomes the first African-American driver to qualify for the Indianapolis 500. During the race, which occurs the following week, Ribbs will be forced to drop out due to engine failure.

20

21

1746 François-Dominique Toussaint L'Ouverture is born into slavery in Haiti. He will lead the revolution in his country against French and English forces to free the slaves. Although he will nominally rule in the name of France, he will in actuality become political and military dictator of the country.

1868 P.B.S. Pinchback and James J. Harris are the first African-American delegates to a Republican convention. They will participate in the nomination of Ulysses S. Grant for President.

1951 The New York branch of the NAACP honors Josephine Baker for her work to combat racism. Baker, the American chanteuse who was acclaimed in Europe, had led a personal crusade to force integration of clubs where she appeared in Miami and Las Vegas. She also campaigned against segregated railroad facilities in Chicago and buses in Oakland.

Josephine Baker

1921 Christopher Perry, who founded the Philadelphia *Tribune* in 1884, dies in Philadelphia, Pa., at the age of 65.

1961 Freedom Riders are attacked in Montgomery, Ala. The third city in which the CORE–sponsored group is attacked, the incident prompts Attorney General Robert F. Kennedy to send U.S. marshals to keep the peace while the governor of Alabama declares martial law and dispatches the National Guard to the troubled area.

1970 The National Guard is mobilized to stop widespread demonstrations and violence at Ohio State University. The interracial student demonstrators demand an end to ROTC programs and greater admissions for African-American students.

1971 Riots in Chattanooga, Tenn., result in one death and 400 arrests as National Guard troops are called to put down the racially motivated disturbances.

22

23

_____

_____

_____

_____

_____

_____

_____

_____

1940 Bernard Shaw is born in Chicago, Ill. He will become a journalist and the principal Washington anchor for Cable News Network, where he will be widely respected for his coverage of world summit meetings, the historic student demonstrations in Beijing, Presidential primaries and elections, and the Gulf War.

1948 Harlem Renaissance poet and author Claude McKay dies in Chicago, Ill. His novel *Home to Harlem* (1928) became the first best-seller written by an African-American.

1959 Benjamin O. Davis, Jr. becomes the first African-American major general in the U.S. Air Force. In doing so, he improves upon the accomplishments of Davis Senior, who was the first African-American general in the U.S. Army.

1967 Langston Hughes, noted poet, dies in New York City. He was the author of the poetry collections *The Weary Blues*,

Not Without Laughter, The Way of White Folks, the autobiographies *The Big Sea* and *I Wonder as I Wander,* and plays and newspaper series. Hughes's ashes will be buried at the Schomburg Center for Research in Black Culture in Harlem.

1966 Bill Cosby, star of *I Spy*, receives an Emmy for best actor in a dramatic series, the first African-American in the category. He will earn a total of four Emmys.

◆ *Bernard Shaw*

1844 Charles Edmund Nash is born in Opelousas, La. He will become the first African-American representative to the U.S. House of Representatives from the State of Louisiana.

1900 Civil War hero Sergeant William H. Carney of the 54th Massachusetts Colored Infantry becomes the first African-American Congressional Medal of Honor winner. He was cited almost 37 years after the Battle of Fort Wagner, where he carried the colors and led the charge after the original standard-bearer was shot.

1921 *Shuffle Along*, the first of a popular series of musicals featuring all-African-American casts, opens at the 63rd Street Music Hall in New York City. The musical is written by Noble Sissle and Eubie Blake and features Florence Mills and a young Josephine Baker in the chorus; William Grant Still and Hall Johnson play in the orchestra.

Charles E. Nash

1961 Twenty-seven Freedom Riders are arrested in Jackson, Miss.

1975 Jackie "Moms" Mabley dies in White Plains, N.Y. Best known as a comedienne, she began her career as a singer at the age of 14 and traveled the vaudeville circuit, appearing in theaters and nightclubs. Making her comedy recording debut in 1960, Mabley appeared on *The Ed Sullivan Show* as well ◆ as in movie roles.

24

Patti LaBelle

1881 Paul Quinn College is chartered in the State of Texas. The college, founded in 1872, had moved from its original site in Austin to Waco in 1877.

1937 Archie Shepp is born in Fort Lauderdale, Fla. He will become a renowned avant-garde jazz saxophonist and play with a variety of jazz greats including John Coltrane, Bobby Hutcherson, and Donald

Cherry. He also will be a composer of jazz instrumental compositions and the play *Lady Day: A Musical Tragedy*.

1944 Patricia Louise Holte is born in Philadelphia, Pa. She will be better known as Patti LaBelle, organizer and lead singer of Patti LaBelle and the Bluebells in 1960. In the 1970's she will reconfigure the group and later reteam with Nona Hendryx and Sara Dash as LaBelle. In 1976, LaBelle will pursue a solo career, gain even more critical and popular acclaim, and win a 1992 Grammy.

1954 Peter Marshall Murray is installed as president of the New York County Medical Society. He is the first African-American physician to head an AMA affiliate.

1991 Hal McRae is named manager of the Kansas City Royals. He is one of two African-American managers serving in major league baseball.

25

1878 Tap-dancing legend Bill "Bojangles" Robinson is born in Richmond, Va.

1905 Dorothy Burnett (later Wesley) is born in Warrenton, Va. She will become a member of Phi Beta Kappa, longtime librarian of the Moorland-Spingarn Research Center, and author of several African-American historical works.

1919 Millionaire Madame C.J. Walker dies. She was the founder of the Madame C.J. Walker Manufacturing Company, the largest African-American hair-care company of its time. After her death, a substantial portion of her business's proceeds will be donated to African-American organizations and scholarships.

1936 Historian and author of *When Harlem Was in Vogue* David Levering Lewis is born.

1943 Leslie Uggams is born in Washington Heights, N.Y. She will make her acting debut on

television's *Beulah* and be a regular on *The Mitch Miller Show* before achieving acclaim in Broadway's *Hallelujah Baby* and TV's *Roots*.

Dorothy Burnett

AARON DOUGLAS, *Building More Stately Mansions,* 1944. Oil on canvas. Permanent collection of Carl Van Vechten Gallery of Fine Arts, Fisk University of Nashville, Tennessee.

26

27

Miles Davis

1899 Aaron Douglas is born in Topeka, Kans. He will become a world-renowned painter and muralist whose work will embrace the African ancestral arts and express pride in the African-American image at a time when doing so was highly unpopular. His most famous works will be *Aspects of Negro Life, Let My People Go, Judgment Day* and *Building More Stately Mansions.*

1907 Elizabeth Keckley, seamstress and confidante to Mary

Todd Lincoln, dies of a paralytic stroke in Washington, D.C. Keckley was the author of *Behind the Scenes or Thirty Years a Slave, and Four Years in the White House* (1868), one of the first insider accounts of a White House Presidency.

1926 Miles Davis is born in Alton, Ill. For over four decades, he will be one of the most innovative and influential jazz trumpeters, known for his hard bop and jazz and fusion accomplishments. Most noted for the albums *Sketches of Spain, Miles Smiles,* and *Kind of Blue,* he will also win three Grammy awards for his albums *We Want Miles, Decoy,* and *Tutu* and be awarded the French Légion d'Honneur in 1991.

1968 Ruth A. Lucas is promoted to colonel in the U.S. Air Force, the first African-American woman to achieve this rank.

1863 Captain André Callioux and his Native Guard Regiment, which had once fought for the Confederacy, charge Port Hudson, La. The Union Army Guard, intent on disproving white contentions that "Negroes" lacked the intelligence for combat, will make six different assaults on the stronghold.

1917 One African-American is killed and hundreds are left homeless in race riots in East Saint Louis, Ill.

Louis Gossett, Jr.

1936 Louis Gossett, Jr. is born in Brooklyn, N.Y. He will make his acting debut at 17 in *Take a Giant Step* and act in numerous stage, film and television roles including Fiddler in *Roots,* for which he will win an Emmy. His portrayal of the tough drill instructor in *An Officer and a Gentleman* will win him an Academy Award as best supporting actor in 1982, the third African-American to win an Oscar for acting.

1941 A race riot begins in East Saint Louis, Ill. After four days of rioting, one African-American will be killed.

1968 The Supreme Court orders schools to present a realistic desegregation plan immediately. The ruling comes almost 13 years to the day after the Court's "all deliberate speed" desegregation order in 1955.

28

29

1944 Gladys Knight is born in Atlanta, Ga. Making her first public appearance at age four, she will win first place on *Ted Mack's Original Amateur Hour* at seven. A member of the Pips since the early 1950's, Knight will remain with the popular group for over 30 years before pursuing a successful solo career.

1974 Cicely Tyson wins two Emmy awards for best actress in a special and best actress in a drama for her portrayal of a strong Southern matriarch in *The Autobiography of Miss Jane Pittman* while Richard Pryor wins an Emmy for his writing contributions on the Lily Tomlin special *Lily*.

1981 Mary Lou Williams dies in Durham, N.C. A jazz pianist who played with Louis Armstrong, Tommy Dorsey, Earl "Fatha" Hines, and Benny Goodman, she formed her own band in 1943. Williams was known for her jazz masses including one, *Mary Lou's Mass*, that was choreographed by the Alvin Ailey American Dance Theater in 1971.

Gladys Knight

1910 Ralph Metcalfe is born in Atlanta, Ga. He will become a world record holder in the 100- and 200-yard dashes and win a bronze medal in the 1932 Olympic Games and gold and silver medals in the 1936 Games. He will also become a four-term congressman representing Illinois's 1st District.

1958 Ernest Green, the only senior among the Little Rock Nine, graduates from Little Rock High School. Green is the only African-American among the 601 students who graduate.

1969 Artist and art educator James V. Herring dies in Washington, D.C. Herring organized the first American art gallery to be directed and controlled by African-Americans on the Howard University campus in 1930, founded and directed the university's art department and, with Alonzo Aden, opened the famed Barnett-Aden Gallery in Washington, D.C., in 1943.

Ralph Metcalfe

1973 Tom Bradley is elected mayor of Los Angeles, Calif. Winning after a bitter defeat four years earlier by incumbent mayor Sam Yorty, Bradley, a Texas native and former Los Angeles Police Department veteran, is the first African-American mayor of the city and will serve an unprecedented five terms.

ROBERT SCOTT DUNCANSON, *Landscape with Rainbow,* 1859. Oil on canvas. National Museum of American Art, Smithsonian Institution, gift of Leonard Granoff.

30

31

Countee Cullen

1822 Denmark Vesey's conspiracy to free the slaves of Charleston, S.C., and surrounding areas is thwarted when a slave betrays the plot to whites. Vesey's bold plan had attracted over 9,000 slaves and freemen of the area including Peter Poyas, a ship's carpenter, Gullah Jack, Blind Phillip, Ned Bennett and Mingo Harth. Later it will be considered one of the most complex and elaborate slave liberation plans ever undertaken.

1903 Countee Cullen is born in New York City. He will attend

NYU, be elected Phi Beta Kappa in 1925, and win poetry prizes throughout his undergraduate years. Among Cullen's most notable poems will be "Yet Do I Marvel," "The Ballad of the Brown Girl," "To the One Who Said Me Nay," the collections *Color, Copper Sun* and the posthumously published *On These I Stand: An Anthology of the Best Poems of Countee Cullen.*

1943 Gale Sayers is born in Wichita, Kans. He will become an outstanding running back and a first-round draft pick of the Chicago Bears in 1965. Elected to the Football Hall of Fame in 1977, he will be the youngest player ever to receive the honor.

1965 Vivian Malone becomes the first African-American to graduate from the University of Alabama, a college that had been one of the last bastions of racial segregation in the South.

1971 Willie Mays scores his 1,950th run.

1870 The first civil rights Enforcement Act, which protects the voting and civil rights of African-Americans, is passed by Congress.

1909 The first NAACP conference is held in New York City with 300 African-Americans and whites in attendance. Ida B. Wells-Barnett, while speaking at the conference, condemns lynching as a "blight upon our nation, mocking our laws and disgracing our Christianity."

1931 Shirley Verrett is born in New Orleans, La. She will become an operatic mezzo-soprano known worldwide for her compelling performance in *Carmen.*

1955 The U.S. Supreme Court passes a second desegregation ruling, demanding "all deliberate speed" be used in the desegregation of public schools.

1987 John Dotson is named publisher of the Boulder, Colo.,

Daily Camera. It is one of many distinctions for the noted journalist, including being the first African-American reporter for *Newsweek* magazine and founding, in the mid-1970's, the Institute for Journalism Education, dedicated to training minority journalists.

Shirley Verrett

1

1835 The Fifth National Negro Convention recommends that blacks remove the word "African" from the titles of their organizations and discontinue referring to themselves as "colored."

1937 Morgan Freeman is born. Making his acting debut in an all-African-American cast of *Hello Dolly* in 1967, Freeman will also have a major role in the television program *The Electric Company* before breaking into movies. He will receive an Academy Award nomination for his supporting role in *Street Smart*, and star in *Clean and Sober* and *Lean on Me*. He will be nominated again for a supporting role in *Glory* and for his starring role in *Driving Miss Daisy*.

1941 The first African-American tank battalion, the 758th, is activated. One year later to the day, the Marine Corps begins enlistment of African-Americans at Camp Lejeune, N.C.

1973 WGPR-TV (Channel 62) in Detroit, Mich., is granted a permit to operate. It is the first television station owned by African-Americans.

Morgan Freeman

2

1868 John Hope is born in Augusta, Ga. He will be the first African-American president of Atlanta Baptist (later Morehouse) College.

1943 The 99th Pursuit Squadron, the first African-American Army Air Corps unit, flies its first combat mission in the Mediterranean, strafing enemy positions on the Italian island of Pantelleria.

1951 Kenneth I. Chenault is born in Mineola (Long Island), N.Y. He will become an attorney and join American Express in 1981, where he will become president of the company's Consumer Card and Financial Services Group in 1989 and one of the highest-ranking African-Americans in corporate America.

1967 The first of three days of race riots occurs in the Roxbury section of Boston. Dozens are injured and more arrested after welfare mothers barricade themselves in protest against welfare policies.

Kenneth I. Chenault

3

4

Charles R Drew MD
USA 35c

1871 Miles Vandehurst Lynk is born near Brownsville, Tenn. A physician at 19, he founds the first African-American medical journal, the *Medical and Surgical Observer,* and will be one of the organizers of what will later become the National Medical Association.

1887 Roland Hayes is born in Curryville, Tenn. A noted concert artist, Hayes will be the first African-American to give a recital in Boston's Symphony Hall. His career will take him throughout the U.S. and to London for a command performance before King George V.

1904 Charles R. Drew, creator of the plasma method of blood preservation, is born in Washington, D.C. He will receive the NAACP's Spingarn Medal for his contributions in 1944 and, in 1981, be posthumously honored by the U.S. Postal Service with a commemorative stamp.

1906 Josephine Baker, singer and entertainer, is born in Saint Louis, Mo. A chorus girl in the 1923 musical *Shuffle Along,* she will travel to Paris, introduce "le jazz hot" in the show *La Revue Nègre,* and will cause a sensation with the Folies Bergères when she performs topless on a mirror, wearing a rubber banana skirt. A World War II Red Cross volunteer, Baker will perform for the Allied troops and in the 1950's she will tour the U.S., fighting for desegregated theaters and restaurants.

1946 In its *Morgan v. Commonwealth of Virginia* ruling, the Supreme Court bars segregation in interstate bus travel.

1922 Samuel L. Gravely, who will become the first African-American admiral in the U.S. Navy, is born in Richmond, Va. He will be the first African-American to command a U.S. warship, the *USS Falgout,* and will also command the *USS Taussig.*

Samuel L. Gravely

1946 Mississippi Valley State University is founded in Itta Bena, Miss.

1972 Angela Davis is acquitted by 11 whites and one Mexican-American of murder, kidnaping, and criminal conspiracy charges brought in connection with a 1970 courthouse shoot-out in San Rafael, Calif.

1989 Four African-Americans win Tony awards for *Black and Blue,* a musical revue featuring classic blues and tap-dance routines. Winners are Ruth Brown (best actress in a musical), Cholly Atkins, Henry LeTang, Frankie Manning, and Fayard Nicholas (best choreography).

1991 Baltimore Orioles manager Frank Robinson is named assistant general manager of the club. He is the third African-American to become an assistant GM, joining Elaine Weddington of the Boston Red Sox and Bob Watson of the Houston Astros.

5

1783 Oliver Cromwell, an African-American soldier who served in the Revolutionary War, receives an honorable discharge signed by George Washington. Cromwell, who will claim to have been with Washington when he crossed the Delaware and in the battles of Yorktown, Princeton, and Monmouth, is cited by Washington as having earned "the Badge of Merit for six years' faithful service."

1872 The Republican National Convention meets in Philadelphia, Pa. The meeting marks the significant participation of three African-American delegates: Robert B. Elliot (chair of the South Carolina delegation); Joseph Rainey, and John R. Lynch of Mississippi, who each make addresses.

1940 The American Negro Theatre is organized in Harlem by Frederick O'Neal, Abram Hill, and members of the McClendon Players. Among the plays it will produce is *Anna Lucasta*, which will be presented on Broadway in 1944 and feature Canada Lee, Ossie Davis, and Ruby Dee.

1956 A three-judge federal court rules that racial segregation on Montgomery city buses is unconstitutional, ending the Montgomery bus boycott.

1973 Doris A. Davis of Compton, Calif., becomes the first African-American female to govern a metropolitan city.

Doris A. Davis

6

1869 Dillard University is chartered in New Orleans, La.

1939 Marian Wright (later Edelman) is born in Bennettsville, S.C. In addition to becoming the first African-American woman admitted to the bar in Mississippi, she will direct the NAACP's Legal Defense and Education Fund in New York and Mississippi and found the Children's Defense Fund in 1973.

1944 The 320th Negro Anti-Aircraft Barrage Balloon Battalion assists in the D-Day invasion in Normandy, France.

1947 Harrison Branch is born in New York City. A student at the San Francisco Art Institute and Yale University School of Art, he will become a professor of art and photographer whose works will be exhibited and collected in the U.S. and Europe and will appear in the landmark photography book *An Illustrated Bio-Bibliography of Black*

Marian Wright Edelman

Photographers, 1940–1988, edited by Deborah Willis Ryan.

1966 James Meredith is wounded by a white sniper on the second day of the Memphis, Tenn.—Jackson, Miss., voter registration march. The march will be continued the next day by Martin Luther King, Jr. and other civil rights groups who cover 260 miles and register almost 4,000 African-Americans.

Meanwhile, Stokely Carmichael, using his newly adopted name of Kwam'e Toure, launches the Black Power movement. Toure will say that the use of the term is not antiwhite but a phrase to denote a political strategy.

DAVID C. DRISKELL, *Sweet Music,* 1978. Collage. Collection the artist.

7

8

Prince

1917 Gwendolyn Brooks is born in Topeka, Kans. She will become the first African-American Pulitzer Prize winner for her 1950 book of poetry, *Annie Allen*.

1930 *The New York Times* capitalizes the word Negro "in recognition of racial self-respect for those who have been for generations in the lowercase."

1931 David C. Driskell is born in Eatonton, Ga. An artist and professor of art at several uni-

versities, Driskell will be acclaimed as one of the foremost art historians and curators of African-American art exhibits.

1943 Nikki Giovanni, poet and author, is born in Knoxville, Tenn. She will be known for her books *Black Feeling, Black Talk*, and *Black Judgement*.

1959 Prince, one of the leading rock artists and producers of the 1980's and 1990's, is born in Minneapolis, Minn. His movie *Purple Rain* (1984) will be hailed by some critics as the best rock movie ever made and earn Prince an Oscar for best original song score and soundtrack album.

1987 Lloyd Richards wins a Tony as best director for the August Wilson play *Fences*. The play wins three other Tony awards, for best play, best performance by an actor (James Earl Jones), and best performance by a featured actress (Mary Alice).

1953 The Supreme Court bans segregation in restaurants in Washington, D.C.

1969 Bill Cosby wins an Emmy for a variety special. It is his fourth Emmy award.

1982 Leroy "Satchel" Paige, a pitcher in the Negro Leagues and the first African-American pitcher in the American League, dies. Paige is heralded as one of the greatest early African-American baseball players in a career that spanned more than 40 years and was enshrined in baseball's Hall of Fame in 1971.

Leroy "Satchel" Paige

9

1877 Meta Vaux Warwick (later Fuller) is born in Philadelphia, Pa. She will become a sculptor who will train at the Pennsylvania Museum and School for Industrial Arts and travel to Paris to study with Auguste Rodin. Her sculptures will be exhibited at the Salon in Paris as well as extensively in the U.S. for 60 years. Her most famous works will include *Ethiopia Awakening, Mary Turner (A Silent Protest Against Mob Violence),* and *The Talking Skull.*

1978 Larry Holmes wins the WBC heavyweight title by defeating Ken Norton in Las Vegas, Nev.

1983 Scott Joplin, noted jazz musician and composer of ragtime music, is the sixth African-American depicted in the U.S. Postal Service's Black Heritage USA commemorative series of postage stamps.

Scott Joplin

Black Heritage USA 20c

10

1794 Richard Allen founds Bethel African Methodist Episcopal Church, the first AME church in the U.S.

1854 James Augustine Healy is ordained as a Catholic priest in ceremonies at Notre Dame cathedral in Paris, France.

1898 Hattie McDaniel is born in Wichita, Kans. A vaudevillian, she will begin her acting career at age 37 in the film *The Golden West.* McDaniel will go on to roles in over 70 films, including *The Little Colonel, Show Boat,* and most notably *Gone With the Wind,* which will earn her an Oscar as best supporting actress in 1940. She will also star in the radio program *Beulah* from 1947 to 1951.

1910 Chester Arthur Burnett is born in Aberdeen, Miss. He will be better know as "Howlin' Wolf," a Delta bluesman whose recordings will inspire English rock bands to adopt his style and material.

Hattie McDaniel

1940 The famed Cotton Club in Harlem closes. Home to some of the most important jazz talents of their day, including Duke Ellington, Lena Horne, and many others, the club falls victim to changing musical tastes and poor attendance.

META WARWICK FULLER, *The Talking Skull,* 1937. Bronze. From the Museum of Afro-American History, Boston, Massachusetts.

11

12

Charles Rangel

1920 Hazel Dorothy Scott is born in Port of Spain, Trinidad. A child prodigy, she will enroll at New York City's Juilliard School and star in nightclubs, Broadway shows, and films. A fixture in jazz society uptown and downtown in New York, most notably for her jazz improvisations on familiar classical works, she will be credited with putting the "swing in European classical music."

1930 Charles Rangel is born in New York City. He will defeat Adam Clayton Powell, Jr. for the latter's Congressional seat in the 16th District and serve on the House Judiciary Commit-

tee hearings on the impeachment of President Richard M. Nixon. He will also chair the Congressional Black Caucus and be a strong advocate in the war on drugs and drug crime as chairman of the House Select Committee on Narcotics Abuse and Control.

1963 Vivian Malone and James Hood, accompanied by U.S. Deputy Attorney General Nicholas Katzenbach, attempt to register at the University of Alabama. They are met by Governor George Wallace, who bodily blocks their entrance to a campus building. When National Guardsmen return later in the day with Malone and Hood to enter the building, Wallace steps aside.

1964 In South Africa, Nelson Mandela is sentenced to life imprisonment for allegedly attempting to sabotage the white South African government.

1840 The World's Anti-Slavery Convention convenes in London, England. Among those in attendance will be African-American Charles Remond, who will refuse to be seated at the meeting when he and the other delegates learn that women are being segregated in the gallery.

1876 A monument is dedicated to Richard Allen in Philadelphia's Fairmont Park. It is the

first known monument erected by African-Americans to honor one of their heroes.

1963 Medgar Evers, field secretary for the Mississippi NAACP, is killed outside his home in Jackson, Miss. He will be widely mourned throughout the civil rights movement and posthumously receive the NAACP's Spingarn Medal.

1967 The U.S. Supreme Court strikes down a Virginia miscegenation law.

1972 The National Black MBA Association is incorporated. An organization of over 2,000 minority holders of advanced business degrees, the organization's mission is to assist the entry of interested minorities into the business community.

Medgar Evers

13

14

1868 Ex-slave Oscar J. Dunn is installed as lieutenant governor of Louisiana. It is the highest executive office held by an African-American to date.

1937 Eleanor Holmes (later Norton) is born in Washington, D.C. A graduate of the Yale University School of Law, Norton will become chairperson of the U.S. Equal Opportunity Commission, the chairperson of the New York City Commission on Human Rights, and a Georgetown University law professor before being elected a nonvoting delegate to Congress representing the District of Columbia.

1967 U.S. solicitor general Thurgood Marshall is appointed associate justice of the Supreme Court by President Lyndon B. Johnson.

1990 Bernadette Locke becomes the first female on-court coach when she is named assistant coach of the University of Kentucky men's basketball team.

Eleanor Holmes Norton

Marla Gibbs

1939 *The Ethel Waters Show*, a variety special, appears on NBC. It is the first time an African-American appears on television.

1941 John Edgar Wideman is born in Washington, D.C. He will become a Rhodes scholar and writer of such fictional works as *Hurry Home*, *Damballah*, and *Philadelphia Fire*.

1946 Marla Gibbs is born in Chicago, Ill. She will become a popular and enduring television personality, notable for her roles in *The Jeffersons* and *227*.

1970 Cheryl Adrienne Brown wins the Miss Iowa pageant and becomes the first African-American to compete in the Miss America beauty pageant.

1989 Congressman William Gray, chairman of the House Democratic Caucus, is elected Democratic Whip of the House of Representatives, the highest ranking leadership position ever held by an African-American in Congress.

15

16

1877 Henry O. Flipper, born into slavery in Thomasville, Ga., becomes the first African-American to graduate from West Point.

1921 Bessie Coleman, a 28-year-old native of Atlanta, Tex., who learned French in order to communicate with instructors, receives a pilot's certificate from the Fédération Aéronautique Internationale in France. She is the first black in the world to become a licensed pilot.

1971 The U.S. Supreme Court upholds the constitutionality of closing Jackson, Miss., swimming pools rather than integrating them. The ruling is considered by many to indicate the Court's resistance to increased integration.

Bessie Coleman

1990 St. Clair Drake dies of a heart attack in Palo Alto, Calif. The noted sociologist and anthropologist was the author of numerous books, including the important *Black Metropolis*, which he coauthored with Horace Cayton. In 1969, he established and served as director of the African and Afro-American Studies Program at Stanford University, a program often imitated by other colleges and universities.

1970 Kenneth Gibson is elected mayor of Newark, N.J. He is the first African-American to serve in the position and the first of a major eastern city. In 1976 he will be elected the first African-American president of the U.S. Conference of Mayors.

1975 Adam Wade hosts the nationally televised game show *Musical Chairs*. He is the first African-American game show host.

1976 Hector Petersen, a 13-year-old Soweto schoolboy, is the first to die in what will become known as the "Children's Crusade," the first nationwide black South African uprising in the 1970's. The violence will last 16 months and result in 570 deaths, 3,900 injuries, and 5,900 detentions.

1991 Natalie Cole's album *Unforgettable* is released. The album consists of her rendition of 24 songs by her father, Nat, and includes the title track, specially remixed to include both father and daughter's voices. It will be her most successful album, selling over 4,000,000 copies, and sweeping the Grammy Awards ceremonies in 1992.

Natalie Cole

17

18

1775 Former slave Peter Salem shoots Major John Pitcairn in the Battle of Bunker Hill. Salem, along with Seasor, Pharaoh, Salem Poor, Barzaillai Lew, and Cuff Whittmore, fights in the battles of Bunker Hill and Breed's Hill. Pitcairn was the major who ordered British soldiers to fire on the Minutemen at Lexington.

1871 James Weldon Johnson is born in Tampa, Fla. He will become a writer (*Autobiography of an Ex-Colored Man*), poet, first African-American admitted to the Florida bar, diplomat, ex-ecutive secretary of the NAACP, and professor.

1928 James Brown is born in Macon, Ga. He will become one of the most influential R & B singers, with a career that spans five decades and includes hits of the 1960's through 1980's ("I Got You," "Cold Sweat," "Living in America"). Incarcerated in 1988 for aggravated assault, Brown will be released in 1991 and return to the recording scene, where he will continue to influence a new generation of artists including Hammer, Prince, and many others.

1967 Six days of rioting end in Newark, N.J., in the worst urban violence since the Watts Riots of 1965.

Salem Poor ✿ *Gallant Soldier*

Wellington Webb

1889 William H. Richardson receives a patent for a baby carriage whose body can be raised from its frame.

1942 Bernard W. Robinson, of Harvard, becomes a Naval Reserve ensign. He is the first African-American to earn a U.S. Navy commission.

1953 Egypt becomes a republic after the forced abdication of King Farouk I.

1966 Samuel Nabrit becomes the first African-American scientist to serve on the Atomic Energy Commission.

1991 City auditor Wellington Webb is elected mayor of Denver, Colo. He is the first African-American to hold the post.

HOWARDENA PINDELL, *Autobiography: Nigeria (Oshogbo, 1973) and Italy (Venice,1971),* 1989. Cibachrome, acrylic, and tempera on museum board. Courtesy the artist.

19

20

_____
_____
_____
_____
_____
_____
_____
_____

_____
_____
_____
_____
_____
_____
_____
_____

1862 Slavery is abolished in U.S. territories by Congress.

1865 Slavery formally ends in Texas when General Gordon Granger arrives in Galveston with Union forces. As news of freedom spreads throughout the state, "Juneteenth" celebrations will come to commemorate emancipation of African-Americans everywhere.

1867 P.B.S. Pinchback urges African-Americans to use their franchise privileges. "The Congress of the United States have conferred upon our People the Elective Franchise and it is our important duty to see that we use it well...."

1914 Ernest Crichlow is born in Brooklyn, N.Y. Studying at the Art Students League, Crichlow will be associated with the Harlem Art Center during the 1930's as a noted painter and illustrator whose objectives will be to advocate social commentary and communication through art.

1918 John H. Johnson is born in Arkansas City, Ark. He will become the editor and publisher of *Ebony* and *Jet* magazines and will be the founder of Johnson Publishing Company, the most successful African-American publishing company in the U.S. He will also own two radio stations (including the first African-American-owned radio station in Chicago) and Fashion Fair Cosmetics.

John H. Johnson

1858 Charles W. Chestnutt is born in Cleveland, Ohio. He will at one time maintain four careers simultaneously—stenographer, lawyer, author, and lecturer. His most famous literary works will be a biography of Frederick Douglass and the short story collection *The Conjure Woman*. In 1928, he will receive the NAACP's Spingarn Medal for his literary accomplishments.

1926 Mordecai W. Johnson becomes the first African-American president of Howard University.

1929 *Hot Chocolates* premieres at the Hudson Theatre in New York City. With music by Fats Waller and lyrics by Andy Razaf, the musical will introduce the songs "Ain't Misbehavin'" and "Black and Blue."

1943 Thirty-four are killed in race riots in Detroit, Mich. Federal troops are called in to control the violence, which stems from African-Americans' frustration over exclusion from civilian defense jobs.

1946 Andre Watts is born in Nuremberg, Germany. He will make his debut as a concert pianist at age nine, have his New York Philharmonic debut in 1963, and become a world-famous classical pianist.

1949 Lionel Richie is born in Tuskegee, Ala. He will be one of the most successful singers/songwriters in contemporary popular music, know for his efforts in pop, R & B, and country music. Once a member of the Commodores, Richie will establish a solo career, win Grammys in 1982 and 1984, and be a featured performer at the closing ceremonies of the 1984 Summer Olympic Games in Los Angeles.

1960 Harry Belafonte wins an Emmy for his variety special *Tonight with Harry Belafonte*. It is the first Emmy awarded to an African-American.

21

22

Col. Benjamin O. Davis, Jr.

1832 Joseph Haynes Rainey is born in Georgetown, S.C. He will become the first African-American representative to the U.S. House of Representatives, where he will serve five terms.

1859 Henry Ossawa Tanner is born in Pittsburgh, Pa. Son of AME bishop Benjamin Tanner, young Tanner will forgo the ministry to take up painting. Constantly facing the tension between racial stereotypes and his art, Tanner will eventually emigrate to France to pursue

his art, considered by many the finest produced by an African-American. He will be known for his commanding use of light and color in his seascapes, scenes of everyday life, and religious paintings.

1945 Colonel Benjamin O. Davis, Jr. becomes the first African-American to command a U.S. Army Air Force base when he takes command of the 477th Composite Group of Godman Field in Kentucky.

1951 PFC William H. Thompson is posthumously awarded the Congressional Medal of Honor. He is the first African-American recipient since the Spanish-American War.

1964 Two white and one African-American civil rights workers, Andrew Goodman, Michael Schwerner, and James Cheney, disappear near Philadelphia, Miss., and are later found murdered.

1909 Katherine Dunham is born in Joliet, Ill. She will become one of the revolutionary forces in modern dance through her introduction and use of African and Caribbean styles. Successful on the stage and in movies, including *Stormy Weather*, in the late 1960's she will form the Katherine Dunham Center for the Performing Arts and in 1983 be awarded Kennedy Center honors.

1937 Joe Louis defeats James (J.J.) Braddock to become heavyweight champion of the world. The fight is won in eight rounds before 45,000 fans, the largest audience to date to witness a fight.

Ed Bradley

1941 Ed Bradley is born in Philadelphia, Pa. A CBS correspondent covering the Vietnam conflict, Bradley will become co-anchor of CBS's *60 Minutes* and win six Emmy awards.

1947 Octavia Butler is born in Pasadena, Calif. She will become a science fiction writer and winner of the Hugo Award for excellence in science fiction writing in 1984.

1949 Ezzard Charles defeats Jersey Joe Walcott to win the world heavyweight championship.

1991 *Kaleidoscope*, an exhibit of the work of over 30 African-American photographers, opens at the Anacostia Museum in Washington, D.C. Among those exhibited are masters Addison Scurlock and Robert Scurlock as well as contemporary photographers Matthew Lewis, Sam Yette, Sharon Farmer, and Brian Jones.

HENRY OSSAWA TANNER, *Florida,* 1894. Oil on canvas. Collection of Walter O. Evans, Detroit, Michigan.

23

24

1893 Willie Sims rides winning horses in five of six races at Sheepshead Bay in Brooklyn, N.Y. Simms will repeat the feat two years later in addition to winning two Kentucky Derbys and two Belmont Stakes.

1926 Langston Hughes's article *The Negro Artist and the Racial Mountain* appears in *Nation* magazine. In it, Hughes expresses African-Americans' bold new confidence to create a new art during the Harlem Renaissance. "We younger Negro artists who create now intend to express our individual dark-skinned selves without fear or shame."

1940 Wilma Rudolph is born in Clarksville, Tenn. A polio victim, she will win three gold medals at the Summer Games in Rome, the first American woman to achieve this feat in a single Olympiad.

1982 The House of Representatives approves the extension of the 1965 Voting Rights Act, despite North Carolina Senator Jesse Helms's attempt to block the House vote. The Senate had approved the extension of the bill five days before the historic House vote.

Wilma Rudolph

1844 Boston African-Americans hold the first of a series of meetings protesting Jim Crow schools.

1896 Booker T. Washington is the first African-American to receive an honorary master of arts degree from Harvard University.

1933 Dramatic soprano Matilda Sissieretta Jones dies of cancer in Providence, R.I. Called "the first Negro prima donna," Jones toured with the Tennesee Jubilee Singers and performed at Carnegie Hall, Madison Square Garden and at the White House in 1892. She was dubbed "Black Patti," a name she reportedly disliked for its allusion to white contemporary, Adelina Patti.

Booker T. Washington

1974 Boston's National Center for Afro-American Artists becomes the first African-American cultural center to be awarded a Ford Foundation grant.

25

26

1876 The most famous Native American uprising, at Little Bighorn, begins in the Dakota territories. Colonel George Armstrong Custer leads three U.S. battalions to their deaths, including Isaiah Dorman, an African-American cavalryman, scout, and intermediary between the Sioux nations and U.S. government who had warned Custer of the hostile Native American presence.

1941 President Franklin D. Roosevelt issues Executive Order 8802 forbidding racial bias in war industries and government service and creating the Federal Employment Practices Committee.

1950 Charles H. Houston is posthumously awarded the NAACP's Spingarn Medal for his legal work with the association's Legal Committee. He is cited as a "stalwart defender of democracy, inspired teacher of youth, and leader in the legal profession…."

1964 Riots erupt in Saint Augustine, Fla., when a mob of 800 whites attacks part of a parade of several hundred African-Americans participating in an integration parade.

1968 Lincoln Alexander of Hamilton West in Ontario, Canada, becomes the first black member of the Canadian Parliament.

1975 Mozambique gains its independence from Portugal. Samora M. Machel, leader of the Mozambique Liberation Front, becomes the republic's first president.

Jamaica Kincaid

1934 W.E.B. Du Bois resigns from the NAACP over the association's policies and strategies. Du Bois had been editor of the association's *Crisis* magazine and director of publicity and research. The resignation brought control of the magazine under the leadership of chief executive Walter White and its new editor and NAACP assistant secretary, Roy Wilkins.

1950 The American Medical Association seats the first African-American delegates at its convention.

1952 The African National Congress begins its Defiance of Unjust Laws campaign in South Africa.

1956 Jazz trumpeter Clifford Brown dies in an auto accident on the Pennsylvania Turnpike. Founder of the Brown-Roach Quintet with Max Roach two years earlier, Brown had built a reputation as one of the finest jazz trumpeters of his day as a major proponent of hard bop.

1978 *Girl*, a single-sentence, two-page short story of a mother's preachy advice to her daughter, appears in the *New Yorker* magazine. Written by Jamaica Kincaid, the story will make her a literary celebrity and will be followed by short story collections and the novels *Annie John* and *Lucy*.

27

28

1919 Archibald H. Grimké, noted lawyer and civil rights advocate who had served as U.S. consul in Santo Domingo and president of the American Negro Academy among other accomplishments, receives the NAACP's Spingarn Medal. An original member of the "Committee of Forty" that helped establish the NAACP, Grimké is honored for his "years of distinguished service to his race and country."

1941 Richard Wright is awarded the Spingarn Medal. He is cited for the power of his books *Uncle Tom's Children* and *Native Son* in depicting "the effects of proscription, segregation and denial of opportunities on the American Negro."

1972 Patricia Roberts Harris, the first African-American U.S. ambassador, is named permanent chairman of the Democratic National Convention. The

Mattoon, Ill., native will later break new ground as Secretary of Health and Human Services and Secretary of Housing and Urban Development.

1989 The Baltimore Orioles beat the Toronto Blue Jays 16–6. Each team is coached by an African-American, Frank Robinson of the Orioles and Cito Gaston of the Blue Jays. Robinson, who will direct his team to an 87–75 season, will be named manager of the year by both AP and UPI.

Frank Robinson

1770 Anthony Benezet and other Quakers open a nonsegregated school for African-American and white children in Philadelphia, Pa.

1927 Anthony Overton, president of Victory Life Insurance Company, receives the NAACP's Spingarn Medal for "his successful business career climaxed by admission of his company as the first Negro organization permitted to do business under the rigid requirements of the State of New York."

1935 Mary McLeod Bethune, founder and president of Bethune-Cookman College, receives the Spingarn Medal from the NAACP. Bethune is honored for speaking out against racism and injustice "in the South as well as in the North, without compromise or fear."

1936 Major Owens, who will succeed Shirley Chisholm as Congressional representative from New York, is born in Memphis, Tenn.

1946 Thurgood Marshall receives the Spingarn Medal for his "distinguished service as a lawyer before the Supreme Court of the United States and inferior courts."

1978 The Supreme Court hands down its *Bakke* decision, ruling that the University of California at Davis Medical College's special admissions program for minority students is illegal. As a result, Allan P. Bakke, a white student, is ordered admitted to the college to prevent what the Court considers reverse discrimination.

29

30

1886 James Van DerZee is born in Lenox, Mass. He will become one of America's foremost photographers and a major chronicler of the visual history of the Harlem Renaissance. His photographic subjects include Marcus Garvey, Madame C.J. Walker, Daddy Grace and many others.

1922 Lloyd Richards is born in Toronto, Canada. He will be the first African-American to direct a Broadway play in modern times (*A Raisin in the Sun*, 1959) and he will become the dean of the Yale School of Drama and artistic director of the Yale Repertory Theatre.

1950 Mabel Keaton Staupers of the National Association of Colored Graduate Nurses receives the Spingarn Medal in honor of her advocacy of integration of African-American graduate nurses into the American workplace.

1988 Motown Records is sold for $61 million to an investment group that includes a venture-capital firm, record executive Jheryl Busby, and others. The company, which was founded by Berry Gordy in 1959, produced some of the biggest rhythm and blues performers of all time including the Supremes, the Temptations, the Four Tops and Marvin Gaye.

Lloyd Richards

1917 Lena Horne is born in Brooklyn, N.Y. She will begin her career at 16 as a chorus girl at the Cotton Club in Harlem, appear in the movies *Cabin in the Sky* and *Stormy Weather* and have a successful Broadway career culminating in her one-woman show. Horne will also be a strong civil rights advocate, refusing to perform in clubs where African-Americans are not admitted and marching during the civil rights movement in the 1960s.

1921 Charles S. Gilpin becomes the first actor to receive the NAACP's Spingarn Medal for his portrayal of Emperor Jones in the Eugene O'Neill play of the same name.

1940 John T. Scott is born in New Orleans, La. He will become a professor of art and a sculptor whose works will be exhibited widely in the U.S. and at the exhibit *Art of Black America in Japan, Afro-American Modernism: 1937–1987*.

Lena Horne

1969 Jacob Lawrence receives the NAACP's Spingarn Medal "in testimony to his eminence among American painters."

1980 Coleman A. Young is awarded the Spingarn Medal for his "singular accomplishments as Mayor of the City of Detroit," a position he had held since 1973.

JOHN T. SCOTT, *Just Another Window for the Blues,* 1991. Kinetic polychrome steel. Courtesy the artist.

1

1863 The Dutch West Indies abolishes slavery.

1898 The Black 10th Cavalry charges Spanish forces at El Caney, Cuba, and relieves Teddy Roosevelt's "Rough Riders."

1899 Thomas Dorsey is born in Villa Rica, Ga. Although he will begin touring with Ma Rainey, he will leave the blues in 1932 to work as a choir director for Pilgrim Baptist Church. A gospel legend, among his most popular songs will be "A Little Talk with Jesus."

1976 Newark mayor Kenneth Gibson is elected as the first African-American president of the U.S. Conference of Mayors.

1991 Former chairman of the Equal Employment Opportunity Commission and judge of the U.S. Court of Appeals, Clarence

Thomas is nominated by President George Bush as associate justice of the Supreme Court to replace retiring justice Thurgood Marshall. Thomas's Senate confirmation hearings will be the most controversial in history and will include charges of sexual harassment by a former employee, Professor Anita Hill.

Clarence Thomas

2

1777 Vermont, not one of the original 13 states, becomes the first U.S. territory to abolish slavery.

1908 Thurgood Marshall is born in Baltimore, Md. He will have the most distinguished legal career of any African-American as the NAACP's national counsel, director-counsel of the organization's Legal Defense and Education Fund, and leader of some of the most important legal challenges for African-Americans' Constitutional rights, including *Brown v. Board of Education* in 1954. In addition to sitting as a circuit judge for the Second Circuit, Marshall will be named U.S. Solicitor General in 1965 and associate justice of the U.S. Supreme Court in 1967, where he will serve for 24 years.

1964 President Lyndon B. Johnson signs the Civil Rights Bill, which includes public accommodation and fair employment sections. The Civil Rights Act prohibits segregation in

Thurgood Marshall

employment, education, and public accommodation on the basis of race, sex, age, national origin or religion.

1990 *Devil in a Blue Dress*, a mystery novel by Walter Mosley set in South-Central Los Angeles, is published. Its realism and strong African-American characters will earn its author enthusiastic praise and a nomination for best novel by the Mystery Writers of America.

3

4

1871 Joseph H. Douglass, grandson of Frederick Douglass, is born in Washington, D.C. A student of the New England Conservatory of Music in Boston, Douglass will become a noted violinist.

1917 Three days of racial riots end in East Saint Louis, Ill. At least 40 and as many as 200 African-Americans are killed and hundreds more are wounded.

1928 Charles Waddell Chestnutt, author of *The Conjure Woman* and other works, is awarded the NAACP's Spingarn Medal for his "work as a literary artist depicting the life and struggle of Americans of Negro descent."

1962 Jackie Robinson, who broke the color line in professional baseball, is the first African-American inducted into the National Baseball Hall of Fame and Museum, in Cooperstown, N.Y.

Joseph H. Douglass

1776 The Declaration of Independence is adopted. A section written by Thomas Jefferson denouncing slavery is deleted.

1779 Colonel Arent Schuyler De Puyster notes the presence of "Jean Baptiste Pointe Du Sable, a handsome Negro, well-educated and settled at Eschikagou." It is the first recorded mention of Du Sable, who settled the area that will become known as Chicago.

1845 Wildfire Lewis is born in Greenwich, N.Y. After living with Chippewa relatives, she will enroll in Oberlin College's preparatory and college program. Changing her name to Mary Edmonia Lewis, she will travel to Boston and abroad where she will become one of the most outstanding sculptors of her day. Among her most-famous works will be *Forever Free, Hagar in Her Despair in the Wilderness* and *Death of Cleopatra.*

1881 Tuskegee Institute opens in Tuskegee, Ala., with Booker T. Washington as its first president.

1963 Marian Anderson and Ralph Bunche receive the first Medals of Freedom from President John F. Kennedy, the creator of the award.

1991 The National Civil Rights Museum officially opens at the Lorraine Motel in Memphis, Tenn., the site of the assassination of civil rights leader Martin Luther King, Jr.

EDMONIA LEWIS, *Hagar,* 1875. Carved marble. National Museum of American Art, Smithsonian Institution, gift of Delta Sigma Theta Sorority, Inc.

5

6

1852 Frederick Douglass delivers his speech "What to the American Slave is Your Fourth of July?": "To him your celebration is a sham…to cover up crimes which would disgrace a nation of savages. There is not a nation of the earth guilty of practices more "shocking and bloody than are the people of the United States at this very hour."

Frederick Douglass

1892 Andrew Beard is issued patent number 478,271 for his rotary engine.

1899 Anna Arnold (later Hedgeman) is born in Marshalltown, Iowa. Hedgeman will be the first woman to serve in the cabinet of a New York City mayor, a special projects coordinator for the Commission on Religion and Race of the National Council of Churches, and recruiter of 40,000 Protestant churchmen to participate in the 1963 March on Washington.

1966 Three nights of rioting in Omaha, Nebr., result in the calling out of the National Guard.

Ida B. Wells
25
Black Heritage USA

1862 Ida B. Wells (later Barnett) is born in Holly Springs, Miss. She will become a journalist and antilynching advocate who, in response to the alarming increase in lynchings of African-Americans, will compile and publish an 1895 statistical study on lynching, *A Red Record*. Wells-Barnett will also be an integral part of the early civil rights movement, participating as a secretary of the National Afro-American Council and member of the "Committee of Forty" that leads to the formation of the NAACP.

1868 Eight-five African-Americans and 70 white representatives meet in Columbia, S.C., at the opening of the state's General Assembly. It is the first and last U.S. legislature with an African-American majority.

1957 Althea Gibson wins the women's singles tennis championship at Wimbledon, in England. She will also team up with Darlene Hard to win the doubles championship. She is the first African-American to win at Wimbledon.

1971 Louis Armstrong dies in New York City. Armstrong had been one of the most popular and influential jazz musicians since his 1929 hit "Ain't Misbehavin'" and had enjoyed an immensely successful performing and recording career.

1990 Jesse Owens is honored on a stamp issued by the U.S. Postal Service. Owens was a four-time Olympic gold medal winner in the 1936 Summer Games in Berlin.

7

8

Margaret Walker

1781 James Armistead, an American slave, infiltrates the headquarters of General Cornwallis and becomes a servant hired to spy on the Americans. In reality, Armistead is a cunning double agent working for French ally General Lafayette and reports on the movements and troop strength of the British. His reports are critical to the surrender of Cornwallis in Chesapeake Bay.

1791 The nondenominational African Church is founded by Richard Allen, Absalom Jones, and Benjamin Rush.

1915 Margaret Walker is born in Birmingham, Ala. Encouraged by Langston Hughes and others, Walker will become a writer best known for her volume of poetry *For My People*, her novel *Jubilee*, and a biography of novelist Richard Wright.

1945 Fern Logan is born in Jamaica (Queens), N.Y. A graduate of Pratt Institute, she studied photography in the mid-1970's with master photographer Paul Caponigro. Among her best-known works are the renowned *Artists Portrait Series* of African-American artists such as Romare Bearden, Roy deCarava, and Jacob Lawrence as well as commanding landscapes and scenes of nature.

1975 *For Colored Girls Who Have Considered Suicide/When the Rainbow is Not Enuf*, a play by 26-year-old Ntozake Shange, premieres in New York City.

1914 William Clarence ("Billy") Eckstine is born in Pittsburgh, Pa. Getting his musical start as a singer with Earl "Fatha" Hines and with his own bop big band that will include Art Blakey, Gene Ammons, and others, Eckstine will settle on a career as a solo singer, where he will achieve widespread admiration.

1943 Faye Wattleton is born in Saint Louis, Mo. She will become the president of Planned Parent Federation of America in 1978 and be known for almost 14 years as an outspoken champion of women's reproductive rights. She will leave Planned Parenthood in 1992 to develop her own talk show devoted to discussions of women's issues.

1966 John H. Johnson wins the Spingarn Medal for his "contributions to the enhancement of the Negro's self-image" through his publications including *Negro Digest*, *Ebony*, and *Jet* magazines, and books such as *Before the Mayflower*, written by historian Lerone Bennett, Jr.

Faye Wattleton

9

10

1901 Jester Hairston is born in Homestead, Pa. Although known for his roles in television's *Amos 'n' Andy* and *Amen*, Hairston will excel as a musician, first with the Eva Jessye Choir and later as assistant conductor of the Hall Johnson Choir. He will also arrange choral music for more than 40 film soundtracks.

1936 June Jordan is born in Harlem. She will become a poet and author of books for children and young adults and will be nominated for the National Book Award in 1972 for *His Own Where*.

1955 E. Frederick Morrow is appointed an administrative aide to President Dwight D. Eisenhower. He is the first African-American to hold an executive position on a White House staff.

1971 Clergyman and activist Leon H. Sullivan is awarded the NAACP's Spingarn Medal for his achievements in transmitting "the social gospel into economic progress for his people."

1987 Percy E. Sutton, former New York State legislator, president of the Borough of Manhattan, founder of Inner City Broadcasting and owner of the Apollo Theatre, receives the NAACP's Spingarn Medal.

Percy Sutton

1875 Mary McLeod Bethune is born in Mayesville, S.C. She will become a noted educator and founder of Daytona Normal and Industrial Institute in Daytona Beach, Fla., in 1904 (now Bethune-Cookman College). In 1935, she will also found the National Council of Negro Women.

1893 Dr. Daniel Hale Williams performs the world's first open-heart surgery at Provident Hospital in Chicago, Ill., when he sutures the pericardium of a stabbing victim.

1941 Ferdinand "Jelly Roll" Morton dies in Los Angeles, Calif. The innovative piano soloist, composer, and arranger claimed to have invented jazz and made a series of recordings for the Library of Congress that immortalized his style. Fifty years after his death, playwright George C. Wolfe presents a well-regarded play on Morton's life, *Jelly's Last Jam*.

"Jelly Roll" Morton

1966 Martin Luther King, Jr. begins a Chicago campaign for fair housing. It is his first foray into a northern city for desegregation activities.

11

12

1905 Niagara Movement meetings begin in Buffalo, N.Y. Started by 29 black intellectuals including W.E.B. Du Bois, the Niagara Movement will renounce Booker T. Washington's accommodation policies set forth in his famed "Atlanta Compromise" speech ten years earlier. The Niagara Movement's manifesto is, in the words of Du Bois, "We want full manhood suffrage and we want it now…. We are men! We want to be treated as men. And we shall win." The movement will be a forerunner of the NAACP.

1915 Mifflin Wistar Gibbs, a multitalented lawyer, politician, and entrepreneur, dies in Little Rock, Ark. Active in the Underground Railroad, he worked with Frederick Douglass and, after success as a clothing retailer, became the publisher and editor of *Mirror of the Times*, the first African-American newspaper in California. The first African-American elected a municipal judge, Gibbs was also active in Republican poli-

tics, serving as a delegate to national conventions and as U.S. consul to Madagascar.

1925 Mattiwilda Dobbs is born in Atlanta, Ga. She will become a coloratura in the 1950's, making her opera debut at La Scala in Milan in 1953 and her U.S. debut with the San Francisco Opera in 1955.

1958 Daisy Bates and the Little Rock Nine, African-American youths who desegregated Central High School in Little Rock, Ark., receive the Spingarn Medal for their "heroism and pioneering roles in upholding the basic ideals of American democracy in the face of continuing harassment and constant threats of bodily injury."

1887 Mound Bayou, an all-African-American town in Mississippi, is founded by Isaiah Montgomery.

1936 Actress Rose McClendon dies of pneumonia in New York City. A student at the American Academy of Dramatic Art in Carnegie Hall, McClendon won fame for her roles in the plays *Deep River*, *In Abraham's Bosom*, and *Porgy*.

She also founded, with Dick Campbell, the Negro People's Theater and, with Campbell and Muriel Rahn, the Rose McClendon Players.

1938 Bill Cosby is born in Philadelphia, Pa. He will become one of the most popular African-American entertainers, first in comedy, where his albums will earn him five Grammy awards, then in Las Vegas and elsewhere. He will later star in the television series *I Spy*, which will be the first of three successful television series.

1967 Five days of rioting begin in Newark, N.J., and spreads to seven other communities.

1991 *Boyz N the Hood*, a film written and directed by John Singleton, premieres. A coming-of-age film set in gang- and violence-ridden South-Central Los Angeles, its positive message will earn Singleton critical acclaim and two Academy Award nominations.

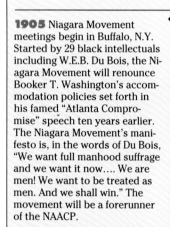

Bill Cosby

PALMER HAYDEN, *Berry Pickers,* 1946–1947. Oil on canvas. Gift of Miriam A. Hayden. From the collection of the Museum of African-American Art, Los Angeles, California.

13

14

1787 The Continental Congress passes the Northwest Ordinance, which, in addition to providing for a government and civil liberties for the new territory, excludes slavery northwest of the Ohio River except as punishment for a crime.

1863 Over 1,200 people, mostly African-Americans, are killed in antidraft rioting in New York City. Rioting begins, in part, when poor whites revolt against military service exemptions that allow for a payment of $300 in lieu of being drafted, a price that they cannot afford. The "Draft Riots" also reflect a growing hostility toward African-Americans, who are seen as the cause of the war.

1928 Robert N.C. Nix, Jr. is born in Philadelphia, Pa. In 1971, he will be the first African-American to serve on the Pennsylvania Supreme Court and, in 1984, the first African-American chief justice

of a state supreme court. Chief Justice Nix will be further honored when he is named president of the Conference of Chief Justices, a national organization of judges and justices in the U.S.

1965 Thurgood Marshall, an Appeals Court judge for three years, is nominated as Solicitor General of the U.S., the first African-American to hold the office.

Robert N. C. Nix, Jr.

1914 Kenneth B. Clarke is born in the Canal Zone, Panama. He will become a noted psychologist who will establish the Northside Center for Child Development in New York City. His pioneering research on the psychological damage to African-American children caused by segregation will be used as part of the basis for the *Brown v. Board of Education* school desegregation decision of the U.S. Supreme Court.

1943 Julius Bledsoe dies in Hollywood, Calif. He was an important stage and film actor whose roles in *Deep River, In Abraham's Bosom,* and the stage and film versions of *Showboat* won him wide acclaim.

1972 Former New York State senator Basil A. Paterson is elected vice-chairman of the Democratic National Committee, the first African-American to hold a leadership position in a national political party.

Ernie Singleton

1990 Ernie Singleton is named president of MCA Records' black music division. As president, Singleton oversees the day-to-day activities of the division and the company's artist roster that includes Bobby Brown, Heavy D. & the Boyz, Gladys Knight, and Patti LaBelle. He, along with Jheryl Busby, president of Motown Records Company, Sylvia Rhone, president of Atco EastWest Records, and Ed Eckstine, president of Mercury Records, are the highest-ranking African-Americans in the record business.

15

16

1968 Ellen Holly integrates daytime television when she appears on ABC's *One Life to Live* as Carla, an African-American "passing" for white. The role is a marked departure for the New York City–born African-American, whose first professional role was with Joseph Papp's New York Shakespeare Festival as the white Desdemona to William Marshall's Othello in 1958. Holly had been a featured player in Papp's company and had played several Shakespearean roles, including Lady Macbeth opposite James Earl Jones in *Macbeth* and Princess Katherine opposite Robert Hooks in *Henry V,* before being signed to the soap opera.

Ellen Holly

Hooks speaks before the convention despite leading candidate Ronald Reagan's refusal to appear at the NAACP convention earlier in the month.

Meanwhile, new violence erupts in the riot-torn Liberty City section of Miami, Fla. Two months after riots that killed 18 and resulted in $100 million in property damage, the violence will leave 40 injured and result in 40 arrests.

1970 James McGhee is sworn in as the first African-American mayor of Dayton, Ohio.

1980 Benjamin Hooks addresses the GOP convention after a lobbying effort and threatened walkout by 121 African-American delegates.

1829 A poem in tribute to the late Philadelphia caterer Robert Bogle is published. Bogle is the first known professional African-American caterer. Among his descendants will be Robert W. Bogle, publisher of the Philadelphia *Tribune,* and Donald Bogle, noted film critic and author of *Black Americans in Film and Television.*

1930 Donald McKayle is born in New York City. McKayle will make his debut, at 22, in *Her Name was Harriet* (a dance tribute to Harriet Tubman) and go on to dance in or choreograph *House of Flowers, The Bill Cosby Special* (1968), the 1970 Academy Awards, the movie version of *The Great White Hope*, and *Sophisticated Ladies* on Broadway.

1932 Mari Evans, author of the poetry collections *I Am a Black Woman* and *Nightstar: 1973–1978*, is born in Toledo, Ohio.

1934 Donald Payne is born in Newark, N.J. In 1988, he will become the first African-American congressman from New Jersey.

1936 The movie *The Green Pastures* premieres in New York's Radio City Music Hall, featuring Eddie "Rochester" Anderson, the Hall Johnson Choir, and Rex Ingram as "De Lawd."

1977 Janelle Penny Commissiong of Trinidad and Tobago is crowned Miss Universe. She is the first black to win the title.

Donald Payne

JOHN RHODEN, *Safari,* 1988. Bronze. Courtesy the artist.

17

18

1862 Congress approves the rights of African-Americans to bear arms to fight in the Civil War and enlist in the Union Army by passing two laws, the Confiscation and Militia acts. Over 186,000 African-Americans will serve in the Union Army, with 38,000 losing their lives.

1911 Frank Snowden is born in York County, Va. He will become the foremost scholar on blacks in ancient history, notable for his books *Blacks in Antiquity: Ethiopians in the Greco-Roman Experience* and *Before Color Prejudice: The Ancient View of Blacks*.

1935 Carol Diahann Johnson is born in the Bronx, N.Y. She will be better know as Diahann Carroll, star of Broadway (*House of Flowers*), television (*Julia*), and films including *Carmen Jones* and *Claudine*, the latter earning her an Academy Award nomination as best actress.

Diahann Carroll

1944 An ammunitions depot at Port Chicago, Calif., explodes, killing 320 men including 202 African-Americans assigned by the Navy to handle explosives. The resulting refusal of 258 African-Americans to return to the dangerous work formed the basis of the trial and conviction of 50 of the men in what will become known as the Port Chicago Mutiny.

1863 The 54th Massachusetts Volunteers charges Fort Wagner in Charleston, S.C. Although the Union forces suffer great losses, Sergeant William H. Carney of Company C exhibits bravery in battle by maintaining the colors high despite three bullet wounds. Although cited for bravery, it will take 37 years for Carney to receive the Congressional Medal of Honor for his actions.

1899 Patent number 629,286 is issued to L.C. Bailey for a folding bed.

W. H. Carney

1964 Riots in Harlem start after a 15-year-old African-American youth is slain by a white policeman. Rioting will continue for five days and spread to the Bedford-Stuyvesant section of Brooklyn.

19

20

1848 The first Women's Rights Convention is held in Seneca Falls, N.Y. The convention is supported by Frederick Douglass of nearby Rochester, N.Y., who attends the meeting and speaks in defense of its organizer, Elizabeth Cady Stanton.

1913 The Tri-State Dental Association is formed in Buckroe Beach, Va. It will be the forerunner to the National Dental Association, an organization dedicated to developing a national forum for African-American dentists in the U.S.

1940 Surgeon Louis T. Wright is presented the Spingarn Medal for his "contribution to the healing of mankind and for his courageous, uncompromising position, often in the face of bitter attack." Among Wright's many accomplishments was being the first African-American surgeon to be admitted to the staff of Harlem Hospital and chairmanship of the board of directors of the NAACP, a position he will hold for 17 years.

1966 The Hough district of Cleveland, Ohio, experiences riots that result in the mobilization of the National Guard by Governor James A. Rhodes, who declares a state of emergency in the city.

1979 Patricia Harris is named Secretary of Health and Human Services. It is her second Cabinet-level appointment.

1934 Henry Dumas, author of *Ark of Bones and Other Stories*, is born in Sweet Home, Ark.

1967 The first National Conference of Black Power opens in Newark, N.J. The four-day meeting is attended by 1,100 African-Americans.

Meanwhile, a night of rioting occurs in Memphis, Tenn.

1973 The National Black Network begins operations. It is the first African-American-owned and -operated radio news network.

1988 In the most formidable attempt ever by an African-American to become President of the U.S., Jessie Jackson receives 1218.5 delegate votes of the 2,082 needed for the Democratic Party's nomination, finishing second to Michael Dukakis. In his second bid for the nomination, Jackson had garnered wide popular support and captured 92% of African-American and 12% of white votes in primary elections and caucuses. The previous night, Jackson had electrified the delegates with a ringing speech encouraging them to "keep hope alive."

♦ *Patricia Harris*

21

22

1896 Mary Church Terrell organizes the National Association of Colored Women in Washington, D.C. It is one of many achievements for Terrell, which include being the first African-American woman to serve on a school's board of education, the first to hold membership in the American Association of University Women, and at age 90, leading the desegregation of Washington, D.C., restaurants, in 1953.

1934 Edolphus Towns is born in Chadbourn, N.C. He will become a longtime civic leader, Brooklyn borough president, congressman from New York's 11th District starting in 1983, and chairman of the Congressional Black Caucus in 1990.

1943 *Stormy Weather* premieres in New York City with Lena Horne, Bill Robinson, Fats Waller, Cab Calloway, the Nicholas Brothers, and Katherine Dunham. A week before the premiere, Horne said of African-American actors,

Edolphus Towns

"All we ask is that the Negro be portrayed as a normal person. A worker in a union meeting, a voter in the polls...or an elected official. Perhaps I'm being naive. Perhaps these things will never be straightened out on the screen itself, but will have to wait until...[they're] solved in real life."

1950 The first victory in the Korean War is aided by African-American troops of the 24th Infantry Regiment, who recapture Yechon after waging a 16-hour battle.

1938 Joe Louis defeats German boxer Max Schmeling in a rematch of their 1936 fight and retains his world heavyweight crown. Because of the Nazi persecution of Jews in Europe and Hitler's disdain for blacks, the fight had taken on mythic proportions, with Louis seen by many as fighting to uphold democracy and the race. He succeeded convincingly, ending the fight in the first round.

1939 Jane Bolin is appointed to the Domestic Relations Court of New York City. She is the first African-American woman judge.

Joe Louis

23

24

1868 The Fourteenth Amendment is ratified, which grants citizenship for African-Americans and provides for federal intervention when state governments are accused of violating an individual's Constitutional rights.

1943 Poet, editor, and author Quincy Troupe is born. Among his books will be volumes of poetry, most notably *Watts Poets*, and an autobiography of Miles Davis.

1968 An alleged black radical ambush of a Cleveland police detail sparks two days of rioting that will result in 11 deaths.

1984 Vanessa Williams, the first African-American Miss America, relinquishes her crown after publication of nude photographs taken before her entry in the pageant. Replacing her is Suzette Charles, first runner-up in the contest.

Suzette Charles

1807 Ira Aldridge is born in New York City. He will be one of America's earliest African-American Shakespearean actors whose fame will come only after leaving the racism of the performing arts in the U.S. and emigrating to Europe.

1893 Charles S. Johnson is born in Bristol, Va. He will become a noted sociologist, founder of the National Urban League's *Opportunity* magazine, and professor at and president of Fisk University.

1921 Billy Taylor is born in Greenville, N.C. He will become a jazz pianist, bandleader, noted jazz educator, and jazz correspondent for CBS's *Sunday Morning*.

1961 Grace Bumbry makes her debut in Richard Wagner's *Tannhauser* at the Bayreuth

Ira Aldridge

Festival in Bavaria. Surrounded by controversy that saw the German press protest the role of Venus being sung by an African-American, Bumbry's performance dispels all doubts as she receives 42 curtain calls during a 30-minute ovation.

1967 Three days of rioting begin in Cambridge, Md., the site of a 1963 confrontation between civil rights demonstrators and white segregationists.

Fᴇʀɴ Lᴏɢᴀɴ, *Moonrise–Beni Hassan (Egypt, Africa)*. Photograph. Collection the photographer.

25

Dennis Hightower

1921 Liberty Life Insurance Company is founded by Frank L. Gillespie. After a 1926 merger with Supreme Life and Casualty of Columbus, Ohio, and Northeastern Life of Newark, N.J., the resulting company will be called Supreme Life Insurance Company and be, at one time, one of the largest African-American-owned insurance companies in the nation.

1930 Nineteen-year-old Josh Gibson is called out of the stands to substitute for the regular catcher for the Pittsburgh Homestead Grays, one of the best-known all-Negro professional baseball teams. Gibson will go on to play 15 years with a variety of Negro teams. His lifetime batting average, .423, will earn him election to the Hall of Fame in 1972.

1990 *Black Enterprise* publisher Earl G. Graves and Los Angeles Lakers star Magic Johnson become the largest minority-controlled Pepsi-Cola franchise in the country when they sign a $60 million agreement to purchase Pepsi-Cola of Washington, D.C.

1991 Dennis Hightower is promoted to president of Disney Consumer Products–Europe/Middle East. Hightower has operating responsibility for all book and magazine publishing, merchandise licensing, children's records and music, film promotion and television sponsorship and manages the company's eight subsidiaries and six offices in Europe and the Middle East.

26

Joseph Jenkins Roberts

1847 Twenty-five years after the first free African-Americans arrive at the colony of Cape Mesurado, the commonwealth of Liberia declares itself an independent republic. Joseph Jenkins Roberts, a Virginia native, becomes its first president.

1865 Catholic priest Patrick Francis Healy passes his final Ph.D. examinations in philosophy at Louvrain in Belgium. He becomes the first African-American to earn a Ph.D.

1916 Spottiswood W. Robinson is born in Richmond, Va. He will pursue a distinguished career in law, in private practice, as a representative of the NAACP Legal Defense Fund, dean of the Howard University Law School, and as a member of the U.S. Commission on Civil Rights. In 1966, he will be named a U.S. Circuit Judge of the D.C. Circuit by President Lyndon B. Johnson, marking the beginning of a successful judicial career.

1918 Two days after she moves into a predominantly, though not exclusively, white Philadelphia neighborhood, an African-American woman's house is stoned. The incident will set off four days of riots in which one African-American and three whites are killed.

1948 President Harry S Truman issues Executive Order 9981, directing "equality of treatment and opportunity" in federal employment and the armed forces.

27

28

1919 Chicago race riots kill 23 African-Americans and 15 whites and injure more than 500, despite the warnings of Ida B. Wells-Barnett to city officials to improve conditions for African-Americans in the city.

Woodie King, Jr.

1937 Woodie King, Jr. is born in Detroit, Mich. A drama critic, producer, and dramatist, he will be best known as the artistic director of the New Federal Theatre at the Henry Street Settlement, for his adaptation of Langston Hughes's *Weary Blues* and *Simply Blues* for the stage, and for producing Ntozake Shange's *For Colored Girls Who Have Considered Suicide/When the Rainbow is Enuf* and *Checkmates*, featuring Denzel Washington.

1984 Reverend C.L. Franklin dies in Detroit, Mich., after a long coma sustained after being shot by a burglar in his home. He was the founder of Detroit's New Bethel Baptist Church, where his radio sermons drew a nationwide audience and where the singing career of his daughter, Aretha, began.

1802 Alexandre Dumas *père* is born in Villiers-Cotterets to a Haitian mulatto, Thomas Alexandre Dumas, and Marie Labouret Dumas, a French woman. He will become an acclaimed author of the French classics *The Three Musketeers*, *The Count of Monte Cristo*, *The Man in the Iron Mask,* and *The Corsican Brothers.*

1903 Maggie Lena Walker founds and becomes the first president of Saint Luke Penny Savings Bank in Richmond, Va. She is the first woman bank president in the nation.

1917 Led by W.E.B. Du Bois and James Weldon Johnson, over 10,000 African-Americans march down Fifth Avenue in New York City to the sound of muffled drums in silent protest of lynchings and other racial indignities that are rampant in the U.S.

James Weldon Johnson
22
Lift ev-'ry voice and sing
Black Heritage USA

EMILIO CRUZ, *Figurative Composition #7,* 1965. Oil on canvas. National Museum of American Art, Smithsonian Institution, gift of Mr. and Mrs. David K. Anderson, Martha Jackson Memorial Collection.

29

30

1909 Chester Himes is born in Jefferson City, Mo. He will become a noted crime novelist whose books *If He Hollers, Let Him Go, Come Back Charleston Blue,* and *Cotton Comes to Harlem* explore the underbelly of the American dream and introduce "Gravedigger Jones" and "Coffin Ed Johnson" to the reading public.

1919 The first convention of the National Association of Negro Musicians is held in Chicago, Ill. NANM's charter members include Clarence Cameron White, who called for formation of the association. R. Nathaniel Dett, Nora Holt, Florence Cole Talbert among others. NANM will be active in furthering African-American music and performers, and award its first scholarship to a young Marian Anderson.

Bernard A. Harris, Jr.

1991 Physician Bernard A. Harris, Jr., becomes a full-fledged astronaut. Harris, who joined NASA's Johnson Space Center in 1987 as a clinical scientist and flight surgeon, is now eligible for future flight assignments.

1822 James Varick is consecrated as the first bishop of the African Methodist Episcopal Church Zion (AMEZ). Varick had formed the first African-American church in New York City in 1796 when forced to sit in segregated seating in the white John Street Methodist Episcopal Church and had established the first AMEZ church in New Haven, Conn.

1885 Eugene Kinckle Jones is born in Richmond, Va. He will become a social worker and first executive secretary of the National Urban League. During his 30-year tenure with the league, he will be instrumental in its expansion to 58 affiliates and a budget of $2.5 million as well as expanding its fellowship program to train social workers.

1967 Eight days of rioting ends in Detroit, Mich. The uprising, the worst of its kind in the 20th century, kills 43 people, injures 2,000, and results in over 5,000 arrests and over 1,400 fires.

1970 Author, television columnist, and Hofstra University professor Louis E. Lomax dies in a car accident near Santa Rosa, N.M.

1988 The first National Black Arts Festival opens in Atlanta, Ga. The biennial festival includes over 50 architectural and art exhibits including the works of Romare Bearden, Edwin Harleston, Camille Billops, David Driskell, and over 140 others.

Eugene Kinckle Jones

31

1

Whitney Young

1874 Patrick Francis Healy, a Jesuit priest, is inaugurated as president of Georgetown University in Washington, D.C. Healy is the first African-American to head a predominantly white university and is credited with the modernization of the university's curriculum and the expansion of its campus.

1921 Whitney Young, Jr. is born in Lincoln Ridge, Ky. He will be dean of Atlanta University's School of Social Work before becoming executive director of the National Urban League. A 1969 recipient of the Presidential Medal of Freedom, Young will speak out against government and business's lack of commitment to African-Americans.

1960 At a New York meeting of the Nation of Islam, the Honorable Elijah Muhammad calls for the creation of a black state in America.

1834 Slavery is abolished in British colonies by the royal assent of the King of England after having been voted by Parliament the previous year.

1879 Mary Eliza Mahoney graduates from the nursing program at the New England Hospital for Women and Children. She is the first African-American to graduate from a nursing school.

1914 Marcus Garvey establishes the Universal Negro Improvement and Conservation Association and African Communities' League, later shortened to UNIA. In New York City six years later to the day, the UNIA will meet in Madison Square Garden as Garvey presents his "Back to Africa" plan and a formal Declaration of Rights for black people worldwide.

1925 The National Bar Association, dedicated to "advance the science of jurisprudence, uphold the honor of the legal profession…and protect the

Marcus Garvey

civil and political rights of all citizens of the several states of the United States," is formally organized in Des Moines, Iowa, by 12 African-American legal pioneers including George H. Woodson, S. Joe Brown, and Gertrude E. Rush.

1963 Arthur Ashe is selected as the first African-American to play on the U.S. Davis Cup tennis team.

2

3

1924 James Baldwin is born in New York City. He will become one of the most prolific and influential African-American authors of fiction (*Go Tell It on the Mountain*, *Another Country*, *Giovanni's Room*), drama (*Blues For Mr. Charlie*, *Amen Corner*), and essay collections (*Notes of a Native Son*, *The Fire Next Time*).

1945 Jewell Jackson (later McCabe) is born in Washington, D.C. She will become president of the Coalition of 100 Black Women, whose mission is to develop a forum for African-American women leaders.

1966 The Charles R. Drew Postgraduate Medical School (later Charles R. Drew University of Medicine and Science) is chartered in Los Angeles, Calif. It is the only African-American-focused medical school west of the Mississippi.

James Baldwin

1967 *In the Heat of the Night*, starring Sidney Poitier and Rod Steiger, premieres.

1982 Jackie Robinson, the first African-American to break the color barrier in major league baseball, is honored by a commemorative stamp issued by the U.S. Postal Service, the fifth in its Black Heritage USA series.

1832 Edward Wilmot Blyden is born in Saint Thomas, West Indies. By the age of 24 he will emigrate to Liberia and become an established author of the pamphlets *A Voice from Bleeding Africa*, in which he attacks slavery, and *A Vindication of the African Race*. Throughout his life, he will be an advocate of African-Americans' returning to their ancestral homes.

1908 A site plan for the town of Allensworth, Calif., is filed with the Tulare County recorder. The town is founded by African-American Allen Allensworth "in order to enable black people to live on an equity [basis] with whites and to encourage industry and thrift in the race."

1960 The Republic of Niger achieves its independence from France.

1972 The Federal Communications Commission upholds a political candidate's right to broadcast paid commercials with racist content if such broadcast presents no danger of violence or incitement to violence.

4

1875 The Convention of Colored Newspapermen is held in Cincinnati, Ohio. The meeting is attended by J. Sella Martin of the *True Republican*, Mifflin W. Gibbs, former publisher of California's *Mirror of the Times* representing the *Pacific Appeal*, Henry McNeal Turner of Philadelphia's *Christian Recorder*, the San Francisco *Elevator*'s L.H. Douglass, and Henry Scroggins of the *American Citizen* (Lexington, Ky.). Chairman P.B.S. Pinchback states the aim of the national organization: "to make colored people's newspapers self-sustaining." At the time of the convention, Martin's *New Era* and Frederick Douglass's *North Star* are among eight African-American newspaper failures.

1890 Sam T. Jack's play *Creoles* opens in Haverhill, Mass. It is the first time African-American women are featured as performers on the stage.

1936 John Woodruff of the University of Pittsburgh wins a gold medal in the 800-meter run at the Olympic Summer Games in Berlin. He, like Jesse Owens (who had won his second medal earlier in the day), will be snubbed by Adolf Hitler, who believes blacks are incapable of athletic achievement.

1980 Maury Wills is named manager of the Seattle Mariners. He is the third African-American to be named a major league manager.

5

1763 William Richmond is born free on Staten Island, N.Y. One of the first African-Americans to attempt winning a title in any sport, Richmond will travel to England to fight, among others, boxing champion Tom Cribb in a losing effort.

1892 Harriet Tubman receives a pension from Congress for her work as a nurse, spy, and scout during the Civil War. She, along with Sojourner Truth, Susie King Taylor and almost 200 other African-American men and women, served as nurses during the war at 11 hospitals in three states.

1938 James Cone, who will become an articulate scholar and author on black theology, is born in Fordyce, Ark. Among his books will be *Black Theology and Black Power* and *Malcolm and Martin and America: A Dream or a Nightmare?*

1984 Evelyn Ashford wins a gold medal in the 100-meter race and Edwin Moses wins a gold medal in the 400-meter hurdles in the Summer Olympic Games in Los Angeles.

Edwin Moses

Evelyn Ashford

JOHN ROZELLE, *It Might as Well Been Yesterday,* 1987. Acrylic, collage and mixed media on paper mounted on canvas. Courtesy the artist. Collection of Quincy and Margaret Troupe, La Jolla, California.

6

7

1965 The Voting Rights Act is signed by President Lyndon B. Johnson in the same room that Abraham Lincoln signed the Emancipation Proclamation. Rosa Parks, Martin Luther King, Jr., and a host of others witness the signing of the act, which suspends the use of literacy tests and calls for federal examiners to ensure fair elections in the South.

1969 *The Learning Tree*, directed by Gordon Parks, Jr., premieres. The film is the first directed by an African-American in modern times.

1973 Stevie Wonder is nearly killed in an automobile accident near Durham, N.C., where he was to perform in a benefit concert. Wonder suffered severe brain contusions and a broken skull and will be in a coma for several days as a result of his injuries. He will reportedly say upon awakening, "I can see, I can see...just kidding."

1988 Once accused by African-American artists of racism, MTV, the 24-hour cable music channel, premieres *Yo! MTV Raps*. It will become one of the station's most popular programs.

Ralph Bunche

1904 Ralph Johnson Bunche is born in Detroit, Mich. A political and social scientist, he will achieve fame as the first African-American Nobel Prize winner (1950) for his role as a UN mediator of the armistice agreements between Israel and her Arab neighbors in the Middle East wars of 1948, for which he will also be awarded the Spingarn Medal (1949).

1936 Roland Kirk is born in Columbus, Ohio. Blind from the age of two, he will begin playing the tenor saxophone professionally in R & B bands before turning to jazz. He will be best known for his ability to play more than one instrument at once, his self-made jazz instruments, and for his creative improvisational skills.

1948 Alice Coachman becomes the first African-American woman to win an Olympic gold medal in the high jump during the Summer Games in London.

1989 Congressman George Thomas "Mickey" Leland, members of his congressional staff and State Department officials die in a plane crash in the mountains near Gambela, Ethiopia. Leland, the Democratic successor to Barbara Jordan, had established the Select Committee on Hunger in 1984 and was chairman of the Congressional Black Caucus during the 99th Congress. A successful campaigner for stronger sanctions against South Africa, Leland was on a visit to a UN refugee camp at the time of his death.

8

9

Julian Dixon

1805 The African Baptist Church is organized in Boston, Mass.

1907 Saxophonist Benny Carter is born in New York City. He will play initially with Fletcher Henderson at age 23 and form his own big band in 1940. Carter will either play, conduc

or write arrangements for Dizzy Gillespie, Duke Ellington, Quincy Jones, and many others. He will also have significant success in scoring the movies *A Man Called Adam*, *Red Sky at Morning*, and *Buck and the Preacher* as well as the *Bob Hope*, *Ironside,* and *Alfred Hitchcock* television programs.

1934 Julian Dixon is born in Washington, D.C. He will be elected to Congress representing California's 28th District in 1978.

Benny Carter

1905 Robert N.C. Nix, Sr. is born in Orangeburg, S.C. An 11-term congressman, he will be the first African-American representative from Pennsylvania.

1936 Jesse Owens wins his fourth gold medal in the Summer Olympic Games in Berlin.

1963 Whitney Houston is born in Newark, N.J. She will achieve fame as a singer with her 1985 debut album, which will sell over nine million copies, have three number-one singles and earn a Grammy for the song "Saving All My Love For You." Her 1987 album "Whitney" will debut at number-one on the charts, a first for a female singer.

1987 Beatrice Foods, International is sold to TLC Group, a New York investment firm led by Reginald Lewis, an African-American businessman and entrepreneur. It is the largest business acquisition ever by an African-American.

Robert N. C. Nix, Sr.

Jesse Owens

STEPHANIE E. POGUE, *Madras Skylight,* 1982. Color etching printed on Arches paper. Courtesy the artist.

10

11

1858 Anna Julia Cooper is born in Raleigh, N.C. She will become an influential African-American intellectual, educator, and founder of Frelinghuysen University.

1909 George W. Crockett, Jr. is born in Jacksonville, Fla. He will become the first African-American lawyer with the U.S. Department of Labor, hearing officer for the newly formed Fair Employment Practices Commission in 1943, active labor and civil rights lawyer and, at 71, representative for the Michigan congressional district left vacant by the resignation of Charles Diggs.

George W. Crockett

1873 John Rosamond Johnson is born in Jacksonville, Fla. He will, with Bob Cole, be part of the famous vaudeville team Cole & Johnson but will best be remembered as a composer who, with his brother James Weldon Johnson providing the lyrics, will write "Lift Every Voice and Sing."

1921 Alex Haley is born in Ithaca, N.Y. He will become an award-winning author, most notably for his authorship with Malcolm X of the latter's autobiography and for *Roots*, which will win a special Pulitzer Prize. *Roots* will be his most successful work, selling over 1 million copies and contributing to a new interest in African-American history.

1925 Carl T. Rowan is born in Ravenscroft, Tenn. He will become one of America's most outspoken journalists. Rowan will also serve in the A.I.D., as a U.S. ambassador during the 1960's, have a syndicated radio commentary program, *The Rowan Report,* and publish his autobiography, *Breaking Barriers*, in 1991.

1948 Amanda Randolph appears on the television series *The Laytons* on the Dumont Network. She and Bob Howard of CBS's *The Bob Howard Show,* which premiered earlier in the summer, are the first African-Americans to be featured in a national network television series.

1965 Rioting starts in the Watts section of Los Angeles. In six days of rioting, the death toll will stand at 34, over 1,300 will be injured, and $35 million in property will be lost.

12

13

1891 Lillian Evans is born in Washington, D.C. As Dame Lillian Evanti (a contraction of her maiden name and that of her husband, Roy W. Tibbs), she will become a world-famous opera star who debuts in France with the Paris Opera and performs in the U.S. and 11 countries on three continents. She will also become one of the founders of the National Negro Opera Company.

1922 Frederick Douglass's home in Washington, D.C., is dedicated as a memorial. The effort is led by Nannie Burroughs, Hallie Q. Brown, and other members of the National Association of Colored Women's Clubs.

1923 Ophelia DeVore-Mitchell is born in Edgefield, S.C. She will be a pioneering force in opening the modeling field to

Lillian Evanti

African-Americans through her founding of the Grace Del Marco Model Agency and the Ophelia DeVore School of Self-Development and Modeling.

1933 Camille Billops is born in Los Angeles, Calif. She will become a painter, archivist, sculptor, ceramicist, and filmmaker and have solo exhibitions in the U.S., Russia, Europe, Africa, and the Far East.

1881 The first African-American nursing school opens at Spelman College in Atlanta, Ga.

1892 The first issue of the Baltimore *Afro-American* is published.

1911 James B. Parsons is born in Kansas City, Mo. After an early career in music, he will become an attorney, superior court judge in Cook County, Ill., an assistant U.S. attorney, and, in 1961, the first African-American appointed to a lifetime federal judgeship in the continental U.S.

1917 Claudia McNeil is born in Baltimore, Md. She will start her career as a singer and tour with Katherine Dunham before finding fame as an actress. Among her most notable roles will be as Lena Younger in both the play and movie versions of *A Raisin in the Sun*.

1948 Kathleen Battle is born in Portsmouth, Ohio. She will become an operatic soprano, winner of Grammy awards in 1987 and 1988, and be considered by many one of the finest modern opera singers.

1963 Noted civil rights and labor leader A. Philip Randolph strongly protests the AFL-CIO Executive Council's failure to endorse the August 28 March on Washington.

Kathleen Battle

14

15

1883 Ernest Everett Just is born in Charleston, S.C. He will become a noted marine biologist, head of the physiology department at Howard University, and recipient of the NAACP's first Spingarn Medal (1915). Plagued by racial prejudice and the limits it imposed on his career, he will write to a friend, "…I have something of value for the human race. I want a chance to do my work. And I do not want to be told over and over again that my place is with my people; that only as a black in a circumscribed arena of the black world must I work."

1938 Niara Sudarkasa is born in Fort Lauderdale, Fla. She will be an anthropologist and ground-breaking educator, becoming the first professor to receive tenure at the University of Michigan, and the first woman president of Lincoln University, a traditionally male African-American college.

1959 Earvin Johnson is born in Lansing, Mich. He will be-

come one of the best point guards in basketball, with skills that will earn him the nickname "Magic." He will join the Los Angeles Lakers in 1980 and lead all NBA guards in rebounds. A member of three NBA All-Star teams, he will be a three-time NBA Most Valuable Player.

*Magic
Johnson*

1900 Riots erupt in New York City as a white plainclothes policeman is killed in a fight with an African-American man. It is the fourth racial riot in the city's history.

1906 At the second meeting of the Niagara Movement at Harpers Ferry, W.E.B. Du Bois demands equal citizenship rights for African-Americans, saying, "We will not be satisfied to take one jot or tittle less than our full manhood rights. We claim for ourselves every single right that belongs to a free-born American, political, civil and social; and until we get these rights we will never cease to protest and assail the ears of America."

1925 Oscar Peterson is born in Montreal (Quebec), Canada. Classically trained on the piano, he will work with top Canadian jazz bands until 1949, when he will first appear in New York City's Carnegie Hall. He will be recognized as a jazz innovator

who forged a synthesis of bop and swing into his own unique style.

1938 Maxine Waters is born in Saint Louis, Mo. A longtime California state legislator, in 1990 she will be the second African-American woman from California elected to the U.S. Congress.

Maxine Waters

16

17

1938 Revolutionary blues singer Robert L. Johnson dies in Greenwood, Miss. The circumstances surrounding Johnson's death are as mysterious as his life, which included learning to play the guitar from Son House and performing in juke joints throughout Mississippi. A revival of interest in his music will occur in the 1990's when a boxed set of 41 of his recordings is issued to critical and popular acclaim.

1987 Charles Wesley dies in Washington, D.C. Noted historian and black college president, he authored over a dozen books on African-American life, including *The Negro in the Americas, The Quest for Equality, Negro Labor in the U.S. 1850–1925, Richard Allen, Apostle of Freedom*, and *The History of the National Association of Colored Women's Clubs*, published when he was 92 years old.

Archibald Grimké

1847 Archibald Henry Grimké is born into slavery on a plantation near Charleston, S.C. His white father, Henry Grimké, was of the famous Grimké family which included abolitionist sisters Sarah and Angelina. After being freed in 1852, Archibald will have a distinguished career as a lawyer (Harvard Law, 1874), political delegate, newspaper publisher (*The Hub* in Boston), and author.

1887 Marcus Garvey is born in St. Ann's Bay, Jamaica. He will become a charismatic black nationalist leader and founder of the UNIA, an organization dedicated to education, racial pride, and African development. He will also found the Black Star line, an African-American-owned steamship company established to link new-world blacks with their African motherland. Garvey and several associates will be tried for mail fraud in connection with the sale of Black Star stock. Garvey will be convicted and serve five years in federal prison.

1931 Residents of Harlem and New York City mourn the death of A'Lelia Walker Robinson. The daughter of hair-care millionaire Madame C.J. Walker, she had distinguished herself as hostess of the "Dark Tower" on Harlem's West 136th Street, a meeting place for Harlem Renaissance poets, philosophers, and artists such as W.E.B. Du Bois, Langston Hughes, and Aaron Douglas, as well as European nobility and members of New York's social register.

Brian V. Jones, *Rushing Water, Rock Creek Park, Washington, D.C.*, 1991. Photograph. Courtesy the photographer.

18

19

1909 Howard Swanson is born in Atlanta, Ga. He will become a classical composer who will study in the U.S. and Paris and will write music for orchestra, solo voice, piano, and chamber ensembles. Among his awards will be a 1951 New York Music Critics Circle Award for his composition *Short Symphony*.

1934 Rafer Johnson is born in Hillsboro, Tex. He will become an Olympic athlete, winning a gold medal in the decathlon in the 1960 Summer Games in Rome and lighting the torch in the 1984 Games in Los Angeles.

1963 James Meredith becomes the first African-American to graduate from Ole Miss. Meredith's admission to the University of Mississippi was among the most controversial of the civil rights movement and included the use of federal troops to protect him.

1977 Steven Biko, one of the most influential black student leaders in South Africa, is ar-

Rafer Johnson

rested in Port Elizabeth on charges of fomenting unrest among blacks in the city through his writings. Biko will reportedly die in police detention less than a month later, supposedly as a result of a hunger strike.

1791 Benjamin Banneker sends a copy of his just-published almanac to the Secretary of State, Thomas Jefferson, along with an appeal on behalf of African-Americans' "humiliating condition (slavery)...one universal father has given being to us all...and...however diversified in situation or color, we are all the same family and stand in the same relation to Him."

1926 Theodore Flowers, known as the "Georgia Deacon," wins the world middleweight title in New York City.

1946 Charles F. Bolden, Jr., is born in Columbia, S.C. A pilot who flew over 100 sorties in Southeast Asia, Bolden will be named an astronaut in 1981. He will become a veteran pilot of several missions, including the Space Shuttle *Atlantis* in 1992, where he will participate as a presenter of a special Academy Award to science-fiction film producer George Lucas.

Charles F. Bolden, Jr.

1950 Mrs. Edith Sampson is the first African-American appointed as a representative to the UN.

1989 Nobel Peace Prize winner Bishop Desmond Tutu is among hundreds of black demonstrators who are whipped and sandblasted from helicopters as they attempt to picnic on a "whites-only" beach near Capetown, South Africa.

20

21

1619 The first group of 20 Africans is brought to Jamestown, Va.

1942 Isaac Hayes is born in Covington, Tenn. He will sing with gospel and R & B groups in his youth and join Stax Records as a backup musician to Otis Redding and others. His successful songwriting collaboration with David Porter at Stax Records will result in hits for Sam & Dave. His solo career will begin in 1969 and bring him wide acclaim. His soundtrack for the movie *Shaft* will earn him an Oscar and two Grammys. He will win a Grammy again in 1972 for *Black Moses.*

1964 The Economic Opportunity Act is signed by President Lyndon B. Johnson. The act initiates what will popularly be called the "War on Poverty."

1989 The first National Black Theater Festival closes in Winston-Salem, N.C. Organized by

Issac Hayes

Larry Leon Hamlin, the festival draws over 20,000 people to performances of African-American classical and contemporary plays by groups such as the Crossroads Theater of New Brunswick, N.J. and the Inner-City Cultural Center of Los Angeles.

1904 William "Count" Basie is born in Redbank, N.J. One of the most influential forces in jazz, he will learn organ technique literally at the feet of Fats Waller and form his own band in Kansas City in the mid-1930's. In 1957, his band will play at a command performance for the Queen of England. He will amass numerous awards, including three Grammys and Kennedy Center Honors in 1981.

1932 Melvin Van Peebles is born in Chicago, Ill. A writer and dramatist, he will produce and direct some of the more important African-American feature films of the 1960's and 1970's, including *Story of a Three Day Pass, Watermelon Man, Sweet Sweetback's Baadasss Song,* and the classic, *Putney Swope.*

1936 Wilt Chamberlain is born in Philadelphia, Pa. Achieving a height of 6'11" in high school, Chamberlain will leave Kansas University in his

William "Count" Basie

third year to play with the Harlem Globetrotters and join the Philadelphia Warriors (later 76ers) in 1959. He will join the L.A. Lakers in 1968 and become a player-coach for the San Diego Conquistadors of the American Basketball Association in 1974. He will be elected to the Basketball Hall of Fame in 1979 and be considered the greatest offensive player in the history of the game.

HALE ASPACIO WOODRUFF, *Old Farmhouse in the Beauce Valley,* 1928. Oil on canvas. Courtesy Ernestine W. Brazeal from the collection of the B.R. Brazeals, Atlanta, Georgia.

22

1831 Responding to a vision commanding him to lead his people to freedom, Nat Turner and a group of seven slaves murder five members of the Travis family. Obtaining weapons and horses while enlisting other slaves, Turner's revolt will last two days, involve 60 to 80 slaves and result in the deaths of at least 57 whites before they go into hiding. Turner will eventually be captured and hanged for his crimes.

1843 Henry H. Garnet issues a call for a slave revolt in "An Address to Slaves of the United States" before a national convention of African-Americans in Buffalo, N.Y. Frederick Douglass is one of the many delegates that condemn Garnet's speech.

1917 John Lee Hooker, who will become a renowned blues singer and guitarist, is born in Clarksdale, Miss.

Henry Highland Garnet

1978 Jomo Kenyatta, president of Kenya, dies of heart failure in his sleep while vacationing in Mobasa, Kenya. He was the leading force in Kenya's independence struggles.

1989 Huey Newton dies in Oakland, Calif. The founder of the Black Panther Party is shot to death outside a crack cocaine house allegedly by a drug dealer whom Newton had robbed.

23

1900 The National Negro Business League is formed in Boston, Mass. Sponsored by Booker T. Washington, the organization is established to stimulate the development of African-American businesses.

1908 Fifty-two nurses, led by Martha M. Franklin, form the National Association of Colored Graduate Nurses. Its formation is the culmination of a two-year effort by Franklin to improve the status of African-American nurses.

1917 A riot occurs in Houston, Tex., when the 24th Infantry seeks revenge on the city's white police after the brutal beating of two of the regiment's soldiers. After two hours of violence, 15 whites, including four policemen, will be killed and 12 more injured. Four soldiers will die as a result of the violence. One hundred and eighteen soldiers will be charged in connection with the riots and 19 executed, most in almost total secrecy, in one of the most infamous court-martials ever involving African-Americans.

24

1854 John VanSurley de-Grasse, M.D., who received his medical degree from Bowdoin College in 1849 and studied in New York and Paris, becomes a member of the Massachusetts Medical Society, a first for an African-American. He will serve in the Army Medical Corps during the Civil War, only one of eight African-Americans to be commissioned as a surgeon. For years deGrasse will be considered the first African-American to receive a medical degree, although he was preceded by Dr. James McCune Smith, who received his degree from the University of Glasgow (Scotland) in 1837 and by Dr. David John Peck, a graduate of Rush Medical College of Chicago in 1847.

1987 Bayard Rustin, longtime civil rights activist, early Freedom Rider, and a key organizer of the 1963 March on Washington, dies in New York City. A Quaker, Rustin was an early organizer of the American Communist Party and a lifelong pacifist who served over two years in a federal penitentiary as a conscientious objector in World War II and on a chain gang in North Carolina for his part in an antisegregation protest. He was best known as a civil rights advocate, first as a founder of the Congress for Racial Equality (CORE), then as a key advisor to a young Dr. Martin Luther King, Jr.

25

Althea Gibson

1925 A. Philip Randolph organizes the Sleeping Car Porters Union.

1927 Althea Gibson is born in Silver, S.C. She will grow to be a pioneer in the field of tennis, becoming the first African-American to play tennis at the U.S. Open in 1950 and at Wimbledon the following year. In 1957, she will win the singles and doubles titles at Wimbledon, another first for an

African-American player. Her later singles title at the U.S. Open in the same year will be repeated in 1958, along with her Wimbledon wins.

1991 African-Americans receive seven Emmy awards, a record number. In addition to director Thomas Carter and choreographer Debbie Allen, four African-American actors (James Earl Jones, Lynn Whitfield, Ruby Dee, and Madge Sinclair) win the statuette. Jones's Emmys for *Gabriel's Fire* and the TV movie *Heatwave* make him the first African-American to win two awards in one year since Cicely Tyson's double awards for *The Autobiography of Miss Jane Pittman* in 1974.

26

27

1900 Hale Woodruff is born in Cairo, Ill. He will study art in the U.S., Paris (at two universities and with Henry Ossawa Tanner), and fresco painting with Diego Rivera in Mexico. Early in his career he will paint still lifes and landscapes, but will later receive important commissions for the *Amistad Murals* at Talladega College. He will also start the influential Atlanta University shows for African-American artists in the 1940's.

1905 George Washington dies in Centralia, Wash. A settler of a vast land claim at the junctions of the Skookumchuck and Chehalis rivers in 1851, Washington endured schemes of white settlers to take his land and the Indian Wars of 1853 to found the town of Centerville (later Centralia), Wash., in 1875.

1960 Jazz saxophonist Branford Marsalis is born in New Orleans, La. He will begin his musical career with Art Blakey & the Jazz Messengers, later play with his brother Wynton's quintet, record with Miles Davis, Dizzy Gillespie, and Sting, and become musical director for *The Tonight Show* in 1992.

Branford Marsalis

1949 Paul Robeson's scheduled singing appearance at the Lakeland picnic grounds in Westchester County, N.Y., is disrupted by a riot instigated and provoked by whites angry at Robeson's political stands.

1963 W.E.B. Du Bois dies at age 95 in Accra, Ghana. He was one of America's foremost scholars, a militant civil rights activist, founding father of the NAACP, and a leading proponent of Pan-Africanism.

Meanwhile, 13 New York–based artists meet to discuss their social responsibility as African-American artists. Among the members of the group are Charles Alston, Romare Bearden, Norman Lewis, Richard Mayhew, and Hale Woodruff. They will take the name Spiral, meet weekly in sometimes spirited discussion of their role as African-American artists in a changing society, and have a single group show before disbanding four years later.

W.E.B. Du Bois
29
Black Heritage USA

1991 Central Life Insurance Company, the last surviving African-American-owned insurance company in the state of Florida, is ordered liquidated by a Florida circuit court judge.

28

29

Martin Luther King, Jr.

1955 Fourteen-year-old Chicago youngster Emmett Till is kidnaped in Money, Miss. Four days later he is found murdered. Two whites will be acquitted of the crime by an all-white jury. The incident will receive national publicity and highlight racism and brutality toward African-Americans.

1963 Over 250,000 African-Americans and whites converge on the Lincoln Memorial during the March on Washington, the largest single protest demonstration in U.S. history. The march, organized to support sweeping civil rights measures, will also be the occasion of Martin Luther King, Jr.'s most famous speech, "I Have a Dream."

1988 Beah Richards wins an Emmy for outstanding guest performance in the comedy series *Frank's Place*. It is one of many acting distinctions for the Vicksburg, Miss., native, including her Academy Award nomination for best supporting actress in *Guess Who's Coming to Dinner?*

1920 Charlie "Bird" Parker is born in Kansas City, Kans. The jazz saxophonist will be one of the leaders of the bebop movement and noted for his works "Ko Ko" and "In the Still of the Night," among others. He will receive numerous awards from *Downbeat* magazine and have the famous Birdland jazz club in New York City named in his honor.

Michael Jackson

1924 Dinah Washington is born in Tuscaloosa, Ala. She will perform with Lionel Hampton from 1943 to 1946 and become one of the most popular R & B singers of the 1950's and early 1960's.

1957 The Civil Rights Act of 1957 is passed by Congress. It is the first civil rights legislation since 1875.

1958 Michael Jackson is born in Gary, Ind. First with the family group the Jackson 5 and later as a solo artist, Jackson will be one of pop and R & B's foremost stars. His solo album *Off the Wall* (1979) will sell 7 million copies worldwide, surpassed only by *Thriller*, his largest-selling album.

1962 Mal Goode becomes the first African-American television news commentator when he begins broadcasting on ABC.

Lᴇᴠ T. Mɪʟʟs, *Something Coming,* 1970. Serigraph. Collection the artist.

30

31

1800 Coachman Gabriel Prosser's plans for a slave revolt in Richmond, Va., are betrayed by a pair of house slaves attempting to save their master. Prosser's plan, which involved over 1,000 slaves, would have resulted in the death of all slave-owning whites, but would have spared Quakers, Frenchmen, elderly women, and children.

1838 The first African-American magazine, *Mirror of Freedom*, begins publication in New York City.

1901 Roy Wilkins is born is Saint Louis, Mo. He will become a civil rights leader, assistant executive secretary of the NAACP under Walter White, and editor of *Crisis* magazine for 15 years. He will become executive secretary of the NAACP in 1955, a post he will hold for 22 years. During his tenure, he will be a champion of civil rights committed to using Constitutional arguments to help obtain full citizenship rights for all African-Americans.

1931 Carrie Saxon Perry is born in Hartford, Conn. In 1987, she will be elected mayor of Hartford, becoming the first African-American woman mayor of a major U.S. city.

1983 Guion Bluford is the first African-American in space when he serves as a mission specialist on *Challenger*.

Guion Bluford

1936 Marva Collins is born in Monroeville, Ala. She will become an innovative educator who will use her pension funds to open Westside Preparatory School in Chicago, dedicated to reversing the educational decline in the city's African-American neighborhoods. Collins's motto for the school is "entrance to learn, exit to serve." Her revolutionary methods and success with some of the city's toughest youngsters will earn her wide acclaim and will be the focus of a 1981 television movie, *The Marva Collins Story*.

1943 The *USS Harmon*, a destroyer escort, is launched. It is named after Mess Attendant 1st Class Leonard H. Harmon, a 1942 Navy Cross recipient.

1962 Joint independence is granted to Trinidad and Tobago. Dr. Eric Williams of the People's National Movement serves the new nations as both prime minister and party leader.

Marva Collins

1983 Brigadier General Hazel W. Jackson retires from the Army Nurse Corps. She was the first African-American woman to achieve the rank of brigadier general and the first African-American to be chief of the Army Nurse Corps.

1991 KQEC-TV of San Francisco begins broadcasting under its new owners, the Minority Television Project. It is the second minority-owned public television station.

1

1912 Samuel Coleridge-Taylor, English-born composer of *Hiawatha's Wedding Feast* and professor of music at Trinity College of Music in London, dies in Croyden, England. Coleridge-Taylor was the most important black composer of his day and toured the U.S. three times, where he played with Will Marion Cook, Clarence Cameron White, and collaborated with Paul Laurence Dunbar in setting several of his poems to music.

1925 Rosa Guy is born in Trinidad. She will become the author of *The Friends*, *Ruby*, and *Edith Jackson*.

1948 William T. Coleman is appointed by Justice Frankfurter as a clerk to the U.S. Supreme Court, the first African-American to hold the position. A Harvard Law School graduate and Army Air Corps veteran, Coleman will again enter public service, first as president of the NAACP Legal Defense and Education Fund

and, in 1975, as Secretary of Transportation under President Gerald Ford.

1970 Dr. Hugh S. Scott of Washington, D.C., becomes the first African-American superintendent of schools in a major U.S. city.

1971 The Pittsburgh Pirates field an all-African-American team in a baseball game against the Philadelphia Phillies.

Rosa Guy

2

1833 Oberlin College is founded in Oberlin, Ohio.

1902 *In Dahomey* premieres at the Old Globe Theater in Boston, Mass. With music by Will Marion Cook and lyrics by poet Paul Laurence Dunbar, it is the most successful musical of its day.

1914 Romare Bearden is born in Charlotte, N.C. A student at NYU, the American Artists School, Columbia University, and the Sorbonne, Bearden's depiction of the rituals and social customs of African-American life will be imbued with an eloquence and power that will earn him accolades as one of the finest artists of the 20th century and a master of collage. Among his honors will be election to the American Academy of Arts and Letters and the National Institute of Arts and Letters, and receiving the President's National Medal of Arts in 1987.

Horace Silver

1928 Horace Ward Martin Tavares Silver is born in Norwalk, Conn. He will become a jazz pianist, bandleader and composer who will initially lead the Jazz Messengers with drummer Art Blakey before forming his own band in 1956. A pioneer of the hard bop style, he will attract to his band the talents of Art Farmer, Donald Byrd, and Blue Mitchell, among others.

1975 In Tallahassee, Fla., Joseph W. Hatcher is sworn in as the state's first African-American supreme court justice since Reconstruction.

WILMER A. JENNINGS, *Landscape*. Oil on canvas. Courtesy Ernestine W. Brazeal from the collection of the B.R. Brazeals, Atlanta, Georgia.

3

_____
_____
_____
_____
_____
_____
_____
_____
_____

1783 Richard Allen, founder of the AME Church, purchases his freedom with his earnings as a self-employed teamster.

1838 Frederick Augustus Washington Bailey escapes from slavery disguised as a sailor. Eventually arriving in New York City, he will take the name Douglass, after the hero of Sir Walter Scott's poem *Lady of the Lake*.

1868 Henry McNeal Turner delivers a speech before the Georgia legislature defending African-Americans' rights to hold state office.

1919 Lincoln Motion Picture Company, owned by African-Americans Noble Johnson and Clarence Brooks, releases its first feature-length film, *A Man's Duty*.

1970 Representatives from 27 African nations, the Caribbean nations, four South American countries, Australia, and the U.S. meet in Atlanta, Ga., for the first Congress of African People.

1990 Jonathan A. Rodgers becomes president of CBS's television stations division, the highest-ranking African-American in network television. Rodgers had been general manager of WBBM-TV, CBS's Chicago station.

Jonathan A. Rodgers

4

_____
_____
_____
_____
_____
_____
_____
_____
_____

1781 Of the 46 settlers of California's second pueblo, Nuestra Señora la Reina de Los Angeles de Porciuncula (later known as Los Angeles), 26 are recorded as blacks or mulattoes.

1848 Lewis Latimer is born in Chelsea, Mass. A one-time draftsman and preparer of patents for Alexander Graham Bell, he will later join the U.S. Electric Company, where he will patent a carbon filament for the incandescent lamp. At his death, he will be eulogized by his coworkers as a valuable member of the "Edison Pioneers," a group of men and women who advanced electrical light usage in the U.S.

1865 Bowie State College is established in Bowie, Md.

Richard Wright

1908 Richard Wright, who will become the author of the best-selling *Native Son* and *Black Boy*, is born in Natchez, Miss.

5

Henry Louis Gates, Jr.

1859 *Our Nig* by Harriet Wilson is published. It is the first novel published in the U.S. by an African-American woman and will be lost to readers for years until reprinted with a critical essay by noted African-American scholar Henry Louis Gates, Jr. in 1983.

1916 Novelist Frank Yerby is born in Augusta, Ga. A student at Fisk University and the University of Chicago, Yerby's early short story "Health Card" will win the O. Henry short story award. He will later turn to adventure novels and become a best-selling author of the 1940's and 1950's with *The Foxes of Harrow*, *The Vixens* and many others. His later novels will include *Goat Song*, *The Darkness at Ingraham's Crest: A Tale of the Slaveholding South*, and *Devil Seed*. In total, Yerby will publish over 30 novels that sell over 20 million copies.

6

1781 African-American Jordan Freeman dies after killing Major William Montgomery in the Battle of Groton Heights.

1892 George "Little Chocolate" Dixon beats Jack Skelly in New Orleans to win the world featherweight title. While some African-American citizens celebrate for two days, the *New Orleans Times-Democrat* says, "It was a mistake to match a Negro and a white man … to bring the races together on any terms of equality even in the prize ring."

1930 Leander Jay Shaw, Jr. is born in Salem, Va. He will become a justice of the Florida State Supreme Court in 1983 and, in 1990, the chief justice, a first in the state and the second African-American chief justice in any state supreme court.

Leander Shaw, Jr.

1988 Lee Roy Young becomes the first African-American Texas Ranger in the police force's 165-year history. Young is a 14-year veteran of the Texas Department of Public Safety.

7

_____
_____
_____
_____
_____
_____
_____
_____
_____

8

_____
_____
_____
_____
_____
_____
_____
_____
_____

1800 The AME Zion Church is dedicated in New York City.

1914 Jean Blackwell Hutson is born in Summerfield, Fla. She will be the longtime curator and chief of the Schomburg Center for Research in Black Culture in New York City, the largest collection on the culture and literature of people of African descent.

1917 Jacob Lawrence is born in Atlantic City, N.J. He will become one of the leading painters in chronicling African-American history and urban life. Among his most celebrated works will be the historical panels *The Life of Toussaint-Louverture* and *The Life of Harriet Tubman*.

1937 Olly Wilson is born in Saint Louis, Mo. He will become a classical composer whose works will be played by the Boston Symphony Orchestra, Oakland City Philharmonic, San Francisco Symphony Orchestra, and many others.

1980 Bessie A. Buchanan, the first African-American woman to be elected to the New York State legislature, dies in New York City. Before her political career, she was a Broadway star who had leading roles in *Shuffle Along* and *Showboat*.

1987 Dr. Benjamin S. Carson, a pediatric neurosurgeon at Johns Hopkins University, leads a surgical team that successfully separates Siamese twins who had been joined at the head.

1968 Black Panther Huey Newton is convicted of voluntary manslaughter in the fatal shooting of an Oakland policeman. He will later begin a 2- to 15-year jail sentence.

Meanwhile, Saundra Williams is crowned the first Miss Black America in a contest held exclusively for African-American women in Atlantic City, N.J.

1990 Marjorie Judith Vincent of Illinois is selected as Miss America in Atlantic City, N.J. The Haitian native, a third-year law student at Duke University, is the fourth African-American to become Miss America.

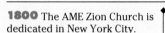

Marjorie Vincent

9

10

1739 Led by a slave named Cato, a slave revolt occurs in Stono, S.C.

1915 A group of visionary scholars, including Carter G. Woodson, George Cleveland Hall, W.B. Hartgrove, Alexander L. Jackson, and James E.

Sonia Sanchez

Stamps, found the Association for the Study of Negro Life and History (ASNLH) in Chicago, Ill. The association is the only organization of its kind concerned with preserving African-American history.

1934 Sonia Sanchez is born in Birmingham, Ala. She will become a noted poet, playwright, short story writer, and author of children's books. She will be most noted for her poetry volumes *We a BaddDDD People*, *A Blues Book for Blue Black Magical Women,* and anthologies she will edit including *We Be Word Sorcerers: 25 Stories by Black Americans*.

1968 Arthur Ashe becomes the first winner of the newly established U.S. Open tennis championships at Forest Hills, N.Y.

1979 Robert Guillaume wins an Emmy award for best actor in a comedy series for *Soap*.

1847 John Roy Lynch is born near Vadalia in Concordia Parish, La. He will serve in the 43rd, 44th and 47th Congresses representing the State of Mississippi as a Republican. He will also preside as temporary chairman over the Republican National Convention of 1884 and deliver the keynote address, the first African-American to do so.

1886 Poet Georgia Douglas Johnson is born in Atlanta, Ga. Among her books will be *Heart of a Woman*, *Bronze*, *An Autumn Love Cycle,* and *Share My Love*. She will be anthologized in Arna Bontemps's *American Negro Poetry* and Davis and Lee's *Negro Caravan*, among others. Her home in Washington, D.C., will be the center for African-American literary gatherings.

1965 Father Divine dies in Philadelphia, Pa. Divine, born George Baker, was the founder of the Peace Mission, a religious group whose followers worshiped Divine as God incarnate on earth.

1973 A commemorative stamp of Henry Ossawa Tanner is issued by the U.S. Postal Service. Part of its American Arts issue, the stamp celebrates the work and accomplishments of Tanner, the first African-American artist elected to the National Academy of Design.

Jacob Lawrence, *On the Way,* 1990. Color lithograph on paper. National Museum of American Art, Smithsonian Institution, gift of the Smithsonian Institution Resident Associate Program.

11

12

Charles Evers

1740 An issue of the *Pennsylvania Gazette* reports on a Negro named Simon who reportedly can "bleed and draw teeth." It is the first mention of an African-American doctor or dentist in the Colonies.

1923 Charles Evers is born in Decatur, Miss. He will be a civil rights worker who will assume the post of field director of the Mississippi NAACP after his brother, Medgar, is assassinated in 1963. He will be elected mayor of Fayette, Miss., in 1969.

1943 Lola Falana is born in Philadelphia, Pa. She will become a dancer, most notably in Broadway's *Golden Boy,* and be a successful performer on television and in Las Vegas, where she will be called "The First Lady of Las Vegas."

1959 Duke Ellington receives the NAACP's Spingarn Medal for his outstanding musical achievements and contributions to the field of music.

1977 Quincy Jones wins an Emmy for outstanding achievement in musical composition for the miniseries *Roots*. It is one of nine Emmys for the series, an unprecedented number.

Jesse Owens

1913 James Cleveland Owens is born in Oakville, Ala. He will be better known as Jesse Owens, one of the greatest track and field stars in history. Owens will achieve fame at the 1936 Summer Olympic Games in Berlin, where he will win four gold medals, dispelling Hitler's notion of the superior Aryan race and the inferiority of black athletes. Among his honors will be the Medal of Freedom, presented to him by President Ford in 1976.

1935 Richard Hunt is born in Chicago, Ill. A graduate of the Art Institute of Chicago, he will later study in Europe and be considered one of the leading sculptors in the U.S. His work will be shown extensively in the U.S. and abroad and his sculptures will be collected by the National Museum of American Art, the Whitney Museum of American Art, the Metropolitan Museum of Art, and the Museum of the Twentieth Century in Vienna.

1974 Eugene A. Marino, SSJ, is consecrated as the first African-American auxiliary bishop in the U.S. He assumes his duties as auxiliary bishop of Washington, D.C.

1986 The National Council of Negro Women sponsors its first Black Family Reunion at the National Mall in Washington, D.C. The reunion, which will grow to encompass dozens of cities and attract over one million people annually, is held to celebrate and applaud the traditional values, history, and culture of the African-American family.

13

14

Alain Locke

1663 The first known slave revolt is planned in Gloucester County, Va. The conspirators, both white servants and black slaves, are betrayed by fellow indentured servants.

1886 Alain Locke is born in Philadelphia, Pa. He will become the first African-American Rhodes scholar and an influential writer, educator, and philosopher. His work in capturing the cultural and social climate of the "New Negro" of the Harlem Renaissance will make him one of the foremost chroniclers of African-American achievement.

1948 Nell Carter is born in Birmingham, Ala. She will become a Broadway sensation as a singer and actress in Broadway's *Bubbling Brown Sugar*, *Ain't Misbehavin'* (for which she will win a Tony), and for five seasons in television's *Gimme a Break*.

1981 Isabel Sanford wins an Emmy award as best comedic actress for *The Jeffersons*.

1891 John Adams Hyman dies in Washington, D.C. He was the first African-American congressman from the State of North Carolina.

Constance Baker Motley

1921 Constance Baker Motley is born in New Haven, Conn. She will achieve many distinctions in her career, including being the only woman elected to the New York Senate in 1964, the only woman Manhattan borough president, and the first African-American woman to be named as a federal court judge in 1966. She will later serve as chief judge of the Southern District of New York.

1964 Leontyne Price and A. Philip Randolph are among the recipients of the Medal of Freedom awarded by President Lyndon B. Johnson.

RICHARD HUNT, *Generation of Points and Arcs,* 1991. Bronze. Courtesy Louis Newman Galleries, Beverly Hills, California.

15

16

1890 Claude McKay is born in Sunnyville, Jamaica. Emigrating to the U.S. in 1912, he will become a poet and winner of the 1928 Harmon Gold Medal Award for Literature. Author of the influential poetry collection *Harlem Shadows*, he will also be famous for the poems "The Lynching," "White Houses," and "If We Must Die," which will be used by Winston Churchill as a rallying cry during World War II.

1928 Julian Edwin Adderly is born in Tampa, Fla. He will be best known as "Cannonball" Adderly, a jazz saxophonist who will play with Miles Davis as well as lead his own band with brother Nat Adderly and musicians such as Yusef Lateef and George Duke.

1963 Four African-American schoolgirls—Addie Collins, Denise McNair, Carol Robertson and Cynthia Wesley—are killed in a bombing at the

Sixteenth Street Baptist Church in Birmingham, Ala. It is an act of violence that galvanizes the civil rights movement.

1978 Muhammad Ali wins the world heavyweight boxing championship for a record third time by defeating Leon Spinks in New Orleans, La.

Claude McKay

1893 The Oklahoma land rush into the territory's Cherokee strip begins. Among the participants is E.P. McCabe, who will establish the all-African-American town of Liberty a few days later. McCabe was also involved in the earlier establishment of the African-American town of Langston, Okla., named for John Mercer Langston, Virginia's first African-American congressman.

1921 Jon Carl Hendricks, who will become an influential singer in the jazz group Lambert, Hendricks and Ross, is born in Newark, Ohio.

1925 Blues great B.B. King is born in Indianola, Miss. Playing his guitar, nicknamed Lucille, King will have over 50 hit blues albums and win a 1970 Grammy for *The Thrill Is Gone.*

1933 *Emperor Jones,* starring Paul Robeson as Brutus Jones, is released by United Artists. It is Robeson's first starring movie role and the first major

B.B. King

Hollywood production starring an African-American with whites in supporting roles.

1989 Debbye Turner, a senior at the University of Missouri Veterinary School, is crowned Miss America. She is the third African-American to win the crown since the pageant began in 1921.

1990 Keenen Ivory Wayans's *In Living Color* wins an Emmy for Outstanding Comedy Series.

17

18

Vanessa Williams

1983 Vanessa Williams, Miss New York State, is named Miss America in Atlantic City, N.J., the first African-American winner in the history of the pageant. Williams will relinquish her crown after a 1984 scandal and later stage a remarkable comeback through a stellar recording career which includes her multimillion-selling album, *The Right Stuff.*

1968 *Julia* premieres on NBC with Diahann Carroll in the title role. It is the first modern television show to star an African-American woman since *Beulah* in the 1950's.

1970 *The Flip Wilson Show* premieres on NBC. Starring the New Jersey comedian born as Clerow Wilson, it is the first prime-time variety show starring an African-American male since the *Nat King Cole Show.*

1973 Illinois becomes the first state to honor Dr. Martin Luther King, Jr.'s birthday as a holiday.

1990 *The Content of Our Character* is published by San Jose State University professor Shelby Steele. The book will attract controversy because of its provocative positions on affirmative action and race relations and win a 1992 National Book Award.

1991 Ground is broken for the Harold Washington wing of the DuSable Museum in Chicago, Ill. Founded by artist and poet Margaret T. Burroughs in 1961, the DuSable is one of the oldest African-American museum in the U.S.

1850 Congress passes the Fugitive Slave Act, a part of the Compromise of 1850. The act offers federal officers a fee for captured slaves.

1895 Booker T. Washington makes a speech at the Cotton States and International Exposition in Atlanta, Ga. Known as the "Atlanta Compromise" speech, Washington advocates acceptance of a subordinate role for African-Americans, espouses peaceful coexistence with white Southerners, and calls agitation over the question of social equality "the extremist folly." The speech, which reportedly leaves some African-American listeners in tears and will incur the wrath of W.E.B. Du Bois and others, secures Washington's reputation among whites as a successor to Frederick Douglass.

1990 Atlanta, Ga., is selected as the site of the XXV Olympiad Summer Games. Mayor Maynard H. Jackson says the 1996 Summer Games will be the "single biggest continuous infusion of economic development to Atlanta in the history of the city under any circumstances." It is the second time the city hosting the games is led by an African-American mayor.

Maynard Jackson

19

20

1931 Brook Benton is born in Camden, S.C. He will amass 16 gold records and be best known for the songs "A Rainy Night in Georgia" and "It's Just a Matter of Time."

1945 Freda Payne is born in Detroit, Mich. She will become a singer whose hits will include "Band of Gold" in 1970.

1989 Gordon Parks's film *The Learning Tree* is selected among the first films to be registered by the National Film Registry of the Library of Congress. The National Film Registry was formed by an act of Congress the previous year to recognize films that are "culturally, historically, or aesthetically significant." Parks's 1969 movie joins other classic films such as *Casablanca*, *Gone With the Wind*, and *The Wizard of Oz*.

Meanwhile, the first issue of *Emerge* magazine goes on sale. *Emerge*, founded by Wilmer C. Ames, Jr., covers domestic and

Gordon Parks, Sr.

international news and issues from an African-American perspective.

1830 The National Negro Convention, a group of 38 free African-Americans from eight states, meets in Philadelphia, Pa., with the express purpose of abolishing slavery and improving the social status of African-Americans. They will elect Richard Allen president and agree to boycott slave-produced goods.

1915 Hughie Lee-Smith is born in Eustis, Fla. He will become a painter known for such surrealistic landscapes as *Man with Balloons*, *Man Standing on His Head* and *Big Brother*.

1984 *The Cosby Show*, starring Bill Cosby, Phylicia Ayers-Allen (now Rashad), and an ensemble of child actors, premieres on NBC. The series, which had been rejected by other network television executives, will become one of the most popular in television history, and help launch the careers of several talented actors, including Rashad, Malcolm

Jamal Warner, Keisha Knight Pullam, and Raven-Symone.

1987 Alfre Woodard wins an Emmy for outstanding guest performance in the dramatic series *L.A. Law*. It is her second Emmy award, her first having been for a supporting role in *Hill Street Blues* in 1984.

The Cosby Show

21

22

1905 Atlanta Life Insurance Company is founded by Alonzo F. Herndon.

1909 Kwame Nkrumah is born in Nkroful, Ghana. A leader in African colonial liberation, Nkrumah will be the first prime minister of Ghana but be forced into exile following a coup.

1967 Walter Washington is nominated by President Lyndon B. Johnson as first mayor of the newly reorganized municipal government of Washington, D.C. In 1974, he will be elected to the post, another first for an African-American.

1989 Army General Colin Powell receives Senate confirmation as Chairman of

General Colin Powell

the Joint Chiefs of Staff, the highest military position in the United States. He is the military's highest-ranking African-American.

1853 George Washington Murray is born near Rembert, S.C. A two-term congressman from his home state, Murray will also be an inventor and holder of eight patents for agricultural tools.

1915 Xavier University of Louisiana opens in New Orleans, the first African-American Catholic college in the U.S.

1941 Chester Lovelle Talton is born in Eldorado, Ark. At 49, he will become the first African-American Episcopalian bishop to be ordained in the western U.S. As suffragan bishop of the diocese of Los Angeles, he becomes the religious leader of Episcopalians in the fourth-largest diocese in the U.S.

1985 Robert Guillaume wins an Emmy for best leading actor in a comedy for *Benson* while *The Cosby Show* wins for best comedy series.

Robert Guillaume

1989 Edward Perkins, the first African-American ambassador to the Republic of South Africa, becomes director-general of the U.S. Foreign Service. The first African-American named to the post, Perkins will be credited with bringing more minorities into the foreign service.

JAMES V. HERRING, *Campus Landscape,* 1924. Oil on canvas. Courtesy Professor and Mrs. David C. Driskell.

23

24

1863 Mary Church (later Terrell) is born in Memphis, Tenn. She will become an educator, civil and woman's rights advocate, and U.S. delegate to the International Peace Conference.

Mary Church Terrell

1926 John Coltrane, brilliant jazz saxophonist and composer who will be considered the father of avant-garde jazz, is born in Hamlet, N.C.

1930 Ray Charles Robinson is born in Albany, Ga. Blind by the age of six, he will study music and form his own band at the age of 24. A recorded performance at the Newport Jazz Festival in 1958 will establish his career as one of the premier soul singers in the U.S. Among Charles's achievements will be three Grammys and Kennedy Center honors in 1986.

1954 Playwright George C. Wolfe is born in Tennessee. He will become critically acclaimed for the controversial plays *The Colored Museum*, *Jelly's Last Jam*, and *Spunk*.

Cardiss Collins

1894 E. Franklin Frazier is born in Baltimore, Md. A noted social scientist and author of such books as *The Negro Family in the U.S.* and *Black Bourgeoisie*, Frazier will have a distinguished career at Howard University as chairman of its sociology department as well as serving as the first African-American president of the American Sociological Society.

1931 Cardiss Robertson (later Collins) is born in Saint Louis, Mo. Elected to the House of Representatives in 1973 after

the death of her husband, George, she will serve in a leadership capacity often in her Congressional career, most notably as chairman of the Energy and Commerce Subcommittee on Commerce, Consumer Protection, and Competitiveness.

1954 Patrick Kelly is born in Vicksburg, Miss. A fashion design student, Kelly will move to Paris, where his innovative and outrageous women's fashion designs, featuring multiple buttons, bows and African-American baby dolls, will win him wide acclaim and make him the first and only American designer admitted to an exclusive organization of French fashion designers.

1957 President Dwight D. Eisenhower sends 1,000 U.S. government paratroopers to Little Rock, Ark., to desegregate schools. The troops will escort nine schoolchildren to Central High School in the first federally supported effort to integrate the nation's public schools.

25

26

Langston Hughes

1861 The Secretary of the Navy authorizes the enlistment of African-Americans in the Union Navy. The enlistees could achieve no rank higher than "boys" and receive pay of one ration per day and $10 per month.

1924 In a letter to his friend Alain Locke, Langston Hughes writes "I've done a couple of new poems. I have no more paper, so I'm sending you one on the back of this letter." The poem, *I, Too*, will be published two years later and be among his most famous.

1962 Sonny Liston knocks out Floyd Patterson in the first round to become the world heavyweight boxing champion.

1991 Pioneer filmmaker Spencer Williams's 1942 movie *Blood of Jesus*, a story of the African-American religious experience, is among the third group of twenty-five films added to the Library of Congress's National Film Registry. Williams, best known for his role of Andy in the television series *Amos 'n' Andy*, was, more importantly, an innovative film director and a contemporary of Oscar Micheaux. Williams's film joins other classics like *Lawrence of Arabia* and *2001: A Space Odyssey*.

1867 Maggie Lena Walker is born in Richmond, Va. She will become a noted businesswoman, civil leader, and founder and president of Saint Luke Penny Savings Bank.

1907 The People's Savings Bank is incorporated in Philadelphia, Pa. Founded by former African-American congressman George H. White, of North Carolina, the bank will help hundreds of African-Americans buy homes and start businesses until the illness of its founder forces its closure in 1918.

1937 Bessie Smith dies in Clarksville, Miss. She was one of the nation's greatest blues singers and was nicknamed "the Empress of the Blues." In 1925, Smith and Louis Armstrong made the definitive rendition of W.C. Handy's "St. Louis Blues," and in 1929 she made her only movie appearance in the movie of the same name.

Maggie Lena Walker

1962 A. Leon Higginbotham, Jr., becomes the first African-American member of the Federal Trade Commission. It is one of the Trenton, N.J., native's many accomplishments, including appointment as a federal district judge and U.S. Circuit Judge of the Third Circuit.

1968 The Studio Museum of Harlem opens in New York City. Conceived by Frank Donnelly and Carter Burden, the Studio Museum will become an influential venue for exhibitions of African-American artists in all media.

EDWARD MITCHELL BANNISTER, *Oak Trees,* 1876. Oil on canvas. National Museum of American Art, Smithsonian Institution, gift of H. Alan and Melvin Frank.

27

28

1875 Branch Normal College opens in Pine Bluff, Ark. A segregated unit of the state university, the college is established by Joseph C. Corbin.

1876 Edward Mitchell Bannister wins a bronze medal for his painting *Under the Oaks* at the American Centennial Exposition in Philadelphia, Pa. The award to Bannister will cause controversy among whites who think African-Americans incapable of artistic excellence.

1934 Greg Morris is born in Cleveland, Ohio. He will become an actor who will have a pioneering feature role in the television program *Mission: Impossible*.

1944 Stephanie Pogue is born in Shelby, N.C. She will become an artist and art professor whose works will be collected by New York City's Whitney Museum of American Art and the Studio Museum of Harlem while she will exhibit widely in

Stephanie Pogue

the U.S., Europe, Japan, and South America.

1967 Washington, D.C.'s Anacostia Museum, dedicated to informing the community of the contributions of African-Americans to U.S. social, political and cultural history, opens its doors to the public.

1988 Several athletes, among them black Canadian sprinter Ben Johnson, are expelled from the Olympic Games for anabolic steroid use. Johnson's gold medal, won in the 100-meter dash, is awarded to African-American Carl Lewis, the second-place finisher.

1785 David Walker, who will become an abolitionist and write the famous "Walker's Appeal," is born in Wilmington, N.C.

1912 W.C. Handy's groundbreaking "Memphis Blues" is published in Memphis, Tenn. The composition was originally entitled "Mr. Crump" and was written for the 1909 political campaign of Edward H. "Boss" Crump.

1945 Todd Duncan debuts with the New York City Opera as Tonio in *Il Pagliacci*. He is the first African-American to sing a leading role with a major American company, almost ten years before Marian Anderson sings with the Met.

1961 Ossie Davis's *Purlie Victorious* opens on Broadway. The play stars Davis, Ruby Dee, Godfrey Cambridge, Alan Alda, and Beah Richards.

Meanwhile, Atlanta's segregated restaurants and other public facilities are peacefully integrated, part of a plan adopted by city officials earlier in the year.

1972 The Secretary of the Army repeals the dishonorable discharges of 167 Brownsville (Tex.) Raid soldiers. The soldiers, members of the 25th Infantry who were involved in a riot with the city's police and merchants, were dishonorably discharged by President Theodore Roosevelt without a trial.

1987 The National Museum of African Art, now a part of the Smithsonian Institution, opens on the Mall in Washington, D.C. Founded by Warren M. Robbins in 1964 as a private educational institution, it is the only museum in the U.S. devoted exclusively to the collection, study, and exhibition of the art of sub-Saharan Africa.

29

30

Bryant Gumbel

1864 At the Battle of New Market Heights, Sergeant Major Christian Fleetwood and 12 other African-Americans fight valiantly for the Union's cause. They will receive the Congressional Medal of Honor for their action the following year.

1916 Henry Green Parks, Jr. is born. He will become an entrepreneur and owner of Parks Sausage Company of Baltimore, Md. In 1969, the company will become the first African-American-owned publicly traded company when it is listed on the over-the-counter market.

1948 Bryant Gumbel is born in New Orleans, La. He will become the editor of *Black Sports* magazine and a successful sportscaster before joining NBC's *Today Show* as the first African-American anchor of a national network morning news/entertainment program.

1935 John Royce Mathis is born in San Francisco, Calif. He will become a romantic pop singer who will amass more that 50 gold and platinum records for such hits as "Misty." He will also have the distinction of having an album on the Billboard pop charts for the longest period, 480 weeks.

1975 Muhammad Ali and Joe Frazier square off in a fight billed as "The Thrilla in Manila." Ali will win the fight and retain his world heavyweight title when, after 14 rounds, Frazier's trainer refuses to let him continue.

1976 *Two Centuries of Black American Art* opens at the Los Angeles County Museum of Art. The exhibit features over 60 lithographers, painters, and sculptors including 19th century masters Joshua Johnston, Edward Bannister, and Henry O. Tanner as well as modern artists Charles White, Romare Bearden, and Elizabeth Catlett. The introduction to the exhibit's catalogue asserts that the assembled artists' work proves that "the human creative impulse can triumph in the face of impossible odds, and at times even because of them."

1

Mary Schmidt Campbell

1851 William "Jerry" Henry, a runaway slave and craftsman who had settled in Syracuse, N.Y., is arrested by a U.S. marshal and scheduled to be returned to slavery. Ten thousand citizens of the city will storm the sheriff's office, free Henry, and aid his escape to Canada via the Underground Railroad.

1886 Kentucky State College is founded in Frankfort, Ky.

1945 Donny Hathaway is born in Chicago, Ill. He will be an influential pop and R & B singer of the 1970's whose hit songs will include "The Ghetto" and "The Closer I Get to You" (with Roberta Flack).

1991 Dr. Mary Schmidt Campbell assumes her duties as dean of New York University's Tisch School of the Arts. A noted art historian, Schmidt had previously served as New York City's commissioner of cultural affairs, director of the Studio Museum of Harlem, and chair of the Smithsonian Institution's Advisory Committee that recommended creation of a national African-American museum.

2

1799 Nat Turner is born in Southampton, Va. Believing himself called by God to free his fellow bondsmen, Turner will become a leader of one of the most famous slave revolts, resulting in the death of scores of whites and involving 60 to 80 slaves.

1898 Otis J. René is born in New Orleans, La. With his younger brother Leon, he will move to Los Angeles, Calif., and establish Exclusive and Excelsior Records in the 1930's. By the mid-1940's, the brothers will be leading independent record producers whose artists will include Nat "King" Cole, Herb Jeffries, and Johnny Otis.

1986 The U.S. Senate overrides President Ronald Reagan's veto of legislation imposing economic sanctions against South Africa. The override is seen as the culmination of efforts by TransAfrica's Randall Robinson, Rep. Mickey Leland, and others begun almost two years earlier with Robinson's arrest before the South African embassy in Washington, D.C.

1989 *Jump Start* premieres in 40 newspapers in the U.S. The comic strip is the creation of 26-year-old Robb Armstrong, the youngest African-American to have a syndicated comic strip. He follows in the footsteps of Morrie Turner, the creator of *Wee Pals*, the first African-American syndicated comic strip.

Otis and Leon René

3

4

Art Shell

1856 T. Thomas Fortune is born in Marianna, Fla. An advocate of full equality for African-Americans, he will found the Afro-American League in 1887, serve as editor of the weekly *New York Globe*, and founder of the *New York Freeman* (later the *New York Age*) and the *Washington Sun*.

1904 Daytona Normal and Industrial School (later Bethune-Cookman College) opens in Daytona Beach, Fla. One of the South's leading institutions for training teachers, founder Mary McLeod Bethune will later say the college was started on "faith and a dollar and a half."

1941 Ernest Evans is born in Philadelphia, Pa. Later adopting the name "Chubby Checker" after the renowned Fats Domino, his best-known recording will be the 1960's "The Twist," which will spark the biggest dance craze since the Charleston in the 1920's.

1949 The first African-American-owned radio station, WERD-AM in Atlanta, Ga., is founded by Jesse Blanton, Sr.

1951 Dave Winfield is born in Saint Paul, Minn. He will be a baseball star with the San Diego Padres, the New York Yankees, and the California Angels.

1974 Frank Robinson is named manager of the Cleveland Indians. He is the the first African-American manager in major league baseball.

1989 Art Shell is named head coach of the Los Angeles Raiders. He is the first African-American coach named to the National Football League in over 60 years.

1934 Malvin Gray Johnson dies in New York City. His deceptively simple paintings, with their warm colors and serene, sensuous charm, had earned him a large and loyal group of admirers during the Harlem Renaissance. His work was exhibited widely, first at the Harmon Exhibition of 1928 and later at the Corcoran Gallery of Art in Washington, D.C., the Texas Centennial Exposition of Art, and the American Negro Exposition, as well as major retrospectives. Among his better-known works are *Roll Jordan Roll* and *Self-Portrait*.

1937 Lee Patrick Brown is born in Wewoka, Oklahoma. He will become one of the top-ranking law-enforcement executives in the U.S., first as Public Safety Commissioner in Atlanta, Ga., then as the first African-American police chief in Houston, Tex., and the second African-American police commissioner for New York City.

1943 Student Nonviolent Coordinating Committee chairman and black nationalist H. Rap Brown is born in Baton Rouge, La.

1944 Dancer Pearl Primus makes her Broadway debut at the Belasco Theater. She will become widely known for blending the African and American dance traditions.

1991 The Harold Washington Library in Chicago, Ill., is dedicated in the memory of its beloved former mayor.

Harold Washington

MALVIN GRAY JOHNSON, *Self-Portrait,* 1934. Oil on canvas. National Museum of American Art, Smithsonian Institution, gift of the Harmon Foundation.

5

6

Yvonne Braithwaite

1878 George B. Vashon dies of yellow fever in Rodney, Miss. He was the first African-American lawyer in the State of New York and an educator and poet whose most famous work was *Victor Ogé* (1854), the first narrative, nonlyrical poem by an African-American writer.

1929 Autherine Lucy (later Foster) is born in Shiloh, Ala. She will be the first African-American student to enroll at the University of Alabama (1956).

1932 Perle Yvonne Watson is born in Los Angeles, Calif. As Yvonne Braithwaite, she will serve as a staff attorney on the McCone Commission investigating the causes of the Watts riots and will become the first African-American woman ever elected to the California state assembly, as well as the first African-American woman from California elected to the House of Representatives. In Congress, she will be a supporter of the Humphrey-Hawkins full-employment bill, serve as the first woman to chair the Congressional Black Caucus, and introduce the Displaced Homemakers Act.

1871 The Fisk Jubilee Singers begin their tour to raise money for the school. Soon they will become one of the most popular African-American folk-singing groups of the late 19th century, performing throughout the U.S. and Europe and raising large sums for Fisk's building program.

1917 Fannie Lou Hamer is born near Ruleville, Miss. She will become a leader of the civil rights movement during the 1960's and a founder of the Mississippi Freedom Democratic Party.

1921 Joseph Echols Lowery is born in Huntsville, Ala. An early civil rights activist, he will become a founder, chairman of the board, and president of the Southern Christian Leadership Conference. He will lead SCLC to great levels of civil rights activism including a 2,700-mile pilgrimage to extend and strength-en the Voting Rights Act, protesting toxic waste sites in African-American communities, and actions against U.S. corporations doing business in South Africa.

1986 Abram Hill dies in New York City. He was the founder of the city's American Negro Theater in 1940, where the careers of Harry Belafonte, Ruby Dee, and Sidney Poitier were launched. Hill's adaptation of the play *Anna Lucasta* premiered on Broadway in 1944 and ran successfully for 900 performances.

1991 Williams College's exhibit of African-American photographers *Black Photographers Bear Witness: 100 Years of Social Protest* opens. The exhibit includes photography by C.M. Battey, James Van Der Zee, Marvin and Morgan Smith, Moneta Sleet, Carrie Mae Weems, and others.

7

Elijah Muhammad

1888 Sargent C. Johnson is born in Boston, Mass. He will be a pioneering artist of the Harlem Renaissance, known for his wood, cast stone, and ceramic sculptures. Among his most famous works will be *Forever Free* and *Mask.*

1891 Archibald John Motley, Jr. is born in New Orleans, La. He will become one of the more renowned painters of the 1920's and 1930's, abandoning mainstream styles of experimental painting for what became his trademark: careful depictions of African-American nightlife. Motley's art will be shown widely throughout his lifetime and in a posthumous one-man retrospective in Chicago in 1991.

1897 Elijah Poole is born in Sandersville, Ga. He will become better know as The Honorable Elijah Muhammad, one of the most influential leaders in the Nation of Islam. Poole will be trained by Master Farad Mohammad, founder of the Nation of Islam, and will lead the organization to become the largest African-American movement since Garveyism.

1934 LeRoi Jones is born in Newark, N.J. He will be better known as Imamu Amiri Baraka, influential playwright, author, and critic of the African-American experience. His works will include the plays *Baptism* and *The Toilet* and fictional and nonfictional works such as *Black Music, Blues People,* and *The System of Dante's Hell.*

8

1930 Faith Ringgold is born in New York City. She will become a multimedia artist whose paintings, face masks, fabric and soft sculptures, and quilts will earn her praise for her reaffirmation of African-American women's values and unique perspective. Among her more important works will be *Marriage Quilt, The Flag is Bleeding* and *Tar Beach,* which will become the basis for a children's book. Her work will be included in numerous group shows and a major 25-year retrospective exhibit in 1991.

1941 Jesse Louis Jackson is born in Greenville, S.C. He will be a civil rights leader and founder of PUSH (People United to Save Humanity) in 1971, an organization that will focus attention on the economic disparity between whites and African-Americans. In 1984 he will

Jessie Jackson

found the "Rainbow Coalition." He will also pursue a political career, running for President of the U.S. in 1984 and 1988 and advocating statehood for the District of Columbia.

ARCHIBALD MOTLEY, JR., *Blues,* 1929. Oil on canvas. Collection of Archie Motley and Valerie Gerrard Browne.

9

10

1806 Benjamin Banneker dies in Oella, Md., one month before his 75th birthday. He was a self-taught mathematician and builder (at 21) of the first striking clock in the U.S. An amateur astronomer, Banneker's calculations for solar and lunar eclipses appeared in 29 editions of his almanacs, published from 1792 to 1797. He was also known for his work as a surveyor for the Federal Territory (later Washington, D.C.) and will be honored for his achievement in 1970 when the District's Banneker Circle, adjoining L'Enfant Plaza, is named in his honor.

1823 Mary Ann Shadd is born in Wilmington, Del. She will become the publisher of Canada's first antislavery newspaper, *The Provincial Freeman*, and the first woman in North America to publish and edit a newspaper.

1962 Uganda achieves its independence from Great Britain.

Benjamin Banneker

Black Heritage USA 15c

Meanwhile, P.B. Young, Sr. dies. Son of the founder of the *True Reformer*, a Littleton, N.C., newspaper, Young will publish the *Norfolk Journal and Guide* and build the paper to the largest weekly circulation of any newspaper south of the Mason-Dixon Line.

1901 Frederick Douglass Patterson is born in Washington, D.C. He will become a veterinarian and founder of the United Negro College Fund.

1917 Innovative jazz pianist and composer of *'Round Midnight* Thelonious Monk is born in Rocky Mount, N.C. Monk will be considered one of the fathers of jazz improvisation and will play with such jazz masters as Coleman Hawkins, Art Blakey, John Coltrane, and Miles Davis. In 1964, he will be featured on the cover of *Time* magazine, only one of three jazz musicians so honored.

1935 George Gershwin's *Porgy and Bess* premieres at the Alvin Theater in New York City with Todd Duncan and Anne Brown in the title roles and tap dancer John Bubbles as Sportin' Life.

1946 Dancer and multi-faceted entertainer Ben Vereen is born in Miami, Fla.

Thelonious Monk

11

12

Art Blakey

1919 Art Blakey is born. Blakey, a jazz drummer credited as one of the creators of bebop, will be best known as the founder of the Jazz Messengers. The band will become a proving ground for some of the best modern jazz musicians, including Horace Silver, Hank Mobley, Freddie Hubbard, Wayne Shorter, Sonny Rollins, Wynton Marsalis, and Branford Marsalis.

1939 Coleman Hawkins records his famous "Body and Soul" in New York City.

1980 Billy Thomas dies of a heart attack in Los Angeles, Calif. He was an actor most notable as the third child to portray Buckwheat in the *Our Gang* comedies, a role he played in some 80 episodes of the popular film series.

1882 Acclaimed concert pianist, composer, arranger, and choral conductor R. Nathaniel Dett is born in Ontario, Canada.

1492 Pedro Alonzo Niño, a Spaniard of African descent, accompanies Christopher Columbus, who claims "discovery" of the New World, landing on what is now Watling Island in the Bahamas.

1904 William Montague Cobb is born in Washington, D.C. He will become a physician, longtime professor of anatomy, and editor of the *Journal of the National Medical Association* from 1949–1977.

Dick Gregory

1908 Ann Petry is born in Old Saybrook, Conn. She will become the author of *The Street* and the juvenile work *Harriet Tubman, Conductor of the Underground Railroad*.

1932 Richard Claxton Gregory is born in Saint Louis, Mo. He will be a comedian, civil rights supporter, and nutrition advocate.

1989 George Beavers, Jr., last surviving founder of Golden State Life Insurance Company of Los Angeles, Calif., dies. Beavers, along with William Nickerson, Jr. and Norman O. Houston, formed the company in 1925, which is the third-largest African-American life insurance company, with $120 million in assets and $5 billion of insurance in force.

13

1902 Prolific poet, librarian, and author of historical and juvenile fiction Arna Bontemps is born in Alexandria, La. Among his best-known works will be the words *God Sends Sunday* and *Black Thunder,* the juvenile books *We Have Tomorrow* and *The Story of the Negro*, and *American Negro Poetry*, which he edited.

1906 J. Saunders Redding is born in Wilmington, Del. He will become a literary and social critic and author of nonfiction works on the African-American experience, such as *To Make a Poet Black, On Being Negro in America,* and *Cavalcade: Negro American Writing from 1760 to the Present*, which he edited with Arthur P. Davis.

1915 Meharry Medical College, founded in 1876, is incorporated in Nashville, Tenn. At the time, there are three other African-American medical schools—Howard University Medical School, opened in 1868,

Arna Bontemps

Shaw Medical School, and the Medical Department of the University of West Tennessee. Four others, Louisville National Medical College, Flint Medical College, Knoxville Medical College and Chattanooga National Medical College, had failed.

1925 Garland Anderson's *Appearances* opens at the Frolic Theatre on Broadway. It is the first full-length play by an African-American on Broadway.

14

1834 Henry Blair of Glen Ross, Md., receives a patent for a corn planting machine.

1864 The first African-American daily newspaper, the *New Orleans Tribune,* is published in both French and English.

1916 Sophomore tackle and guard Paul Robeson is excluded from the Rutgers football team when Washington and Lee University refuse to play against an African-American. The exclusion will be temporary and the young Robeson will go on to be named a football All-American twice.

1958 The District of Columbia Bar Association votes to accept African-Americans as members.

1964 Dr. Martin L. King, Jr. is announced as the 1964 recipient of the Nobel Peace Prize for his civil rights activities. King is the second African-American to win the Peace Prize.

15

16

_____
_____
_____
_____
_____
_____
_____
_____
_____

Wyomia Tyus

1890 The Alabama Penny Savings Bank is founded in Birmingham, Ala., by W.R. Pettiford with $2,000 in capital. Although so strapped for funds in its initial months that its officers will not draw salaries, the bank will prosper so well that during the panic of 1893, it will remain open when larger, white banks in Birmingham fail.

1957 The Sickle Cell Disease Research Foundation opens in Los Angeles, Calif. It is the forerunner to a national association and over 50 local chapters dedicated to provide education, screening, counseling, and research in the genetic disease that affects over 50,000 individuals, mostly African-Americans.

1964 Bob Hayes wins a gold medal for the 100-meter dash in the 1964 Olympic Games in Tokyo with a time of ten seconds, equaling the world record.

1968 Wyomia Tyus becomes the first person to win a gold medal in the 100-meter race in two consecutive Olympic games.

1991 Judge Clarence Thomas is confirmed as the 106th associate justice of the U.S. Supreme Court, its second African-American.

1849 George Washington Williams is born in Bedford Springs, Pa. He will be an early African-American historian and founder of two African-American newspapers, *The Commoner* in Washington, D.C., and Cincinnati's *The Southern Review*.

1859 Osborne Perry Anderson, a freeman, is one of five African-Americans in John Brown's raid on the U.S. arsenal at Harpers Ferry, Va. Anderson survives the attack, will serve in the Civil War, and become the author of a book on the raid, *A Voice from Harpers Ferry*.

1932 Chi Eta Phi sorority is founded in Washington, D.C. Aliene Carrington Ewell and 11 other women establish the nursing society, which will grow to 72 chapters in 22 states, the District of Columbia, and Liberia and eventually admit men and women.

1940 Benjamin O. Davis, Sr. becomes the first African-American brigadier general in the U.S. Army.

1968 Tommie Smith and John Carlos hold up their fists in a Black Power salute during the 1968 Summer Olympic Games in Mexico City. Their actions will come to symbolize the Black Power movement in sports and will result in their suspension from the games two days later.

Gen. B. O. Davis, Sr.

SARGENT CLAUDE JOHNSON, *Mask,* ca. 1930–1935. Copper on wood base. National Museum of American Art, Smithsonian Institution, gift of International Business Machines Corporation.

17

18

Mae Jemison

1817 Samuel Ringgold Ward is born on the Eastern Shore of Maryland. He will be considered one of the finest abolitionist orators, known for his fiery speeches in the U.S., Canada, and Great Britain.

1956 Mae C. Jemison is born in Decatur, Ala. She will grow up in Chicago and become a physician, serve in the Peace Corps in Africa, and practice medicine in Los Angeles, before being selected for the astronaut training program in 1987.

1984 Legendary jazz and blues singer Alberta Hunter dies in New York City. She

achieved fame in Chicago jazz clubs in the 1920's, toured Europe in the 1930's and, after over 20 years' anonymity as a nurse, returned to performing in 1977.

1991 The 100th episode of *A Different World* airs on NBC. The acclaimed show, a spin-off of *The Cosby Show* that stars Jasmine Guy, Kadeem Hardison, and an ensemble of young African-American actors, is directed by Debbie Allen.

Debbie Allen

1926 Chuck Berry is born in Saint Louis, Mo. He will become one of the foremost legends in rock 'n' roll, whose songs "Johnny B. Goode," "Go, Johnny, Go," and "Sweet Little Sixteen" will sell millions of copies and inspire many later performers, both white and African-American.

1961 Wynton Marsalis is born in New Orleans, La. A jazz trumpeter from the famous Marsalis family, which includes father Ellis and brothers Branford and Delfayo, he will, at 19, become a member of Art Blakey's Jazz Messengers and in 1984 be the first musician to win Grammys for jazz and classical music recordings simultaneously.

1968 Bob Beamon wins an Olympic gold medal in the Mexico City Summer Games. His long jump of 29' 2½" betters the world record by over 21".

1973 *Raisin,* a musical adaptation of the Lorraine Hansberry play *A Raisin in the Sun,* opens

Wynton Marsalis

on Broadway. It marks the debut of Debbie Allen in the role of Beneatha Younger and will act as the catalyst for her further success in the movie and television series *Fame,* a revival of *Sweet Charity,* a successful career as a choreographer, and director of television's *A Different World.*

1990 Filmmaker Charles Burnett's 1977 movie *Killer of Sheep* is among 25 films added to the Library of Congress's National Film Registry. Burnett's film joins other significant films such as *All About Eve, The Godfather,* and *Top Hat.*

19

20

1924 *From Dixie to Broadway* premieres at the Broadhurst Theatre in New York City. The music is written by Will Vodery, an African-American, who arranged music for the Ziegfeld Follies for 23 years and will later be given a three-year contract with the Fox Film Company in Hollywood.

1936 Johnnetta Betsch (later Cole) is born in Jacksonville, Fla. She will have a distinguished career as an educator and administrator and become the first African-American woman to head Spelman College.

1944 Peter Tosh is born in Westmorland, Jamaica. He will become a founding father of reggae music.

1946 The first exhibition of the work of Josef Nassy, an American citizen of Dutch-African descent, is held in Brussels. The exhibit consists of 90 paintings and drawings Nassy created while in a Nazi-controlled internment camp during World War II.

1981 The Martin Luther King, Jr. Library and Archives opens in Atlanta, Ga. Founded by Coretta Scott King, the facility is the largest repository in the world of primary resource materials on Dr. Martin Luther King, Jr., nine major civil rights organizations, and the American civil rights movement.

1983 Grenadan Prime Minister Maurice Bishop is assassinated after refusing to share leadership of the New Jewel Movement with his deputy, Bernard Coard. This event will indirectly lead to the invasion of Grenada by the U.S. and six Caribbean nations.

1895 Rex Ingram is born near Cairo, Ill. He will attend medical school and earn a Phi Beta Kappa key but foresake medicine for the stage, becoming a powerful actor on the stage and screen, most notably as "De Lawd" in the 1936 film *The Green Pastures.* He will also appear in *Cabin in the Sky* and *Anna Lucasta.*

1898 North Carolina Mutual Life and Provident Association is organized by seven African-Americans: John Merrick, Dr. Aaron M. Moore, P.W. Dawkins, D.T. Watson, W.G. Pearson, E.A. Johnson, and James E. Shepard. Each invests $50 in the company, which will grow to become North Carolina Mutual Life Insurance Company and have over $211 million in assets and over $8 billion of insurance in force by 1991.

1924 The "First Colored World Series" of baseball is held in Kansas City, Mo. The series, which pits the Kansas City Monarchs against the Hillsdale team from Darby, Pa., is won by the Monarchs, five games to four, and was organized by Rube Foster.

Rex Ingram

RICHARD MAYHEW, *Sonata in G Minor,* 1987. Oil on canvas. Courtesy Sherrie Washington Gallery, Detroit, Michigan.

21

_____

_____

_____

_____

_____

_____

1832 Maria W. Stewart, an African-American women's rights and abolitionist speaker, says in her farewell address "…for it is not the color of the skin that makes the man or woman, but the principle formed in the soul."

1872 John H. Conyers, Sr. becomes the first African-American admitted to the U.S. Naval Academy.

Dizzy Gillespie

1917 Famed jazz trumpeter John Birks ("Dizzy") Gillespie is born in Cheraw, S.C. He will, with Charlie Parker and Thelonius Monk, be the founder of the revolutionary bebop movement. Gillespie will be the first jazz musician to travel abroad under the auspices of the U.S. government and he will tour to acclaim throughout Europe, the Middle East, and Latin America as well as be a favorite in the U.S.

1979 The Black Fashion Museum is opened in Harlem by Lois Alexander to highlight the achievements and contributions of African-Americans to fashion.

1989 Bertram M. Lee and Peter C.B. Bynoe sign an agreement to purchase the National Basketball Association's Denver Nuggets for $54 million. They become the first African-American owners of a professional basketball team.

22

_____

_____

_____

_____

_____

_____

Spike Lee

1854 James Bland is born in Flushing, N.Y. He will write over 700 songs including "Oh, Dem Golden Slippers" and "Carry Me Back to Old Virginny." The latter song will be selected in 1940 as the state song of Virginia, the state's legislators little knowing the identity and race of its composer.

1936 Bobby Seale is born in Dallas, Tex. He will become a radical political activist and cofounder, with Huey Newton, of the Black Panther Party.

1986 In an interview with the _Washington Post_, Spike Lee says, "Movies are the most powerful medium in the world and we just can't sit back and let other people define our existence, especially when they're putting lies out there on the screen."

1991 Thirty African-American delegates conclude a three-day visit to the Republic of South Africa at the invitation of the African National Congress. While there, TransAfrica's Randall Robinson charges President Bush with failing to exert his influence to end black township strife and Congresswoman Maxine Waters vows to press U.S. cities and states to maintain sanctions against the republic.

23

24

Thurgood Marshall

1775 The Continental Congress prohibits the enlistment of blacks in the Army.

1783 Virginia emancipates slaves who fought for independence during the Revolutionary War.

1847 William Leidesdorff brings his ship *Sitka* from Sitka, Alaska, to San Francisco, Calif. Earlier in the year, the Danish West Indies native had launched the first steamboat ever to sail in San Francisco Bay. The ventures were one of

many activities for Leidesdorff, which included appointment as U.S. vice-counsel, property acquisition in San Francisco, and membership on the city council. After his death, the City of San Francisco will name a street in his honor.

1945 Branch Rickey of the Brooklyn Dodgers signs Jackie Robinson to the club's Triple A farm team, the Montreal Royals. In a little under 18 months, Robinson will be called up to the majors, the first African-American to play major league baseball.

1951 The NAACP pickets the Stork Club in support of Josephine Baker, who had been refused admission to the club a week earlier. After a city-convened special committee calls Baker's charges unfounded, Thurgood Marshall will call the findings a "complete and shameless whitewash of the long-established and well-known discriminatory policies of the Stork Club."

1935 Langston Hughes's play *Mulatto* opens on Broadway. It will have the longest run of any play by an African-American until Lorraine Hansberry's *A Raisin in the Sun.*

1936 The Boston *Chronicle* blasts the soon-to-be-released movie *The Big Broadcast of 1937* for featuring a white pianist who appears in the movie while Teddy Wilson actually plays the music: "This form of racial discrimination and falsification of acts ... is frequently duplicated by many whites in their daily dealings with Negroes ... Negro farm hands and laborers in other fields of industry produce billions of dollars of wealth, but the white landowners and sweat shop operators get all the profit."

1942 In recognition of the influence of so-called race music, *Billboard* creates its first ratings chart devoted to African-American music, *The Harlem Hit Parade.* The number-one record is "Take It & Git" by

Andy Kirk and His Twelve Clouds of Joy, featuring Mary Lou Williams on piano.

1948 Frizzell Gray is born in Baltimore, Md. Better known as Kweisi Mfume, an adopted African name that means "Conquering Son of Kings," he will be elected a congressman from Maryland's 7th District in 1986.

Kweisi Mfume

25

26

1926 *Crisis* magazine, led by editor W.E.B. Du Bois, awards its first prizes in literature and art. Among the winners will be Arna Bontemps's poem "Nocturne at Bethesda," Countee Cullen's poem "Thoughts in a Zoo," Aaron Douglas's painting *African Chief* and a portrait by Hale Woodruff.

1976 Clarence "Willie" Norris, the last surviving member of the Scottsboro Boys, is pardoned by Governor George Wallace. Norris had spent 15 years in prison for allegedly raping a white woman and had been a fugitive since fleeing parole in Alabama in 1946.

1983 Mary Frances Berry, professor of history and law at Howard University, and two other members of the Civil Rights Commission are fired by President Ronald Reagan. Considered a champion of minority concerns on the Commission, Berry will charge the administration with attempting to "shut up" criticism. She will later sue and be reinstated.

1988 Two units of the Ku Klux Klan and eleven individuals are ordered to pay $1 million to African-Americans who were attacked during a brotherhood rally in predominantly white Forsythe County, Ga.

1990 Evander Holyfield knocks out James "Buster" Douglas in the third round of their twelve-round fight to become the undisputed world heavyweight champion. Holyfield's record stands at 25–0, with 21 knockouts.

Edward W. Brooke

1919 Edward William Brooke III is born in Washington, D.C. After serving in World War II and obtaining a law degree from Boston University, he will be elected attorney general of the State of Massachusetts and serve a term of four years before being elected to the U.S. Senate as a Republican in 1966, the first African-American elected since Reconstruction. In the Senate, Brooke will oppose President Nixon's policies in Southeast Asia, advocate low-income housing, and oppose quotas to meet affirmative action goals. Among his awards will be the NAACP's Spingarn Medal in 1967.

1962 Louise Beavers, who starred in more than 100 films, including *Imitation of Life*, *The Jackie Robinson Story*, and *Mr. Blandings Builds his Dream House*, dies in Los Angeles, Calif.

1980 Ten African-American Roman Catholic bishops issue a pastoral letter asserting that "the Church must seize the initiative to 'share the gift of our blackness with the Church in the U.S.'"

27

28

Ruby Dee

1821 A play produced by the African Grove Company, the first African-American theater company, is reviewed in the New York *National Advocate* newspaper. The paper sarcastically comments that "they have generously made a partition at the back of the house for the accommodations of whites," a reference to the segregated seating practices of white theaters of the day.

1891 Charles H. Garvin, the first African-American physician commissioned in World War I, is born in Jacksonville, Fla.

1917 Oliver Tambo, longtime leader and president of the African National Congress, is born in Bizania, South Africa.

1927 Ruby Dee is born in Cleveland, Ohio. She will become one of the foremost actresses in America, beginning her career on Broadway in the early 1940's. Married to actor Ossie Davis, Dee's most notable stage roles will include *A Raisin in the Sun*, *Purlie Victorious,* and *The Taming of the Shrew* as well as work in numerous television series and movies including *Raisin*, *Do the Right Thing*, and *Jungle Fever*.

1954 Benjamin O. Davis, Jr. becomes the first African-American general in the history of the U.S. Air Force.

1914 Omega Psi Phi fraternity is incorporated. Founded in 1911 by three students, Frank Coleman, Oscar J. Cooper and Edgar A. Love and their faculty adviser, Ernest Everett Just, the fraternity will grow to have over 90,000 members in chapters throughout the U.S. and abroad.

1965 Earl Bostic, popular jazz alto saxophonist and winner of the 1959 Playboy Jazz poll, dies

Ernest E. Just

Earl Bostic

in Rochester, N.Y. The Tulsa, Oklahoma native had begun his career in the Midwest and, after studying music and playing with bands in the South, landed in New York City as a soloist with Lionel Hampton's big band, among others. He was best known as a leader of his own groups, which attracted jazz greats like John Coltrane and Stanley Turrentine, and for his popular recordings, including "Flamingo" and "Cherokee."

CHARLES ETHAN PORTER, *Still Life.* Oil on canvas. The Fine Arts Collection of the Hartford Steam Boiler Inspection and Insurance Company, Hartford, Connecticut.

29

30

1902 The Dinwiddie Quartet from Virginia is the first African-American singing group on record when they record six single-sided discs, including "Down at the Old Camp Ground," on the Victor Talking Machine Company's Monarch label.

William Otis Walker

1969 Johnson Products Company of Chicago, Ill., the largest African-American hair-care products manufacturer, is incorporated. Founded by George Johnson in 1954, in 1971 it will become the first African-American-owned company listed on the American Stock Exchange.

1974 Muhammad Ali defeats George Foreman in Zaire to regain his heavyweight crown in a fight billed as "The Rumble in the Jungle." In addition to the fight's being the first heavyweight title fight held in Africa, it is the 14th anniversary of Ali's professional boxing debut.

1981 William Otis Walker, publisher of the *Cleveland Call & Post*, dies. He was the first African-American to hold a post in the Ohio Cabinet, in 1963, and was national chairman for Black Republicans for Reagan and Bush in 1980.

Richard Arrington

1954 The Defense Department announces that all units in the armed forces are now integrated. The announcement comes six years after President Harry S Truman issued Executive Order 9981.

1976 Joseph H. Evans is elected president of the United Church of Christ, the first African-American to hold the post.

1979 Richard Arrington is the first African-American to be elected mayor of Birmingham, Ala.

1989 Frank Mingo, CEO of the Mingo Group, dies in New York City. He, along with D. Parke Gibson, Barbara Proctor of Proctor and Gardner, and Tom Burrell of Burrell Advertising, was one of the pioneering advertising executives who specialized in targeting African-American consumers.

1991 Led by President Robert L. Johnson, BET Holdings, Inc., the parent company of Black Entertainment Television, sells 4.2 million shares of stock in an initial public offering on the New York Stock Exchange. BET is the first African-American company listed on the "Big Board."

31

1

1895 Frederick Douglass Memorial Hospital and Training School for Nurses is founded in Philadelphia, Pa., by Nathan F. Mossell, M.D.

1900 Ethel Waters is born in Chester, Pa. She will become a famous blues singer, the first woman to perform W.C. Handy's "St. Louis Blues," and an actress known for her roles in the movie *Cabin in the Sky* and such stage plays as *Member of the Wedding*, for which she will be nominated for a New York Drama Critics Award.

1935 John Henry Lewis wins the world light heavyweight crown in Saint Louis, Mo., by defeating Bob Olin. He will be the first American-born light heavyweight champion to retire undefeated.

Ethel Waters

1950 Earl Lloyd is the first African-American to play in an NBA game when he plays with the Washington Capitols, who are defeated by the Rochester Royals 78–70.

1910 The first edition of *Crisis* magazine is published by the NAACP with W.E.B. Du Bois as its editor.

1927 Florence Mills dies in New York City after being hospitalized for an appendectomy. She was one of the most popular entertainers of her day, appearing in *Shuffle Along* and *From Broadway to Dixie* as well as having successful tours in the U.S. and Europe.

1929 Grambling State University is founded in Grambling, La.

1940 In the foreword to his book *The Negro in Art*, Howard University professor Alain Locke introduces the most extensive retrospective of African-American art published to date. The selections appearing in the book span almost 300 years and include the work of 100 black artists from Europe and the U.S. including Joshua Johnston, Edward Bannister, Henry O. Tanner, Romare Bear-den, Hale Woodruff, Palmer Hayden, Allan Crite, James A. Porter, and James Lesesne Wells, among others.

1945 The first issue of *Ebony* magazine is published in Chicago, Ill. The second publication of John H. Johnson's fledgling company, *Ebony* will be the catalyst for a communications empire that will eventually include magazines, book publishing, and radio.

W. E. B. DuBois

HARRISON BRANCH, *Ajijie, Mexico.* Silver gel contact print. Courtesy the photographer, Corvallis, Oregon.

2

3

1930 Ras Tafari Makonnen is crowned Negus of Ethiopia, taking the name Haile Selassie. His coronation will signify to thousands of Jamaicans and Garveyites in the U.S. the fulfillment of the prophesy of their leader, Marcus Garvey.

1954 Charles C. Diggs becomes the first African-American representative to Congress from Michigan. He, along with William Dawson of Illinois and Adam Clayton Powell, Jr. of New York, comprise the largest number of African-Americans to date in Congress in the 20th century. Diggs will leave Congress in 1980 after being convicted of mail fraud and being censured by Congress.

1982 Katie B. Hall is elected the first African-American congressional representative from Indiana.

1983 President Ronald Reagan signs a bill to establish a federal holiday in honor of Dr. Martin Luther King, Jr.'s birthday. It is the culmination of the efforts by many civil rights organizations and entertainers to name King's birthday as a national holiday.

Katie B. Hall

1905 Artist Lois Mailou Jones is born in Boston, Mass. She will win her first award in 1926 and have major exhibitions at the Harmon Foundation, the Salon des Artistes Français in Paris, the National Academy of Design, and many others. Despite her long career, she will not have a major retrospective of her work until the Museum of Fine Arts in Boston mounts a show in her honor in 1973.

1933 Louis Wade Sullivan is born in Atlanta, Ga. He will become the founder and first dean of the Morehouse School of Medicine and Secretary of Health and Human Services, the highest-ranking African-American in the Bush Administration.

1953 Jeffrey Banks is born in Washington, D.C. He will become an influential fashion designer and the youngest designer to win the prestigious Coty Award, for his outstanding fur designs.

Lois Mailou Jones

1983 Reverend Jesse Jackson announces his candidacy for President of the U.S. Although unsuccessful in this and a later 1988 campaign, Jackson will win many Democratic state primaries. His candidacy will win him national attention and a platform for increased representation by African-Americans in the Democratic Party.

4

Rayford Logan

1969 Howard N. Lee and Charles Evers are elected the first African-American mayors of Chapel Hill, N.C., and Fayette, Miss., respectively.

1971 Elgin Baylor announces his retirement from the Los Angeles Lakers. After 14 years in the NBA, Baylor had scored 23,149 points, the third highest in the league, and was the fifth-highest career rebounder.

1982 Rayford Logan dies in Washington, D.C. He was an educator, historian, and author of numerous books on African-

Americans, including the *Dictionary of American Negro Biography.* Among his honors was a 1980 NAACP Spingarn Medal.

1988 Bill and Camille Cosby make a $20 million gift to Spelman College. In his remarks to newly inaugurated President Johnnetta B. Cole, Cosby states, "I want Johnnetta Cole to understand the love that Camille and I have for this college, the love we have for women who, in spite of odds against them, come to this school to challenge themselves, to challenge the school, then to challenge what we call 'the outside world.'"

Meanwhile, the Martin L. King, Jr. Federal Building is dedicated in Atlanta, Ga. It is the first federal building in the nation to bear the name of the slain civil rights leader.

5

1956 The *Nat King Cole Show* premieres. The 15-minute show starring the popular singer will run until June 1957 and reappear in July in a half-hour format. The first network variety series hosted by an African-American star, it was cancelled due to lack of support by advertisers.

1968 Eight African-American males and the first African-

Shirley Chisholm

American female, Shirley Chisholm, are elected to the U.S. Congress. Including previously elected Massachusetts senator Edward Brooke, it is the largest number of African-American representatives to serve in Congress since the 44th Congress of 1875–1877.

1974 George Brown of Colorado and Mervyn Dymally of California are the first African-American lieutenant governors elected in the 20th century, while Walter Washington becomes the first African-American to be elected mayor of the District of Columbia, and Harold Ford is elected to Congress from Tennessee, the first African-American from the state.

1989 The first memorial to the civil rights movement in the U.S. is dedicated at a ceremony in Montgomery, Ala. The memorial was commissioned by the Southern Poverty Law Center, a legal and educational organization located in Montgomery.

6

7

1884 Author and abolitionist William Wells Brown dies in Chelsea, Mass. An escaped slave, Brown's autobiography sold 10,000 copies, a record in his day. Brown also wrote the first known travelogue by an African-American and authored the 1853 work *Clotel; Or The President's Daughter: A Narrative of Slave Life in the United States*, the first fictional work published by an African-American.

1973 Coleman Young is elected the first African-American mayor of Detroit, Mich.

1976 FCC Commissioner Benjamin Hooks is elected NAACP executive director by the organization's board of directors. He will serve the organization for 16 years, retiring in 1992. Of his tenure he says, "We have maintained the integrity of this organization and kept our name out front and on the minds of those who would turn back the clock."

Benjamin C. Hooks

1990 Harvey Gantt, former mayor of Charlotte, N.C., loses his Senate race to incumbent Jesse Helms and the opportunity to become the first African-American senator from the South since Reconstruction.

Meanwhile, Barbara-Rose Collins and Maxine Waters are elected to Congress from their home districts in Michigan and California, respectively, while Eleanor Holmes Norton is elected as a nonvoting delegate from the District of Columbia.

1950 Alexa Canady is born in Lansing, Mich. She will become, at age 30, the first African-American woman neurosurgeon in the U.S.

1962 Augustus "Gus" Hawkins is elected to the U.S. House of Representatives from California. He is the first African-American from the state to serve in Congress, a position he will hold for 28 years.

1967 Carl Stokes of Cleveland, Ohio, and Richard Hatcher of Gary, Ind., become the first African-American mayors of these major U.S. cities.

1972 Reverend Andrew Young of Atlanta and Barbara Jordan of Houston become the first southern African-Americans elected to Congress since Reconstruction.

1989 David Dinkins is the first African-American elected mayor of New York City.

1990 The National Football League withdraws its plans to hold the 1993 Super Bowl in Phoenix due to Arizona's refusal to honor Dr. Martin Luther King, Jr.'s birthday.

1991 Los Angeles Lakers superstar Magic Johnson announces his retirement from professional basketball after learning he has tested positive for the AIDS virus.

David Dinkins

8

9

Harvey Gantt

1938 Crystal Bird Fauset is elected to the Pennsylvania House of Representatives. She is the first African-American women elected to a state legislature.

1966 Frank Robinson of the Baltimore Orioles, the American League's batting and home-run champion, is named the league's Most Valuable Player.

1983 W. Wilson Goode of Philadelphia, Pa., Harvey Gantt of Charlotte, N.C., and James A. Sharp, Jr. of Flint, Mich., are the first African-Americans elected mayor of their respective cities.

Dorothy Dandridge

1868 The Howard University Medical School opens with eight students.

1923 Dorothy Dandridge is born in Cleveland, Ohio. She will try vaudeville and a stint at the Cotton Club before finding her most noteworthy success as an actress. She will appear in such works as *Porgy and Bess* and minor movie roles before her big break in a series of low-budget movies including *Tarzan's Perils*. While simultaneously maintaining a singing career, Dandridge will have her greatest success in *Carmen Jones* opposite Harry Belafonte, Pearl Bailey, Diahann Carroll, and Brock Peters, which will earn her an Academy Award nomination, a first for an African-American actress.

1925 Oscar Micheaux's movie *Body and Soul* is released. It marks the film debut of Paul Robeson.

1982 Sugar Ray Leonard retires from professional boxing because of a recurring eye problem sustained in a welterweight title match.

1990 Freedom Bank in New York City, one of the largest African-American-owned banks in the nation, is declared insolvent. Its losses in 1988–1989 totaled $4.7 million, and it was expected to lose $2 million in 1990. A last-minute effort to revive the bank by raising funds from the local Harlem community will fail to meet the government-imposed deadline.

CLAUDE CLARK, Sr., *Growing Dahlias,* 1953. Oil on canvas. Courtesy the artist, Oakland, California.

10

11

1930 Clarence Pendleton is born in Louisville, Ky. He will become the first African-American chairman of the U.S. Civil Rights Commission in 1981, where he will oppose affirmative action and busing to achieve school desegregation.

1961 Andrew Hatcher is named associate press secretary to President John F. Kennedy. He is the highest-ranking African-American appointed to date in the executive branch.

1968 Ida Cox, blues singer of such songs as "Wild Women Don't Have the Blues," dies in Knoxville, Tenn.

1989 The Rhythm and Blues Foundation presents its first lifetime achievement awards in Washington, D.C. Among the honorees are bluesmen Charles Brown, Ruth Brown, Percy Sledge ("When a Man Loves a Woman"), and Mary Wells ("My Guy").

Andrew Hatcher

1915 Claude Clark, Sr. is born near Rockingham, Ga. He will study at the Philadelphia Museum of Art, the Barnes Foundation, and the University of California, Berkeley, and become a renowned artist whose studies of urban life and social realism will be exhibited widely, including at the New York World's Fair of 1939, the Sorbonne, the Oakland Museum, the Museum of African-American Art in Los Angeles and in the major group exhibits *Hidden Heritage: Afro-American Art 1800–1950* and *Two Centuries of Black American Art.*

1928 Ernestine Anderson is born in Houston, Tex. Her introduction to jazz singing will begin at age 12 at the Eldorado Ballroom in Houston. She will perform with Russell Jaquet, Johnny Otis, and Lionel Hampton and be known for her warm, blues-influenced vocals.

1979 The Bethune Museum and Archives is established in Washington, D.C. The goal of

Martin Luther King, Sr.

the museum, which is housed in the Mary McLeod Bethune Council House, is to serve as a depository and center for African-American women's history.

1984 Reverend Martin Luther King, Sr. dies of a heart attack in Atlanta, Ga. Better known as "Daddy King," he was the father of famed civil rights leader Martin Luther King, Jr. and was himself an early civil rights leader. The elder King was pastor of Ebenezer Baptist Church in Atlanta, the center for much of his son's civil rights activity.

12

13

1779 Twenty slaves petition New Hampshire's legislature to abolish slavery. They argue that "the god of nature gave them life and freedom upon the terms of most perfect equality with other men; that freedom is an inherent right of the human species, not to be surrendered but by consent."

1882 Lane College is founded in Jackson, Tenn.

1896 Moses Williams is awarded the Congressional Medal of Honor for bravery in the Battle of Cuchillo Negro Mountains, in New Mexico.

1922 Sigma Gamma Rho sorority is founded in Indianapolis, Ind., by Mary Lou Allison, Bessie Mae Downey, Hattie Mae Annette Dulin, Nannie Mae Gahn, Dorothy Hanley, Cubena McClure, and Vivian White.

1941 Opera instructor Mary Cardwell Dawson and coloratura Lillian Evanti establish the

National Negro Opera Company in Pittsburgh, Pa., to provide more opportunities for African-Americans to sing and study opera. The company's first opera, Verdi's *Aïda*, will be staged the following August at the annual meeting of the National Association of Negro Musicians. In its 21-year history, its performers will include Evanti, Minto Cato, and Robert McFerrin.

Mary Caldwell Dawson

Whoopi Goldberg

1910 Painter and printmaker Wilmer Angier Jennings is born in Atlanta, Ga. A graduate of Morehouse College and student of Hale Woodruff, Jennings was employed by the Public Works for Art Project and Works Progress Administration in the 1930's, where he painted murals and landscape paintings, and produced prints.

1940 The Supreme Court rules in *Hansberry v. Lee* that whites cannot bar African-Americans from white neighborhoods. The Supreme Court's ruling in the case, brought by wealthy real-estate

broker Carl Hansberry of Chicago, allows the Hansberry family, including 10-year-old daughter Lorraine, to move into a white neighborhood.

1949 Caryn Johnson is born in New York City. She will grow up in the ghettos of New York, overcome drug addiction and poverty, and become known as Whoopi Goldberg, multitalented comedian and actress and Academy Award winner for *Ghost* in 1991.

1956 The Supreme Court upholds a lower court decision banning segregation on city buses in Montgomery, Ala. The Court establishes grounds for challenging bus segregation in nine states that have violated the 15th Amendment.

Meanwhile, dancer Geoffrey Holder begins a contract with the Metropolitan Opera. Holder will dance in 26 performances, including *Aïda* and *La Perichole*, and his career will include dance, acting, and art collecting.

HENRY OSSAWA TANNER, *Street in Tangier,* ca. 1910. Oil on fiberboard. National Museum of American Art, Smithsonian Institution, gift of James and Shirley Gordon.

14

1900 In Washington, D.C., a small group meets to form the Washington Society of Colored Dentists. It is the first society of African-American dentists in the U.S.

1915 Booker T. Washington, educator, orator, and founder of Tuskegee Institute, dies on the college's campus. He was one the most famous African-American educators and leaders of the 19th century, whose message of acquiring practical skills and emphasizing self-help over political rights was popular among whites and segments of the African-American community. His 1901 autobiography, *Up From Slavery*, which details his rise to success despite numerous obstacles, became a best-seller and further enhanced his public image as a self-made man. As popular as he was in some quarters, Washington was aggressively opposed by critics such as W.E.B. Du Bois and William Monroe Trotter.

1920 *The New York Times* and *Tribune* call Charles Gilpin's portrayal of Brutus Jones in *The Emperor Jones* "a performance of heroic stature." Gilpin had premiered in the play earlier in the month with the New York–based Provincetown Players, which will influence his being named one of the ten most important contributors to the American theater of 1920 and the 1921 recipient of the NAACP's Spingarn Medal.

15

1805 Explorers Lewis and Clark reach the mouth of the Columbia River. Accompanying them on their expedition is a slave named York, who, while technically Clark's valet, distinguished himself as a scout, interpreter, and emissary to the Native Americans encountered on the expedition.

1969 The Amistad Research Center is incorporated as an independent archive and research library. The center collects original source materials on the history of the nation's ethnic minorities and race relations in the U.S.

1976 Plains Baptist Church, home church of President Jimmy Carter, votes to admit African-American worshipers. The church had been under pressure to admit African-Americans since Reverend Clennon King had announced his intentions to join the congregation.

Mickey Leland

1989 President George Bush signs a bill to rename a Houston, Tex., federal building after George Thomas "Mickey" Leland, the Houston congressman who died in a plane crash earlier in the year.

16

17

1873 W.C. Handy is born in Florence, Ala. He will be best known as a composer and blues musician and will earn the nickname "Father of the Blues." Among his most noteworthy compositions will be "Memphis Blues," "St. Louis Blues," and "Beale Street Blues." He will also form a music publishing company with Harry Pace and become one of the most important influences in African-American music. His 1941 autobiography, *Father of the Blues*, will be a sourcebook and reference on this uniquely African-American musical genre.

1930 Chinua Achebe is born in Ogidi, Nigeria. He will become the internationally acclaimed author of the novel *Things Fall Apart*, among others.

1967 A one-man showing of 48 paintings by Henry O. Tanner is presented at the Grand Central Galleries in New York City. The presentation of the canvases, not in the best of condition, is criticized by *The New York Times* as an "injustice to a proud man."

W.C. HANDY
Father of the Blues
6¢
UNITED STATES

1978 Two FBI agents testify before the House Select Committee on Assassinations that the bureau's long-term surveillance of Dr. Martin Luther King, Jr. was based solely on J. Edgar Hoover's "hatred of the civil rights leader" and not on the civil rights leader's alleged communist influences or linkages with radical groups.

1979 Jamaican-born Arthur Lewis, along with Theodore Schultz, is named the recipient of the Nobel Memorial Prize in Economic Sciences for "pioneering research into economic development ... with particular consideration of the problems of developing countries."

1980 Howard University's WHMM-TV starts broadcasting. It is the first African-American-owned public-broadcasting television station.

Itabari Njeri

1990 Itabari Njeri receives the American Book Award for Outstanding Contribution in American Literature for her book *Every Good-bye Ain't Gone*. Also honored is poet Sonia Sanchez, who receives a lifetime achievement award.

18

19

1900 Howard Thurman is born in Daytona Beach, Fla. A theologian who studied at Morehouse with Martin L. King, Sr., he will found the interracial Church of Fellowship of All Peoples. The first African-American to hold a full-time faculty position at Boston University (in 1953), Thurman will write 22 books and become widely regarded as one of the greatest spiritual leaders of the 20th century.

1969 The National Association of Health Services Executives is incorporated. NAHSE's goal is to elevate the quality of health-care services rendered to poor and disadvantaged communities.

1977 Robert Edward Chambliss, a former KKK member, is convicted of first-degree murder in connection with the 1963 bombing of the 16th Street Baptist Church in Birmingham, Ala., that killed four African-American teenage girls.

1980 Wally "Famous" Amos's signature panama hat and embroidered shirt are donated to the National Museum of American History's Business Americana collection. It is the first memorabilia added to the collection by an African-American entrepreneur and recognizes the achievement of Amos, who built his company from a mom-and-pop enterprise to a $250 million cookie manufacturing business.

1797 Isabella Baumfree is born in New York. She will live in New York City after being freed in 1827 by the New York State Emancipation Act. After a divine revelation in 1843, she will change her name to Sojourner Truth and begin speaking for emancipation and woman's rights. During the Civil War, she will help freedmen in the North and later tour and lecture on better educational opportunities for African-Americans.

Sojourner Truth

1915 William "Billy" Strayhorn is born in Dayton, Ohio. He will write his first song, "Lush Life," when he is 16 while working as a soda jerk in Pittsburgh, Pa. He will join Duke Ellington as a co-composer, assistant arranger, and pianist, where he will collaborate with Ellington for 28 years on some of the band's greatest hits. Among Strayhorn's compositions will be "Satin Doll," and "Take the 'A' Train."

Wally "Famous" Amos

1921 Roy Campanella is born is Philadelphia, Pa. He will become one of the first African-American baseball players signed to major league ball after Jackie Robinson breaks the color line. Campanella will play for the Brooklyn Dodgers and be the National League's Most Valuable Player in 1951, 1953, and 1955.

1955 Carmen de Lavellade begins a contract for three seasons as a dancer with the Metropolitan Opera.

20

21

Pauli Murray

1910 Pauli Murray is born. A lawyer and author of *Song in a Weary Throat, Proud Shoes*, and *Dark Testament and Other Poems*, she will also be a powerful theologian and the first African-American woman priest to be ordained in the Episcopal Church.

1923 Garrett A. Morgan receives a patent for his three-way traffic signal. The device, which will revolutionize traffic control, is one of many inventions for the Paris, Ky., native, which include a hair-straighten-

ing process and the gas mask.

1939 Morgan State College is established in Baltimore, Md., succeeding Morgan State Biblical College, founded in 1857.

1973 The gravesite of Mary Seacole, a Jamaican nurse who served in the Crimean War, is restored in England. Traveling to the battlefield at her own expense when her expert services are rejected by English authorities and Florence Nightingale, Seacole opened her own nursing hotel, which she operated by day, serving as a volunteer with Nightingale at night. Seacole's skills saved the lives of many soldiers wounded during the war or infected with malaria, cholera, yellow fever, and other illnesses.

1981 The Negro Ensemble Company's production of Charles Fuller's *A Soldier's Play* opens at the Theatre Four. The play will win a New York Drama Critics Award for best American play and the Pulitzer Prize.

1784 James Armistead is cited by French General Lafayette for his valuable service to the American forces in the Revolutionary War. Armistead, who was born into slavery 24 years earlier, had worked as a double agent for the Americans while supposedly employed as a servant of British General Cornwallis.

1865 Shaw University is founded in Raleigh, N.C.

1878 Marshall "Major" Taylor is born in Indianapolis, Ind. He will become an international cycling star who will be the first native-born African-American to win a national sports title. During his career, Taylor will win over 100 professional races and one-on-one matches in the U.S. and nine other countries.

1984 TransAfrica's Randall Robinson, D.C. congressional delegate Walter Fauntroy, and U.S. Civil Rights Commissioner Mary Frances Berry are arrested at a sit-in at the South

Randall Robinson

African Embassy in Washington, D.C. Their demonstration against apartheid will be repeated and spread to New York City, Los Angeles, Chicago, and other cities, and involve such notables as Jesse Jackson, Arthur Ashe, Harry Belafonte, and Stevie Wonder. Their efforts will play a large part in the passage of the Antiapartheid Act of 1986, which will impose economic sanctions against South Africa.

HORACE PIPPIN, *The Old Mill,* 1930. Oil on wood. Private collection.

22

23

1965 Muhammad Ali defeats Floyd Patterson. Ali, a recent convert to the Muslim faith, taunts the former champ and ends the fight in 12 rounds to win the world heavyweight title.

1968 A portrait of Frederick Douglass appears on the cover of *Life* magazine. The cover story, "Search for a Black Past," will be the first in a four-part series of stories in which the mag-

Bob Watson

azine examines African-American history and pride. Articles feature a review of slavery and reconstruction, a history of Oklahoma towns founded by African-Americans, a review of the last 50 years of struggle and interviews with Jesse Jackson, Julian Bond, Eldridge Cleaver, Dick Gregory, and others.

1986 Twenty-four-year-old George Branham wins the Brunswick Memorial World Open. It is the first time an African-American wins a Professional Bowlers Association title.

1988 Bob Watson is named assistant general manager of the Houston Astros, the team where he began his professional career in 1965. One of a select few African-American assistant general managers in the sport, Watson's spikes hang in the Baseball Hall of Fame for scoring baseball's 1,000,000th run in 1976.

Mike Garrett

1934 *Imitation of Life* premieres in New York City. Starring Claudette Colbert, Louise Beavers, and Fredi Washington,

it is the story of a white woman and an African-American woman who build a pancake business while the latter's daughter makes a desperate attempt to pass for white.

1965 Mike Garrett, a University of Southern California running back with 4,876 total yards and 3,221 yards rushing, is announced as the Downtown Athletic Club's Heisman Trophy winner of 1965. He is USC's first Heisman Trophy winner. He will go on to play eight years in the pros, first with the Kansas City Chiefs and later with the San Diego Chargers, and be elected to the National Football Hall of Fame in 1985.

1988 Al Raby, the civil rights leader who convinced Martin Luther King, Jr. to bring his movement to Chicago, dies of a heart attack.

24

25

Ron V. Dellums

1883 Edwin Bancroft Henderson is born in Washington, D.C. He will become a pioneering physical education instructor, coach, and organizer of the Negro Athletic Conference, Interscholastic Athletic Association, and the Colored Inter-Collegiate Athletic Association. Inducted into the Black Sports Hall of Fame in 1974, he will be widely considered "the Father of Black Sports."

1935 Ron V. Dellums is born in Oakland, Calif. He will become a Berkeley city councilman, where he will be a vocal champion for minority and disadvantaged communities. In 1970, he will stage a successful campaign for the U.S. Congress, and will distinguish himself there as a forceful opponent of the war in Vietnam and racism in the U.S. Among his leadership roles will be Chairman of the District of Columbia Committee.

1938 Oscar Robertson is born in Charlotte, Tenn. An outstanding college and professional basketball player, "The Big O" will gain notoriety with the Milwaukee Bucks, winning a 1971 NBA championship with teammate Kareem Abdul-Jabbar and holding a record of 9,888 assists that will stand until broken by Magic Johnson in 1991.

1922 Marcus Garvey electrifies a crowd at Liberty Hall in New York City as he states the goals and principles of the Universal Negro Improvement Association (UNIA): "We represent peace, harmony, love, human sympathy, human rights and human justice ... we are marshalling the four hundred million Negroes of the world to fight for the emancipation of the race and for the redemption of the country of our fathers."

1935 Namahyoke Sokum Curtis, who led a team of 32 African-Americans to nurse yellow fever victims during the Spanish-American War, dies. She will be buried in Arlington National Cemetery.

1941 Annie Mae Bullock is born in Nutbush, Tenn. She will meet Ike Turner in the early 1950's at a Saint Louis club. Soon after, she will begin singing with his band on occasional engagements, and in 1959, form the Ike and Tina Turner Revue. After separating from Ike and the band, she will build an even more successful career on her own, which will include the multiplatinum album *Private Dancer* and five Grammy awards.

1955 The Interstate Commerce Commission bans segregation in interstate travel. The law affects buses as well as terminals and waiting rooms.

Tina Turner

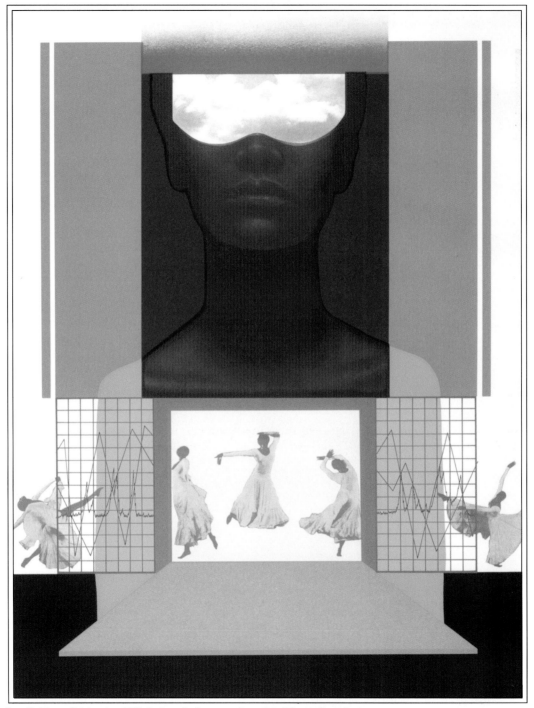

Lᴇᴠ T. Mɪʟʟs, *Celebration,* 1982. Serigraph. Courtesy the artist, Atlanta, Georgia.

26

27

1866 Rust College is founded in Holly Springs, Miss.

1890 Savannah State College is founded in Savannah, Ga.

1968 O.J. Simpson is named Heisman Trophy winner for 1968. A running back for the University of Southern California, Simpson amassed a total of 3,187 yards in 18 games and scored 33 touchdowns in two seasons. He will play professional football with the Buffalo Bills and the San Francisco 49ers and be equally well known as a sportscaster and actor.

O.J. Simpson

1942 Johnny Allen Hendrix is born in Seattle, Wash. He will be best known as Jimi Hendrix, pioneering rock guitarist and leader of the influential rock group the Jimi Hendrix Experience. His career will be highlighted by musical brilliance and severe drug abuse; he will die in 1970 of strangulation related to a drug overdose. His music will influence such groups as Earth, Wind and Fire, Living Colour, and Sting.

1951 Sixteen-year-old Hosea Richardson becomes the first licensed African-American jockey to ride on the Florida circuit.

1968 Eldridge Cleaver, minister of information for the Black Panther Party, becomes a fugitive from justice as a parole violator when he fails to return to prison.

1989 Jennifer Lawson assumes her duties as Executive Vice President for National Programming and Promotion Services at the Public Broadcast-

Charles Johnson

ing Service. The Alabama native is the chief programming executive for PBS, determining which programs are seen on the network. She is the first woman to hold such a position at a major television network.

1990 Charles Johnson wins the National Book Award for his novel *Middle Passage*. He is the fourth African-American to win the award, formerly called the American Book Award.

28

29

1907 Artist Charles Alston is born in Charlotte, N.C. After studying at Columbia University and Pratt Institute, he will travel to Europe and the Caribbean, execute murals for Harlem Hospital and Golden State Mutual Life Insurance Company in Los Angeles, earn the National Academy of Design Award, and the First Award of the Atlanta University Collection's 1942 show for his gouache *Farm Boy.*

1929 Berry Gordy is born in Detroit, Mich. He will become the founder and president of Motown Records, the most successful African-American-owned record company. Gordy's "Motown Sound" will become synonymous with the 1960's and will launch the careers of Diana Ross and the Supremes, the Temptations, Stevie Wonder, Smokey Robinson and the Miracles, the Jackson 5, and many others.

1961 The Downtown Athletic Club awards the Heisman Trophy to Ernie Davis, a halfback from Syracuse University. He is the first African-American to win the award. Davis was his team's leading ground gainer for three seasons and had 823 yards rushing on 150 carries and 15 touchdowns in his senior year. He also broke Jim Brown's career rushing and total-yards-gained records.

1981 Pam McAllister Johnson is named as publisher of Gannett's *Ithaca (N.Y.) Journal.* She is the first African-American woman to head a general circulation newspaper in the U.S.

1908 Adam Clayton Powell, Jr. is born in New Haven, Conn. Son of the famed minister of Harlem's Abyssinian Baptist Church, the younger Powell will be a civil rights activist, using mass meetings and strikes to force employment reforms. In 1944, Powell will be elected to Congress and begin what will be considered a controversial congressional career. Among his early actions will be the desegregation of eating facilities in the House and a unrelenting fight to end discrimination in the armed forces, employment, housing, and transportation. Later in his career, his questionable activities while chairman of the Committee on Education and Labor will result in his expulsion from Congress, re-election and eventual return to his seat.

Adam Clayton Powell

1935 Two-term congressman from North Carolina Henry Plummer Cheatham dies in Oxford, N.C. Cheatham was the only African-American member of Congress during the 1890 term.

1989 The space shuttle *Discovery* lands after completing a secret military mission. The mission was led by Air Force Colonel Frederick D. Gregory, the first African-American commander of a space shuttle mission.

30

1

1912 Gordon Parks, Sr. is born in Fort Scott, Kans. He will become a photographer for *Life* magazine, director of *The Learning Tree* and *Shaft,* and be called a "Twentieth-Century Renaissance man" by the NAACP, who will award him its Spingarn Medal in 1972.

1924 Shirley Anita St. Hill (later Chisholm) is born in Brooklyn, N.Y. She will begin her political career at the age of 40 when she is elected to the state assembly. In 1968, she will be the first African-American woman elected to Congress. She will run for President in 1972 and continue her Congressional duties until 1982.

1933 Sam Gilliam is born in Tupelo, Miss. He will become an artist known for his unique manipulation of materials that result in painted sculpture or suspended paintings. His work will be shown at the 36th Venice Biennale as well as in the exhibit *African-American Artists 1880–1987.*

1953 Albert Michael Espy is born in Yazoo City, Miss. In 1987, he will be sworn in as the state's first African-American congressman since John Lynch more than 100 years before.

1962 Bo Jackson is born in Bessemer, Ala. The 1985 Heisman Trophy winner will be one of the few professional athletes to play in two sports—football and baseball.

1965 Judith Jamison makes her debut with Alvin Ailey's American Dance Theatre in Chicago, dancing in Talley Beatty's *Congo Tango Palace.* Jamison will rejoin the company in 1989 as its artistic director.

1990 Ruth Washington, longtime publisher of the *Los Angeles Sentinel*, dies. Following the death of her husband, Chester, Washington acted as publisher of the weekly newspaper, founded in 1933, for sixteen years.

Alvin Ailey

1935 Lou Rawls is born in Chicago, Ill. A successful R & B, blues, and jazz singer, he will record over 30 albums including *Unmistakably Lou*, a 1977 Grammy winner for best R & B vocal performance. He will also be a strong supporter of African-American colleges, as host of the annual UNCF telethon since 1984.

1940 Richard Pryor is born in Peoria, Ill. Raised in a brothel owned by his grandmother, Pryor will try music as a drummer before his big comedy break on *The Ed Sullivan Show* and a series of successful, Grammy–winning comedy albums. Pryor will also make movies, most notably *Stir Crazy* and *Silver Streak*. Pryor will also battle drug abuse and illness in his career, including his near death from burns inflicted while freebasing cocaine and a battle against multiple sclerosis.

1955 Rosa Parks defies the segregated transportation ordinance in Montgomery, Ala., by riding in the front of a bus. Her actions will spark a 382-day bus boycott and signal the beginning of the modern American civil rights movement.

1989 Dancer and choreographer Alvin Ailey dies in New York City. Ailey began his professional career with Lester Horton, founded, and was the sole director of the Alvin Ailey American Dance Theater in 1958. Initially performing four concerts annually, he took the company to Europe on one of the most successful tours ever by an American dance troupe. Among his honors were the NAACP's Spingarn Medal (1977) and Kennedy Center Honors.

2

3

1866 Harry T. Burleigh, singer and composer, is born in Erie, Pa. While at the National Conservatory of Music in New York City, he will meet and form a lasting friendship with Anton Dvořák. The Spingarn Medal recipient will be known for his arrangements of the spiritual "Deep River."

1908 John Baxter "Doc" Taylor dies of typhoid pneumonia at age 26. Taylor had been a record-setting quarter miler and the first African-American Olympic gold medal winner in the 4 x 400-meter medley in the 1908 London games.

1912 Henry Armstrong is born in Columbus, Miss. Better known as "Hammering Hank," Armstrong will become the only man to hold three boxing titles at once in the featherweight, welterweight, and lightweight divisions.

1975 Ohio State running back Archie Griffin becomes the first person ever to win the Heisman Trophy twice when he is awarded his second trophy in New York City. He amassed a career record of 5,176 yards and 31 consecutive 100-yard-plus games. He will play for the Cincinnati Bengals and be elected to the National Football Hall of Fame in 1986.

1989 André Ware of the University of Houston becomes the first African-American quarterback to win the Heisman Trophy.

Archie Griffin

1841 Returning from an extended visit to Great Britain, abolitionist Charles Remond sails home with an "Address from the People of Ireland" including 60,000 signatures urging Irish-Americans to "oppose slavery by peaceful means and to insist upon liberty for all regardless of color, creed, or country."

1847 Frederick Douglass and Martin R. Delany publish the *North Star* newspaper, one of the leading abolitionist newspapers of its day.

1979 Charles White, a running back with the University of Southern California, is named the Heisman Trophy winner for 1979. White, who gained a career regular season total of 5,598 yards, will play for the Los Angeles Rams.

1990 *Black Art—Ancestral Legacy: The African Impulse in African-American Art* opens at the Dallas Museum of Art. U.S. and Caribbean artists represented among the more than 150 works include Richmond Barthé, John Biggers, Aaron Douglas, Malvin Gray Johnson, Sargent Johnson, and Houston Conwill.

RICHMOND BARTHÉ, *Mary,* 1945. Bronze. Courtesy Eric Silver, Great Neck, New York.

4

5

1783 George Washington's farewell address to his troops is held at Fraunces Tavern in New York City. The tavern is owned by Samuel "Black Sam" Fraunces, a wealthy West Indian of African and French descent who aided Revolutionary forces with food and money.

1833 The American Anti-Slavery Society is founded in Philadelphia by James Barbados, Robert Purvis, James McCrummell, James Forten, Sr., John B. Vashon and others.

1909 The New York *Amsterdam News* is founded by James Anderson. Originally priced at two cents, it will grow to a circulation of almost 35,000 by 1990.

1927 Duke Ellington debuts at the Cotton Club in Harlem.

1982 Herschel Walker, a University of Georgia running back who amassed an NCAA record of 5,097 yards in three seasons, is named the Heisman Trophy

Samuel Fraunces

winner. He will go on to play with the New Jersey Generals of the U.S. Football League as well as in the NFL with the Minnesota Vikings.

1990 The Watts Health Foundation reports revenues in excess of $100 million for the first year in its history. Established in 1967, the Foundation grew from its initial site on riot-torn 103rd Street to serve over 80,000 residents of the Greater Los Angeles area with its HMO, United Health Plan, and its numerous community-based programs. Led by CEO Dr. Clyde Oden, it is the largest community-based health care system of its kind in the nation.

1784 African-American poet Phillis Wheatley dies in Boston. Born in Africa and brought to the U.S. as a slave at the age of eight, Wheatley was quick to learn both English and Latin. Her first poem was published in 1770 and she continued to write poetry and eulogies. A 1773 trip to England secured her success there, where she was introduced to English society. Her book, *Poems on Various Subjects, Religious and Moral*, was published late that year. Married for six years to John Peters, Wheatley and her infant daughter died hours apart in a Boston boarding house where she worked.

1931 James Cleveland is born in Chicago, Ill. He will sing his first gospel solo at the age of eight in a choir directed by famed gospel pioneer Thomas Dorsey. He will later sing with Mahalia Jackson, The Caravans, and other groups before forming his own group, The Gospel Chimes, in 1959. His recording of "Peace Be Still" with the

James Cleveland Singers and the 300-voice Angelic Choir of Nutley, N.J., will earn him the title "King of Gospel."

1935 The National Council of Negro Women is established by Mary McLeod Bethune in Washington, D.C.

1955 The Montgomery bus boycott begins as a result of Rosa Parks's refusal to ride in the back of a city bus four days earlier. The boycott will last a little over a year and be the initial victory in the civil rights struggle of African-Americans in the U.S.

1981 Marcus Allen, tailback for the University of Southern California, wins the Heisman Trophy. Six years later, Tim Brown of the Notre Dame "Fightin' Irish" will win the award.

6

1871 P.B.S. Pinchback is elected president pro tem of the Louisiana Senate and acting lieutenant governor. He is the first African-American to serve in these positions in state government.

1875 The 44th Congress of 1875–1877 convenes with a high of eight African-Americans taking office. They are Senator Blanche K. Bruce of Mississippi plus congressmen Jeremiah Haralson, Ala.; Josiah T. Walls, Fla.; John R. Lynch, Miss.; John A. Hyman, N.C.; Charles E. Nash, La.; and Joseph H. Rainey and Robert Smalls of S.C.

1949 Blues legend Huddie "Leadbelly" Ledbetter dies in New York City.

Frantz O. Fanon

1961 Dr. Frantz O. Fanon, noted author of *Black Skins, White Masks* and *Wretched of the Earth*, dies in Washington, D.C.

7

1931 Comer Cottrell is born in Mobile, Ala. In 1970, he will become founder and president of Pro-Line Corporation, the largest African-American-owned business in the southwest, which he will start with $600 and a borrowed typewriter. An entrepreneur with a wide range of interests, Cottrell will also become the first African-American to own a part of a major league baseball team, the Texas Rangers, in 1989.

1941 During the Japanese attack on Pearl Harbor, Dorie Miller, a messman aboard the battleship *Arizona* who had never been instructed in firearms, heroically downs three Japanese planes before being ordered to leave the ship. Miller will be awarded the Navy Cross for his bravery.

Meanwhile, the exhibit *American Negro Art, 19th and 20th Century* opens at the Downtown Gallery in New York City. Included in the exhibit is work by Robert Duncanson, Horace Pippin, Eldzier Cortor, Richmond Barté and others.

1978 Billy Sims is awarded the Heisman Trophy at the annual awards dinner sponsored by the Downtown Athletic Club. The running back from the University of Oklahoma is the sixth junior to win the award.

1981 John Jacobs is named president of the National Urban League.

Dorie Miller

VINCENT SMITH, *Black Family,* 1972. Oil on canvas with collage. Collection of Columbus Museum of Art, Columbus, Ohio.

8

9

Kurt Schmoke

1925 Sammy Davis, Jr. is born in New York City. A vaude-villian at the age of four, Davis will debut on Broadway in *Mr. Wonderful* and later have success in the films *Porgy and Bess, Ocean's Eleven,* and *Robin and the Seven Hoods*. He will make over 40 albums and receive numerous gold records.

1977 Earl Campbell, a running back with the University of Texas, is awarded the Heisman Trophy. Campbell will play for the Houston Oilers and be elected to the National Football Hall of Fame in 1990. On this same day, Heisman awards go to Mike Rozier of the University of Nebraska in 1983 and Barry Sanders of Oklahoma State in 1988.

1987 Kurt Schmoke is inaugurated as the first African-American to be elected mayor of Baltimore, Md.

1991 Tap dancing legends Fayard and Harold Nicholas and six others receive Kennedy Center Honors in Washington, D.C.

Sammy Davis, Jr.

1919 Roy deCarava is born in New York City. He will become a leading photographer of the African-American experience. The first African-American photographer to be awarded a Guggenheim Fellowship, his first book, *The Sweet Flypaper of Life*, will be a collaboration with poet Langston Hughes. He will also found and direct Kamoinge Workshop for African-American photographers in 1963.

1922 Redd Foxx is born in Saint Louis, Mo. His off-color records and concerts will catapult him to fame and his own television show, *Sanford & Son,* and a later series, *The Royal Family,* his last before his sudden death in 1991.

1976 Tony Dorsett is awarded the Heisman Trophy. Dorsett, a running back for the University of Pittsburgh, amassed a total of 6,082 total yards and will go on to play with the Dallas Cowboys and in the Super Bowl.

1989 Craig Washington wins a special congressional election in Texas's 18th District to fill the seat vacated by the death of Mickey Leland.

Redd Foxx

10

11

Otis Redding

1846 Norbert Rillieux invents the evaporating pan, which revolutionizes the sugar industry.

1910 Smarting from the humiliation of seeing the Ty Cobb–led Detroit Tigers tie the Negro Havana Stars in a six-game series 3–3, the *Indianapolis Freeman* states: "the American scribes refused to write on the matter, it cut so deep and was kept quiet." Not quiet enough, however, to prevent a ban on Negro teams, even the Cuban–named clubs, from playing whites.

1964 Martin Luther King, Jr. receives the Nobel Peace Prize. In his acceptance speech he dramatically rejects racisim and war and reaffirms his commitment to "unarmed truth and unconditional love."

1967 Otis Redding, the R & B singer famous for his recording of "The Dock of the Bay," is killed in a plane crash.

1926 Willie Mae Thornton is born in Montgomery, Ala. She will be better known as "Big Mama" Thornton, a blues singer whose recording of "Hound Dog" in 1952 will be mimicked by Elvis Presley, much to the latter's success.

1940 Lev T. Mills, who will become an artist and chairman of the art department at Spelman College, is born in Tallahassee, Fla. His prints and mixed-media works will be collected by the Victoria & Albert and British Museums in London and the High Museum in Atlanta and include glass mosaic murals for an Atlanta subway station and the atrium floor of Atlanta's City Hall.

1980 George Rogers, South Carolina running back, is awarded the Heisman Trophy. He achieved 21 consecutive 100-yard games with the Gamecocks and led the nation in rushing.

12

13

1899 Boston native, dentist, and avid golfer George F. Grant receives a patent for a wooden golf tee. Grant's invention will revolutionize the manner in which golfers swing at the ball.

1918 Famed jazz singer Joe Williams is born in Cordele, Ga. Williams will sing for seven years in Count Basie's band, where he will record such hits as "Every Day I Have the Blues."

1929 Vincent Smith is born in New York City. Smith will exhibit his works on four continents and be represented in the collections of the Museum of Modern Art, the National Museum of American Art, and the National Museum of Afro-American Artists in Boston.

1941 Dionne Warwick is born in East Orange, N.J. Warwick will sing in a gospel trio with her sister Dee Dee and cousin Cissy Houston, begin her solo career in 1960 singing the songs of Burt Bacharach and Hal

David, and be a three-time Grammy winner.

1963 Kenya achieves its independence from Great Britain with Jomo Kenyatta as its first prime minister.

1975 The National Association of Black Journalists is formed in Washington, D.C. Among its founding members are Max Robinson, who will become the first African-American anchor of a national network news program, and Acel Moore, a future Pulitzer Prize winner.

1903 Ella Baker is born in Norfolk, Va. A civil rights worker who will direct the New York branch of the NAACP, Baker will be executive director of the Southern Christian Leadership Conference in the 1960's during student integration of lunch counters in the South. She also will play a key role in the formation of the Student Nonviolent Coordinating Committee and its voter registration drive in Mississippi.

1913 Archibald Lee Wright is born in Benoit, Miss. Better known as Archie Moore, he will become a boxer and win the light heavyweight crown in 1952.

Dionne Warwick

1944 The first African-American women complete officer training for the WAVES. They had been admitted to the corps two months earlier.

1981 Popular African-American comedian Dewey "Pigmeat" Markham dies of a stroke. He was famous late in his life for his "here come de judge" routine popularized in television's *Laugh-In.*

14

15

John Mercer Langston

1799 George Washington, first President of the U.S., dies at Mount Vernon, Va. A slaveholder, he stipulates in his will that his slaves are to be freed upon the death of his wife, Martha, who will die three years later.

1829 John Mercer Langston is born in Louisa County, Va. He will have a distinguished career as an attorney, educator, recruiter of soldiers for the all-African-American 54th and 55th Massachusetts and 5th Ohio regiments, dean of the law school and president of Howard University, diplomat, and U.S. congressman.

1920 Clark Terry is born in Saint Louis, Mo. He will be a trumpeter and flügelhorn player who will be known for his association with Duke Ellington in the 1950's, his innovative flügelhorn sound, and unusual mumbling scat singing.

1945 Stanley Crouch is born in Los Angeles, Calif. He will become a drummer, poet, and writer for *The Village Voice*. Among his books will be *Notes of a Hanging Judge*, published in 1990.

1972 Johnny Rodgers, a running back with the University of Nebraska, is awarded the Heisman Trophy. Rodgers gained a total of 5,586 yards for the Cornhuskers in three years.

1644 A Dutch land grant is issued to Lucas Santomee, son of Peter Santomee, one of the first 11 Blacks brought to Manhattan. Among the land granted to Santomee and the original 11 is property in Brooklyn and Greenwich Village.

1706 A slave named Onesimus arrives in the home of Cotton Mather. The slave's experience and explanation of African inoculation will result in Mather's encouragement of Dr. Zabdiel Boylston to inoculate for smallpox in Boston in 1721.

J. Bruce Llewellyn

1870 The Colored Methodist Episcopalian Church is established.

1943 Fats Waller dies outside Kansas City, Mo. The self-taught piano player began recording at age 18 and one year later was one of a small group of African-American pianists to make piano rolls for the growing player piano industry. Waller's first solo recording in 1926 led to his own radio show and three tours of France. Waller was known for such popular songs as "Ain't Misbehavin'," "I'm Gonna Sit Right Down and Write Myself a Letter," and "Honeysuckle Rose." He also wrote music for the stage and the movies, most notably "Stormy Weather."

1985 Businessman J. Bruce Llewellyn and former basketball star Julius Erving become owners of Philadelphia Coca-Cola Bottling, the fourth-largest African-American business in the U.S.

JOSHUA JOHNSON, *Portrait of a Man* (also called *Portrait of a Cleric*), ca. 1805–10. Oil on canvas. Courtesy Bowdoin College Museum of Art, The Hamlin Fund, Brunswick, Maine, .

16

17

Andy Razaf

1895 Andy Razafkeriefo (Razaf) is born in Washington, D.C. He will become an important lyricist and musical collaborator with Eubie Blake and Fats Waller. His most famous songs will include "Ain't Misbehavin'," "Honeysuckle Rose," and the lyrics to "Stompin' at the Savoy." He will be inducted into the Songwriters' Hall of Fame in 1972.

1834 George Ruffin is born in Richmond, Va. He will be the first African-American to obtain a law degree from Harvard University and will be a lifelong champion for African-American suffrage and equality.

1859 Shields Green and John Anthony Copeland, two of five African-American conspirators, are hanged for their participation in John Brown's raid on Harpers Ferry. Copeland will be led to the gallows shouting "I am dying for freedom. I could not die for a better cause. I had rather die than be a slave."

1976 Andrew Young is appointed ambassador to the UN by President Jimmy Carter.

1971 Congressman Charles Diggs, Jr. resigns from the U.S. delegation to the UN in protest of the Nixon Administration's African policies.

1975 Noble Sissle dies in Tampa, Fla. A protégé of James Reese Europe, Sissle traveled with the famous bandleader to Europe as the drum major in the 369th Regimental Band and teamed as lyricist with Eubie Blake to form the famous songwriting team of Sissle and Blake. Together with Flourney Miller and Aubrey Lyles, Sissle and Blake wrote *Shuffle Along* and other musicals. A founding member of the Negro Actor's Guild, Sissle was a successful orchestra and bandleader in his own right, touring Europe in the 1930's and with the USO during World War II.

1991 Michael Jordan, outstanding guard for the Chicago Bulls who led his team to their first-ever NBA championship, is named 1991 *Sports Illustrated* Sportsman of the Year. Jordan's likeness will appear on the December 23rd issue of the magazine in the form of a full-color holographic stereogram, a first for a mass-market publication.

Noble Sissle

18

19

1852 George H. White is born in Rosindale, N.C. He will become a lawyer, state legislator, and, in 1896, the only African-American member of the U.S. House of Representatives, where he will be the first to introduce an antilynching bill. White will also found the town of Whitesboro, N.J., as a haven for African-Americans escaping Southern racism.

1865 Congress ratifies the 13th Amendment, abolishing slavery.

1917 Ossie Davis is born in Cogdell, Ga. While he will be best known as an actor in such plays as *Jeb* (where he will meet his wife, Ruby Dee) and *Purlie Victorious* and films like *Let's Do It Again*, *Do the Right Thing*, and *Jungle Fever*, he will be a playwright, screenwriter, and director (*Cotton Comes to Harlem*). In 1969, he will win an Emmy for his role in *Teacher, Teacher* and will be a featured performer in television's *Evening Shade*.

Ossie Davis

1971 Jesse Jackson announces the formation of Operation PUSH (People United to Save Humanity), a new African-American political and economic development organization. Jackson, who resigned from Operation Breadbasket, the economic arm of the SCLC, says, "the problems of the 1970's are economic so the solution and goal must be economic."

1989 Ernest Dickerson wins the New York Film Critics Circle Award for best cinematography for the movie *Do the Right Thing*.

1798 Portrait painter Joshua Johnston places an ad in the *Baltimore Intelligencer* describing himself as "a self-taught genius." Johnston, a freeman, will paint portraits of some of the most successful merchant families in Maryland and Virginia. Only three of his subjects will be African-Americans, among them *Portrait of an Unknown Man* and *Reverend Daniel Coker*.

1875 Carter G. Woodson is born in New Canton, Va. A founder of the Association for the Study of Negro Life and History, of the *Journal of Negro History*, and Negro History Week, Woodson will write many books on African-American history, the most popular of which, *The Negro in Our History*, will be used extensively in high schools throughout the U.S.

1933 Cicely Tyson is born in New York City. She will pursue a modeling career, appearing on the covers of both *Vogue* and *Harper's Bazaar* at the age

Cicely Tyson

of 23. She will later pursue acting and win acclaim for her roles on the stage and on television as well as in the movies *Sounder* (for which she will be named best actress by the National Society of Film Critics and receive an Academy Award nomination) and *The Autobiography of Miss Jane Pittman*, for which she will win two Emmys.

ROBERT SCOTT DUNCANSON, *Landscape with Lake*, 1864. Oil on canvas. National Museum of American Art, Smithsonian Institution, gift of Charles Mandell.

20

21

1854 Walter F. Craig is born in Princeton, N.J. He will become a violinist, organizer of Craig's Celebrated Orchestra, and, in 1886, the first African-American to be admitted to the Musicians Protective Union.

1893 Paul Laurence Dunbar publishes *Oak and Ivy*. Unable to afford the $125 publishing costs, he accepts a loan from a white friend. The loan will be quickly repaid through book sales, often to passengers in the elevator of the Dayton, Ohio, building where he worked.

1981 *Dreamgirls* opens on Broadway at the Imperial Theater. The musical, which chronicles the rise of a black female group in the 1960's, stars Jennifer Holliday, Ben Harney, and Cleavant Derricks. Holliday, Derricks, and choreographer Michael Peters will earn Tony awards for their work in the musical.

1983 In a basketball game against the Seattle Supersonics, Philadelphia 76er Julius Erving scores his 25,000th career point. He becomes only the ninth professional basketball player to achieve this mark.

Paul Laurence
Dunbar

American poet

10 cents U.S. postage

1872 Robert Scott Duncanson dies in Detroit, Mich. Duncanson avoided painting in an ethnic style, favoring still lifes and landscapes including *Mount Healthy, Ohio, Blue Hole, Little Miami River,* and *Falls of Minnehaha.*

1959 Delorez Florence Griffith is born in Los Angeles, Calif. As Florence Griffith Joyner, she will bring glamour to women's track and field. A world-class runner, "FloJo" will win three gold medals (in the 100-meter, 200-meter and 400-meter races) at the 1988 Summer Olympic Games in Seoul and a silver medal in the 1600-meter relay.

1986 While seeking a tow for his disabled car in Howard Beach (Queens), N.Y., Michael Griffith is struck by an automobile and killed as he attempts to escape from a mob of whites who were beating him. The incident will spark a controversy that will further divide factions in New York City, already

Florence Griffith Joyner

troubled by racially motived violence.

1988 Jesse Jackson, in a speech in Chicago, urges the use the term "African-American": "Every ethnic group in this country has reference to some land base, some historical cultural base. African-Americans have hit that level of maturity."

22

23

1883 Arthur Wergs Mitchell is born near Lafayette, Ala. He will become the first African-American Democrat elected to Congress, representing Illinois for four terms. In 1937, after being forced from first-class train accommodations in Arkansas to ride in a shabby Jim Crow car, Mitchell will sue the railroad and eventually argue unsuccessfully before the Supreme Court that interstate trains be exempt from Arkansas's "separate but equal" laws.

1905 James A. Porter is born in Baltimore, Md. An artist, chair of the department of art at Howard University and one of the earliest scholars of African-American art, Porter will exhibit his works widely in the U.S., Europe, and Africa.

1939 Jerry Pinkney is born in Philadelphia, Pa. He will become an award-winning illustrator of children's books and numerous U.S. postage stamps

featuring notable African-Americans.

1980 Samuel R. Pierce, Jr., a New York City lawyer and former judge, is named to President Reagan's Cabinet as Secretary of Housing and Urban Development.

1989 The art exhibit *Afro-American Artists in Paris: 1919–1939* closes at the Bertha and Karl Leubsdorf Gallery on the Hunter College campus in New York City. The exhibit of eight artists including William Harper, Lois Mailou Jones, Archibald Motley, Jr., Henry O. Tanner, and Hale Woodruff, among others, powerfully illustrated the results achieved by African-American artists when they were able to leave the confines and restrictions imposed upon them by race in the U.S.

Madame C.J. Walker

1815 Henry Highland Garnet is born in New Market, Md. He will become a noted clergyman and abolitionist. He will also be the first African-American to deliver a sermon before the House of Representatives.

1867 Sarah Breedlove is born in Delta, La. She will be better known as Madame C.J. Walker, the first female African-American millionaire whose hair-care, toiletry, and cosmetics products revolutionized the standard of beauty for African-

American women. Her philanthropy and generosity will make her a popular figure of the early 1900's.

1935 Esther Mae Jones is born in Galveston, Tex. She will begin her career as a blues singer at 13 as "Little" Esther Phillips, taking her name from a billboard for the gasoline company. Problems with drugs and alcohol will cause her to interrupt her career a number of times. She will record several memorable songs including "And I Love Him" and "Release Me."

1990 Wendell Scott dies in Danville, Va. He was a prominent African-American in early stock car racing, finishing among the top five drivers in 20 Grand National events and winning 128 races in the sportsman division.

24

_____
_____
_____
_____
_____
_____
_____

1853 Octavia Victoria Rogers Albert is born in Oglethorpe, Ga. Albert is best known for her book *House of Bondage*, an informal narrative of slaves' lives 15 years after manumission.

1898 Irvin C. Mollison is born in Chicago, Ill. In 1945, he will be appointed the first African-American judge of the Customs Court.

1936 Count Basie makes his New York debut at the Roseland Ballroom.

1954 In a session with the Miles Davis All-Stars, Thelonius Monk records "Bag's Groove," which many will regard as his finest solo performance.

Theologian Howard Thurman

The true meaning of Christmas is expressed in the sharing of one's graces in a world in which it is so easy to become callous, insensitive, and hard. Once this spirit becomes part of a man's life, every day is Christmas, and every night is freighted with anticipation of the dawning of fresh, and perhaps holy, adventure.

—Howard Thurman
The Mood of Christmas

25

_____
_____
_____
_____
_____
_____
_____

1776 Oliver Cromwell and Prince Whipple are among soldiers who cross the Delaware River with George Washington to attack the Hessians in Trenton, N.J., in the Revolutionary War.

1835 Benjamin Tucker Tanner is born in Pittsburgh, Pa. Father of famed painter Henry O. Tanner, he will become an AME bishop and editor of the *Christian Recorder* and founder in 1884 of the *AME Church Review*, a leading magazine of the day.

1907 Cabel "Cab" Calloway is born in Rochester, N.Y. A versatile jazz bandleader and singer who will popularize scat singing, his song "Minnie the Moocher" will be the first million-selling jazz record. Calloway will also appear in the movie *Porgy and Bess* as well as perform as a singer in the touring companies of *Porgy* and *Hello Dolly*.

1932 "Little Richard" Penniman is born in Macon, Ga. He will be known for his flamboyant singing style, which will be influential to many R & B and British artists.

1951 Harry T. Moore, a Florida NAACP official, is killed by a bomb in his home in Mims, Fl. Active in expanding the African-American vote in Florida and in desegregating the University of Florida, Moore will be posthumously awarded the NAACP's Spingarn Medal for 1952.

Cab Calloway

26

27

Dr. Maulana Karenga

1849 David Ruggles dies in Northampton, Mass. Often called the first African-American bookseller for his bookstore established in 1834, Ruggles was an early abolitionist, speaker, and writer as well as a "conductor" on the Underground Railroad.

1894 Jean Toomer is born in Washington, D.C. The grandson of P.B.S. Pinchback, Toomer will become the author of the influential *Cane*.

1908 Jack Johnson wins the heavyweight title in Australia, defeating Tommy Burns. After avoiding fighting Johnson for

over a year, Burns will later say of his loss, "Race prejudice was rampant in my mind. The idea of a black man challenging me was beyond enduring. Hatred made me tense."

1931 Lonnie Elder is born in Americus, Ga. He will be known as an author, playwright (*Ceremonies in Dark Old Men*), and screenwriter (*Sounder, A Woman Called Moses*).

1966 Kwanzaa, originated by Dr. Maulana Karenga, is first celebrated by a small number of African-American families in Los Angeles, Calif., to "restore and reaffirm our African heritage and culture." Kwanzaa, a Kiswahili word meaning first or first fruit, will celebrate over the next seven days the Nguzo Saba, or seven principles, of Umoja (Unity), Kujichagulia (Self-determination), Ujima (Collective Work and Responsibility), Ujamaa (Cooperative Economics), Nia (Purpose), Kuumba (Creativity), and Imani (Faith).

1873 William A. Harper is born in Cayuga, Canada. A student at the Art Institute of Chicago, he will study with Henry O. Tanner and be considered one of the most gifted African-American artists of the early 20th Century.

1892 Livingstone and Biddle College (now Johnson C. Smith) play the first African-American intercollegiate football game.

1904 Monroe Nathan Work marries Florence Evelyn Hendrickson of Savannah, Ga. Greatly assisted by his wife, Work will publish *The Negro Year Book*, an annual encyclopedia of African-American achievement. He will later publish a *A Bibliography of the Negro in Africa and America* (1928), with over 17,000 entries. Reviewers will laud it as "absolutely indispensable" and call it "a monument of which any race may well be proud." It will be reprinted in 1965.

1956 After a boycott by African-Americans that lasted more than six months, segregation is outlawed on Tallahassee, Fla., buses.

WILLIAM A. HARPER, *Patio,* 1908. Oil on canvas. The Evans-Tibbs Collection, Washington, D.C.

28

29

1829 Elizabeth "Mumbet" Freeman dies. Freeman, born into slavery, ran away from her owners after mistreatment by her master's wife. She petitioned successfully for her freedom, citing her knowledge of the Bill of Rights and the new constitution of the Commonwealth of Massachusetts in her argument that all men were created equal, thereby justifying her petition for freedom. Her victory effectively abolished slavery in Massachusetts. Freeman was the great-grandmother of W.E.B. Du Bois, one of America's most renowned scholars, leaders, and fighters for civil rights.

1905 Earl "Fatha" Hines is born in Duquesne, Pa. He will be considered the "Father of Modern Jazz Piano."

1954 Denzel Washington is born in Mount Vernon, N.Y. He will become an actor, playing Dr. Phillip Chandler for six seasons on television's *St. Elsewhere* and have a successful movie career that will include roles in *A Soldier's Story* and an Oscar–winning performance in *Glory*.

1977 Karen Farmer becomes the first African-American member of the Daughters of the American Revolution when she traces her ancestry back to William Hood, a soldier in the Revolutionary War.

Earl Hines

Kelly Miller

1925 At 67, Anna Julia Cooper receives her doctorate from the University of Paris. Officials of the French Embassy present the degree to her at ceremonies at Howard University. Cooper had been a noted college and secondary school educator and will continue to teach and work for educational improvement for African-Americans until her death at 105.

1939 Kelly Miller dies in Washington, D.C. The first African-American to be admitted to Johns Hopkins University (in 1887), and later a longtime professor and dean at Howard University, Miller was a noted writer, essayist, and newspaper columnist who opposed the accommodations policies of Booker T. Washington. He was best known, however, as a champion for educational development for African-Americans, dramatically increasing enrollment at Howard and founding a "Negro-Americana Museum and Library," which became Howard's Moorland-Spingarn Research Center.

1952 Noted jazz bandleader Fletcher Henderson dies in New York City. Henderson worked early in his career with Harry Pace of Black Swan Records and, in 1924, started playing at the Roseland Ballroom, the same year he added New Orleans trumpeter Louis Armstrong to the band. Armstong's short tenure helped it evolve from a dance to a jazz band and established Henderson as the founding father of the big band movement in jazz.

30

31

Bo Diddley

1928 Ellas Bates McDaniel is born in Magnolia, Miss. Better known as Bo Diddley, he will be a blues composer and performer who will influence a generation of musicians including such groups as the Rolling Stones and the Doors. A favorite of President John F. Kennedy, who invited Diddley to play in the White House in 1962, he will be inducted into the Rock 'n' Roll Hall of Fame in 1987.

1935 Marian Anderson makes a historic appearance in New York City's Town Hall. Fresh from a triumphant tour in Europe, Anderson will be hailed by New York critics as one of the "great singers of our time." Her performance will mark a new era in the Philadelphian's long and successful career.

1952 Tuskegee Institute reports there were no lynchings during the year for the first time in the 71 years it has been keeping such records.

1842 Josiah T. Walls is born near Winchester, Va. He will become, in 1871, Florida's first African-American congressman.

1916 Frederick Douglass "Fritz" Pollard of Brown University becomes the first African-American running back named to the All-American team.

1930 Odetta Holmes is born in Birmingham, Ala. She will become a famous folksinger who will sing all over the world and at major peace and civil rights meetings, including the 1963 March on Washington.

1948 Donna Summer is born in Boston, Mass. She will be the reigning "Queen of Disco" music in the 1970's, known for her renditions of "Bad Girls" and "Last Dance."

Odetta Holmes

1953 Hulan Jack is inaugurated as Manhattan borough president, the first African-American to hold the post.

1964 In a speech before a group of young people, Malcolm X urges them "to see for yourself and listen for yourself and think for yourself. This generation, especially of our people, have a burden, more so than any other time in history. The most important thing we can learn to do today is think for ourselves."

1984 The first nationally broadcast telethon for the United Negro College Fund raises $14.1 million. the telethon will become an annual fundraising drive that will support more than 40 historically African-American institutions of higher learning and draw widespread individual and corporate support.

BIOGRAPHIES

Great-granddaughter of an African-American college president and granddaughter of an AME minister, Paula L. Woods obtained her BA in English and Black studies before obtaining a master's degree from UCLA and turning to business, where she has spent the last fifteen years as a successful marketing executive and consultant. *I, Too, Sing America* gives her an opportunity to blend her interest in African American history with communications skills used in the firm she co-founded with her partner, Felix H. Liddell.

I, Too, Sing America brings Felix H. Liddell back to his first love, art, after nearly two decades as a successful businessman and owner of his own consulting firm. "Had I been exposed in my youth to·the outstanding African-American art we've selected for *I, Too, Sing America*, I might have continued in my artistic training" says the Chicago native who turned down a scholarship to the Art Institute to pursue a business career, obtaining a bachelor's degree from Loyola University in Chicago and an MBA from Lake Forest Graduate School of Management.

Public Relations
George Benson, Jerry Ohlinger
Dorothy Height, Courtesy of
NCNW, Inc.
Aretha Franklin, Frank Driggs
Collection
Emmanuel Cleaver, Office of the
Mayor, City of Kansas City
Sarah Vaughan, Frank Driggs
Collection
Benjamin Mays, Schomburg
Center for Research in Black
Culture, The New York Public
Library, Astor, Lenox and Tilden
Foundation
Pearl Bailey, Reproduction from
the Collections of the Library of
Congress
Naomi Sims, Courtesy Naomi Sims
Beauty Products, LTD
William Grant Still, Frank Driggs
Collection

APRIL
Charles White, Schomburg Center
for Research in Black Culture,
The New York Public Library,
Astor, Lenox and Tilden
Foundation
Maya Angelou, Photo: © Susan
Mullally Weil
Booker T. Washington Cabin,
National Philatelic Collection,
Smithsonian Institution
Matthew Henson, Stamp design ©
1986 United States Postal Service
Billy Holliday, Reproduction from
the Collections of the Library of
Congress
Percy Julian, Schomburg Center
for Research in Black Culture,
The New York Public Library,
Astor, Lenox and Tilden
Foundation
Marian Anderson, Reproduction
from the Collections of the
Library of Congress
Arthur Ashe, © Allsport, Photo:
Tony Duffy
Roy Wilkins, Courtesy, NAACP
Public Relations
August Wilson, Yale Repertory
Theatre, Photo: William B.
Carter
Sidney Poitier, Courtesy Verdon-
Cedric Productions, Inc.
Howardena Pindell, Photo:

Amy Stromsten
A. Philip Randolph, Stamp design
© 1989 United States Postal
Service
Kareem Abdul-Jabbar,
© Allsport, Photo: Mike Powell
Alice Walker, Photo: Jeff Reinking
James Earl Jones, Courtesy
Lorimar Television, Inc.
Lee Elder, Courtesy Rose Elder
& Associates, Inc.
Charles Mingus, Frank Driggs
Collection
Ella Fitzgerald, Schomburg Center
for Research in Black Culture,
The New York Public Library,
Astor, Lenox and Tilden
Foundation
William L. Dawson,
Reproduction from the
Collections of the Library of
Congress
Coretta King, Reproduction from
the Collections of the Library of
Congress
Gloria Naylor, Courtesy American
Program Bureau
Duke Ellington, National Philatelic
Collection, Smithsonian
Institution
Jesse E. Moorland, Schomburg
Center for Research in Black
Culture, The New York Public
Library, Astor, Lenox and Tilden
Foundation

MAY
Gwendolyn Brooks, Schomburg
Center for Research in Black
Culture, The New York Public
Library, Astor, Lenox and Tilden
Foundation
Ralph Abernathy, Reproduction
from the Collections of the
Library of Congress
Jimmy Winkfield, © 1902 Churchill
Downs Incorporated, Kinetic
Corporation
William Stanley Braithwaite,
Reproduction from the
Collections of the Library of
Congress
Charles Gilpin, Reproduction from
the Collections of the Library of
Congress
William Hastie, Schomburg Center
for Research in Black Culture,

The New York Public Library,
Astor, Lenox and Tilden
Foundation, Photo: Fabian
Bachrach
Canada Lee, Reproduction from
the Collections of the Library of
Congress
Jackie Robinson, Stamp design ©
1983 United Postal Service
Fred Shuttlesworth, Reproduction
from the Collections of the
Library of Congress
Mervyn Dymally, Office of
Congressman Mervyn Dymally
Stevie Wonder, Courtesy Motown
Record Company LP
Clara Stanton Jones, Courtesy
Clara Stanton Jones
Henry Johnson, Reproduction
from the Collections of the
Library of Congress
Reggie Jackson, Courtesy
California Angels
Malcolm X, Reproduction from the
Collections of the Library of
Congress
Josephine Baker, Frank Driggs
Collection
Bernard Shaw, Courtesy Cable
News Network
Charles E. Nash, Schomburg
Center for Research in Black
Culture, The New York Public
Library, Astor, Lenox and Tilden
Foundation
Pattie LaBelle, Courtesy MCA
Records, Photo: Marc Raboy
Dorothy Burnett, Schomburg
Center for Research in Black
Culture, The New York Public
Library, Astor, Lenox and Tilden
Foundation
Louis Gossett, Jr., Schomburg
Center for Research in Black
Culture, The New York Public
Library, Astor, Lenox and Tilden
Foundation
Gladys Knight, Courtesy MCA
Records, Photo: Mathew Rolston
Countee Cullen, Reproduction
from the Collections of the
Library of Congress
Shirley Verrett, Courtesy IMG
Artists, Photo: Christian Steiner

JUNE
Morgan Freeman, Photo:

Vanessa Adams
Kenneth I. Chenault, Courtesy
American Express Consumer
Card and Financial Services
Group
Charles R. Drew, Stamp design ©
1981 United States Postal Service
Samuel L. Gravely, Official U.S.
Navy Photograph
Doris A. Davis, Courtesy of Doris
A. Davis
Marion Wright Edelman, Photo: ©
Rick Reinhard 1990
Prince, Courtesy Paisley Park
Productions
Leroy "Satchel" Paige, National
Baseball Library, Cooperstown,
N.Y.
Scott Joplin, National Philatelic
Collection, Smithsonian
Institution
Hattie McDaniel, Schomburg
Center for Research in Black
Culture, The New York Public
Library, Astor, Lenox and Tilden
Foundation
Medgar Evers, Courtesy NAACP
Public Relations
Marla Gibbs, Courtesy Office of
Marla Gibbs
Bessie Coleman, Schomburg
Center for Research in Black
Culture, The New York Public
Library, Astor, Lenox and Tilden
Foundation
Natalie Cole, Courtesy Elektra
Entertainment, Photo: George
Hurrell
Wellington Webb, Office of the
Mayor, City of Denver
John H. Johnson, Johnson
Publishing Company, Inc.
Col. Benjamin O. Davis, Jr., USAF
Photographic Collection
National Air & Space Museum,
Smithsonian Institution
Ed Bradley, Courtesy of CBS,
Photo: Tony Esparza
Wilma Rudolph, U.S. Olympic
Committee
Booker T. Washington, New York
Public Library Picture Collection
Jamaica Kincaid, Courtesy Farrar,
Straus and Giroux, Photo © 1990
Sigrid Estrada
Frank Robinson, Courtesy
Baltimore Orioles

Lloyd Richards, Yale Repertory Theatre, Photo: Gerry Goodstein

Lena Horne, Frank Driggs Collection

JULY

Clarence Thomas, National Geographic Society/Supreme Court Historical Society

Thurgood Marshall, National Geographic Society/Supreme Court of the United States

Joseph H. Douglass, Reproduction from the Collection of the Library of Congress

Jean Baptiste DuSable, National Philatelic Collection, Smithsonian Institution

Ida B. Wells, Stamp design © 1990 United States Postal Service

Margaret Walker, Schomburg Center for Research in Black Culture, The New York Public Library, Astor, Lenox and Tilden Foundation

Faye Wattleton, UPI Bettman

Percy Sutton, Inner City Broadcasting

"Jelly Roll" Morton, Frank Driggs Collection

Bill Cosby, Courtesy the Brokaw Company

Robert N.C. Nix, Jr., Pennsylvania Supreme Court, Photo: Bachrach Photography

Ernie Singleton, Courtesy MCA Records

Ellen Holly, Courtesy © 1992 Capital Cities/ABC, Inc.

Donald Payne, Photo: Bill Epps

Diahann Carroll, Franks Driggs Collection

W.H. Carney, Schomburg Center for Research in Black Culture, The New York Public Library, Astor, Lenox and Tilden Foundation

Patricia Harris, Jimmy Carter Library

Edolphus Towns, Office of Edolphus Towns

Joe Louis, Photo: Jerry Ohlinger

Suzette Charles, Miss America Organization

Ira Aldridge, Reproduction from the Collections of the Library of Congress

Dennis Hightower, Courtesy Disney Consumer Products

Joseph Jenkins Roberts, Schomburg Center for Research in Black Culture, The New York Public Library, Astor, Lenox and Tilden Foundation

Woodie King, Jr., Courtesy Woodie King, Jr.

James Weldon Johnson, Stamp design © 1988 United States Postal Services

Bernard A. Harris, Jr., Courtesy of NASA

Eugene Kinckle Jones, Schomburg Center for Research in Black Culture, The New York Public Library, Astor, Lenox and Tilden Foundation

Whitney Young, Schomburg Center for Research in Black Culture, The New York Public Library, Astor, Lenox and Tilden Foundation

AUGUST

Marcus Garvey, Reproduction from the Collections of the Library of Congress

James Baldwin, Reproduction from the Collections of the Library of Congress

Edwin Moses, © Allsport, Photo: David Cannon

Evelyn Ashford, © Allsport, Photo: Steve Powell

Ralph Bunche, Schomburg Center for Research in Black Culture, The New York Public Library, Astor, Lenox and Tilden Foundation

Benny Carter, Frank Driggs Collection

Jesse Owens, U.S. Olympic Committee

Robert N.C. Nix, Sr., Reproduction from the Collections of the Library of Congress

Lillian Evanti, Schomburg Center for Research in Black Culture, The New York Public Library, Astor, Lenox and Tilden Foundation

Kathleen Battle, UPI/Bettmann

Magic Johnson, © Allsport, Photo: Tim Defrisco

Maxine Waters, Office of

Congresswoman Maxine Waters

Archibald Grimké, Schomburg Center for Research in Black Culture, The New York Public Library, Astor, Lenox and Tilden Foundation

Rafer Johnson, United States Olympic Committee

Charles F. Bolden, Jr., Courtesy of NASA

Isaac Hayes, Courtesy © American International Pictures Export Corp.

WIlliam "Count" Basie, Frank Driggs Collection

Henry Highland Garnett, Schomburg Center for Research in Black Culture, The New York Public Library, Astor, Lenox and Tilden Foundation

Althea Gibson, Reproduction from the Collections of the Library of Congress

Branford Marsalis, Courtesy Columbia, Photo: Timothy White

W.E.B. DuBois, Stamp design © 1992 United States Postal Service

Martin Luther King, Jr., Reproduction from the Collections of the Library of Congress

Michael Jackson, Courtesy Epic Records

Guion Bluford, Courtesy of NASA

Marva Collins, Courtesy Marva Collins

SEPTEMBER

Rosa Guy, Courtesy Dell Publishing

Horace Silver, Frank Driggs Collection

Jonathan A. Rodgers, Courtesy CBS Photography, Photo: Marty Silverstein

Richard Wright, Reproduction from the Collections of the Library of Congress

Henry Louis Gates, Jr., Courtesy of Duke University

Leander Shaw, Jr., Florida Supreme Court

Marjorie Vincent, © 1991 Miss America Pageant, Photo: Kathleen A. Frank

Sonia Sanchez, Photo: Marion Ettinger

Henry O. Tanner, National Philatelic Collection, Smithsonian Institution

Charles Evers, Reproduction from the Collections of the Library of Congress

Jesse Owens, Stamp design © 1990 United States Postal Service

Alain Locke, Schomburg Center for Research in Black Culture, The New York Public Library, Astor, Lenox and Tilden Foundation

Constance Baker Motley, Schomburg Center for Research in Black Culture, The New York Public Library, Astor, Lenox and Tilden Foundation

Claude McKay, Schomburg Center for Research in Black Culture, The New York Public Library, Astor, Lenox and Tilden Foundation

B.B. King, MCA Records, Inc.

Vanessa Williams, Miss America Organization

Maynard Jackson, Office of the Mayor, City of Atlanta

Gordon Parks, Sr., Schomburg Center for Research in Black Culture, The New York Public Library, Astor, Lenox and Tilden Foundation

The Cosby Show, Courtesy NBC

General Colin Powell, Department of Defense

Robert Guillaume, Courtesy Office of Robert Guillaume

Mary Church Terrell, Reproduction from the Collections of the Library of Congress

Langston Hughes, Reproduction from the Collections of the Library of Congress

Maggie Lena Walker, Schomburg Center for Research in Black Culture, The New York Public Library, Astor, Lenox and Tilden Foundation

Stephanie Pogue, Photo: Robert Hall

Bryant Gumbel, NBC News Today

OCTOBER

Mary Schmidt Cambell, Courtesy New York University, Tisch School of the Arts

Otis and Leon René, Frank Driggs Collection

Art Shell, Courtesy Los Angeles Raiders, Photo: Messenchmidt

Elijah Muhammad, Schomburg Center for Research in Black Culture, The New York Public Library, Astor, Lenox and Tilden Foundation

Jesse Jackson, National Organization of the Rainbow Coalition

Benjamin Banneker, Stamp design © 1980 United States Postal Service

Thelonious Monk, Frank Driggs Collection

Art Blakey Frank Driggs Collection

Dick Gregory, Schomburg Center for Research in Black Culture, The New York Public Library, Astor, Lenox and Tilden Foundation

Arna Bontemps, Reproduction from the Collections of the Library of Congress

Wyomia Tyus, United States Olympic Committee

Gen. B.O. Davis, Sr., Dept. of the Army, Media Services

Mae Jemison, Courtesy NASA

Debbie Allen, Courtesy Wolf Kastellar

Wynton Marsalis, Frank Driggs Collection

Rex Ingram, Schomburg Center for Research in Black Culture, The New York Public Library, Astor, Lenox and Tilden Foundation

Dizzy Gillespie, Reproduction from the Collections of the Library of Congress

Spike Lee, Forty Acres and A Mule, Photo: David Lee

Thurgood Marshall, Reproduction from the Collections of the Library of Congress

Edward W. Brooke, The United States Senate, Senate Historical Office

Ruby Dee, Reproduction from the Collections of the Library of Congress

Ernest E. Just, Courtesy Omega Psi Phi Fraternity, Inc.

Earl Bostic, Frank Driggs Collection

William Otis Walker, P.W. Publishing

Richard Arrington, Office of the Mayor, Birmingham, Alabama

Ethel Waters, Reproduction from the Collections of the Library of Congress

NOVEMBER

W. E. B. DuBois, Schomburg Center for Research in Black Culture, The New York Public Library, Astor, Lenox and Tilden Foundation

Lois Mailou Jones, Schomburg Center for Research in Black Culture, The New York Public Library, Astor, Lenox and Tilden Foundation

Rayford Logan, Schomburg Center for Research in Black Culture, The New York Public Library, Astor, Lenox and Tilden Foundation

Shirley Chisholm, Photo: Dev O'Neill

Benjamin C. Hooks, Courtesy NAACP Public Relations

David Dinkins, Office of the Mayor, The City of New York, Photo: Joan Vitale Strong

Harvey Gantt, Gantt Huberman Architects

Dorothy Dandridge, Schomburg Center for Research in Black Culture, The New York Public Library, Astor, Lenox and Tilden Foundation

Andrew Hatcher, Courtesy John F. Kennedy Library

Martin Luther King, Sr., Reproduction from the Collections of the Library of Congress

Mary Caldwell Dawson, Schomburg Center for Research in Black Culture, The New York Public Library, Astor, Lenox and Tilden Foundation

Whoopi Goldberg, Jerry Ohlinger

Booker T. Washington, National Philatelic Collection, Smithsonian Institution

W.C. Handy, National Philatelic Collection, Smithsonian Institution

Itabari Njeri, Courtesy Vintage

Contemporaries, Photo: Jeffrey

Wally "Famous Amos", Courtesy Wally Amos

Sojourner Truth, Schomburg Center for Research in Black Culture, The New York Public Library, Astor, Lenox and Tilden Foundation

Pauli Murray, Photo: Ralph Norman

Randall Robinson, © 1990 Courtesy Marvin T. Jones & Assoc.

Bob Watson, Courtesy Houston Astros

Mike Garrett, Courtesy University of Southern California

Tina Turner, Frank Driggs Collection

O.J. Simpson, NBC Sports

Charles Johnson, Courtesy of Macmillan, Photo: Jerry Bauer

DECEMBER

Alvin Ailey, Reproduction from the Collections of the Library of Congress

Archie Griffin, Courtesy Ohio State University

Frantz Fanon, Courtesy Grove Press

Dorie Miller, Official U.S. Navy Photograph

Kurt Schmoke, Office of the Mayor, City of Baltimore

Sammy Davis, Jr., Frank Driggs Collection

Redd Foxx, Schomburg Center for Research in Black Culture, The New York Public Library, Astor, Lenox and Tilden Foundation

Otis Redding, Frank Driggs Collection

Lou Rawls, Frank Driggs Collection

Dionne Warwick, Frank Driggs Collection

John Mercer Langston, Schomburg Center for Research in Black Culture, The New York Public Library, Astor, Lenox and Tilden Foundation

J. Bruce Llewellyn, Courtesy of Mr. J. Bruce Llewellyn

Noble Sissle and Eubie Blake, Frank Driggs Collection

Andy Razaf, Frank Driggs Collection

Ossie Davis, Reproduction from the Collections of the Library of Congress

Cicely Tyson, Jerry Ohlinger

Paul Laurence Dunbar, National Philatelic Collection, Smithsonian Institution

Florence Griffith Joyner, Jerry Ohlinger

Madame C.J. Walker, Schomburg Center for Research in Black Culture, The New York Public Library, Astor, Lenox and Tilden Foundation

Howard Thurman, Courtesy Howard Thurman Educational Trust

Cab Calloway, Frank Driggs Collection

Dr. Maulana Karenga, Courtesy Maulana Karenga

Earl Hines, Frank Driggs Collection

Bo Diddley, Frank Driggs Collection

Odetta Holmes, Schomburg Center for Research in Black Culture, The New York Public Library, Astor, Lenox and Tilden Foundation